1001
UNFORGETTABLE
QUOTES
ABOUT
GOD, FAITH, & THE BIBLE

RON RHODES

Cover by Dugan Design Group, Bloomington, Minnesota

Cover photo © Reddogs / Fotolia

1001 UNFORGETTABLE QUOTES ABOUT GOD, FAITH, AND THE BIBLE
Copyright © 2011 by Ron Rhodes
Published by Harvest House Publishers
Eugene, Oregon 97402
www.harvesthousepublishers.com

Library of Congress Cataloging-in-Publication Data
Rhodes, Ron.
1001 unforgettable quotes about God, faith, and the Bible / Ron Rhodes.
p. cm.
Includes bibliographical references and index.
ISBN 978-0-7369-2848-9 (pbk.)
1. Religion—Quotations, maxims, etc. 2. God—Quotations, maxims, etc. 3. Faith—Quotations, maxims, etc. 4. Bible—Quotations. I. Title. II. Title: One thousand and one unforgettable quotes about God, faith, and the Bible
PN6084.R3R46 2010
200—dc22

2010015982

Printed in the United States of America

11 12 13 14 15 16 17 18 / VP-NI / 10 9 8 7 6 5 4 3 2 1

In memory of Bob Hawkins, Sr.

ACKNOWLEDGMENTS

There is not a day that passes that I am not thankful to God for my wife, Kerri, and our two children, David and Kylie. Life is good, and life is rich because of these three.

I also continue to be thankful for the privilege of working with Bob Hawkins, Jr., president of Harvest House Publishers, and his fine staff of friendly professionals. They are a great team to work with.

INTRODUCTION

Writing *1001 Unforgettable Quotes About God, Faith, and the Bible* has been an uplifting experience for me. I love to read! I am the bookworm in our family. When I read good Christian books, I always have a yellow marker handy to highlight sentences I want to remember. I've been doing this for decades, and should you ever have the opportunity to visit my personal library, you will find plenty of books that are so marked.

I occasionally go back to some of these books and flip through the pages, rereading the highlighted words. I do this to re-experience the blessing. I personally find this to be an inspirational boost to my spiritual life.

When it came time to write this book, I was overjoyed to go to virtually all of these books and siphon out the "best of the best" of these many highlighted words of wisdom. I also availed myself of other books compiled by thoughtful Christians that contain collections of memorable quotes uttered by notable Christians of the past. From these various sources, I have gleaned many pearls of Christ—words not only full of rich context but spoken with eloquence and wit.

You will notice that along with each quote is a brief section titled "Bible Truth Behind the Quote." I felt it would be especially useful to you if I provided the biblical wisdom that lies behind each quotation. This makes the book especially useful for short devotionals or quiet times. You might contemplate one or two quotes a day along with the Bible truths that motivated them.

For your convenience, I've included a brief topical index at the end of the book. This will make for easier navigation.

As you peruse the pages of this book, my prayer is that the quotes would not only be a source of deeply insightful knowledge based on the writings of present and past Christians but also be an uplifting spiritual experience for you. We can all learn a lot from such quotes. May the Lord bless you as you read this book!

Abundant Living

— 1 —

The whole secret of abundant living can be summed
up in this sentence: "Not your responsibility
but your response to God's ability."

—*Carl F.H. Henry (1913-2003), American evangelical theologian*

Bible Truth Behind the Quote:
Paul, who knew he was weak in himself, said, "I can do all things through him who strengthens me" (Philippians 4:13). God's power is "made perfect" in human weakness (2 Corinthians 12:9).

Acronym to Remember

— 2 —

Is there a...

S—Sin to avoid?
A—Action to do?
F—Faith to exercise?
E—Example to follow?
P—Promise to claim?
A—Attitude to change?
C—Challenge to meet?
K—Key to victory in my
life today?

—*Mark Littleton, author, former pastor*

Bible Truth Behind the Quote:
Scripture is profitable for teaching, reproof, correction, and training in righteousness (2 Timothy 3:15-17). Asking applicable questions of the scriptural text yields powerful results.

AGING

— 3 —

Seek that your last days be your best days.

—*Ralph Venning (1622-1674), author, clergyman*

Bible Truth Behind the Quote:
An aging Paul, near death, said: "I have fought the good fight, I have finished the race, I have kept the faith" (2 Timothy 4:7). Paul served the Lord right up till the end.

— 4 —

We must both, I'm afraid, recognize that, as we grow older,
we become like old cars—more and more repairs and
replacements are necessary. We must just look forward to
the fine new machines (latest Resurrection model) which
are waiting for us, we hope, in the Divine garage.

—*C.S. Lewis (1898-1963), author, professor, Oxford University*

Bible Truth Behind the Quote:
Our current bodies will wear out like tents, but our future resurrection bodies will be like sturdy buildings that won't wear out (2 Corinthians 5:1-5).

ANGELS

— 5 —

The angels are the dispensers and administrators of the
divine beneficence toward us; they regard our safety,
undertake our defense, direct our ways, and exercise
a constant solicitude that no evil befall us.

—*John Calvin (1509-1564), French reformer*

Bible Truth Behind the Quote:
Angels are "ministering spirits" who render specific acts of service to God's people (Hebrews 1:14).

— 6 —

The angels keep vigil for our safety, take upon
themselves our defense, direct our ways, and take
care that some harm may not befall us.

—*John Calvin (1509-1564), French reformer*

Bible Truth Behind the Quote:
"He will command his angels concerning you to guard you in all your ways" (Psalm 91:11; see also 2 Kings 6:17).

ANGER

— 7 —

Speak when you're angry and you'll make
the best speech you'll ever regret.
—*Henry Ward Beecher (1813-1887),*
Congregationalist clergyman

Bible Truth Behind the Quote:
Short-tempered people do foolish things (Proverbs 14:17), including causing quarrels (Proverbs 30:33).

— 8 —

When anger enters the mind, wisdom departs.
—*Thomas à Kempis (1380-1471), author,* The Imitation of Christ

Bible Truth Behind the Quote:
A quick-tempered person is a fool (Proverbs 12:16). Those who control their anger are wise (Proverbs 14:29).

— 9 —

Satan's most successful maneuver in churches and Christian
organizations is to get people angry at one another, to attack and
insult our brothers and sisters, thus splitting the body of Christ.
—*James Dobson (born 1936), founder of Focus on the Family*

Bible Truth Behind the Quote:
Satan and demons promote anger, bitterness, jealousy, and division among believers (2 Corinthians 2:5-11; Ephesians 4:26-27; James 3:13-16). Christians should seek to "maintain the unity of the Spirit in the bond of peace" (Ephesians 4:3).

— 10 —

Oh, the hard, cruel thoughts which men have toward
one another when they are angry! They kill and slay
a thousand times over. These hasty sins are soon
forgotten by us, but they are not forgotten by God.
—*Charles Spurgeon (1834-1892), pastor, New Park Street Chapel, London*

Bible Truth Behind the Quote:
"We must all appear before the judgment seat of Christ" (2 Corinthians 5:10). Even our thoughts will be judged (1 Corinthians 4:5).

— 11 —

Anger is a weed; hate is the tree.
—*Augustine (354-430), bishop of Hippo*

Bible Truth Behind the Quote:
Anger is lesser than hate, but Christians ought to be rid of both (Matthew 5:43-44; Ephesians 4:31; Colossians 3:8).

— 12 —

Don't get angry at the person who acts in ways that
displease you. Give him the smile he lacks. Spread
the sunshine of your Lord's limitless love.
—*Joni Eareckson Tada (born 1949), founder of Joni and Friends*

Bible Truth Behind the Quote:
"This is the will of God, that by doing good you should put to silence the ignorance of foolish people" (1 Peter 2:15).

— 13 —

Irritation in the heart of the believer is always
an invitation to the devil to stand by.
—*Anonymous*

Bible Truth Behind the Quote:
"Do not let the sun go down on your anger, and give no opportunity to the devil" (Ephesians 4:26-27).

— 14 —

If you hug to yourself any resentment against anybody else,
you destroy the bridge by which God would come to you.
—*Peter Marshall (1902-1949), Scottish-American preacher*

Bible Truth Behind the Quote:
Jesus warned: "If you forgive others their trespasses, your heavenly Father will also forgive you, but if you do not forgive others their trespasses, neither will your Father forgive your trespasses" (Matthew 6:14-15). We should always seek reconciliation with others (5:24).

ANXIETY

— 15 —

The beginning of anxiety is the end of faith, and
the beginning of faith is the end of anxiety.
—*George Müller (1805-1898), director of orphanages in Bristol, England*

Bible Truth Behind the Quote:
Instead of anxiety, we ought to turn our burdens to the Lord in prayer with faith, and we will then enjoy the "peace of God" (Philippians 4:6-7). "You keep him in perfect peace whose mind is stayed on you, because he trusts in you" (Isaiah 26:3).

APOLOGY

— 16 —

A stiff apology is a second insult.
—*Gilbert Keith Chesterton (1874-1936), English author, apologist*

Bible Truth Behind the Quote:
We ought to let go of grudges (Leviticus 19:18) and forgive others without measure (Matthew 18:21-22). We should show love to all people, even our enemies (Matthew 5:44).

APOSTASY

— 17 —

Apostasy must be called what it is—spiritual adultery.
—*Francis Schaeffer (1912-1984), theologian, philosopher, pastor*

Bible Truth Behind the Quote:
We ought always to be faithful (Proverbs 3:3; 2 Timothy 3:14), even in small matters (Luke 16:10), and stay true to the Lord in all things (Philippians 1:27). Spiritual adultery is the primary focus of the book of Hosea.

ATHEISTS

— 18 —

I never behold the heavens filled with stars that I do not
feel I am looking in the face of God. I can see how it
might be possible for a man to look down on the earth
and be an atheist, but I cannot conceive how he could
look up into the heavens and say there is no God.
—*Abraham Lincoln (1809-1865), sixteenth president of the United States*

Bible Truth Behind the Quote:
"The heavens declare the glory of God, and the sky above proclaims his handiwork" (Psalm 19:1).

— 19 —

Sometimes when I'm faced with an unbeliever, an atheist,
I am tempted to invite him to the greatest gourmet dinner
that one could ever serve, and when we finished eating that
magnificent dinner, to ask him if he believes there's a cook.
—*Ronald Reagan (1911-2004), fortieth president of the United States*

Bible Truth Behind the Quote:
God's "invisible attributes, namely, his eternal power and divine nature, have been clearly perceived, ever since the creation of the world, in the things that have been made" (Romans 1:20).

ATTITUDE

— 20 —

I am convinced that life is 10 percent what happens to me and 90 percent how I react to it. And so it is with you...We are in charge of our attitudes.

—*Charles Swindoll (born 1934), pastor, Stonebriar Community Church*

Bible Truth Behind the Quote:
One of the best ways to control your attitude is to walk in dependence on the Holy Spirit. The fruit of the Holy Spirit is love, joy, peace, patience, kindness, goodness, faithfulness, gentleness, and self-control (Galatians 5:22-23)—all key components of a good attitude.

— 21 —

If you can't change circumstances, change the way you respond to them.

—*Tim Hansel (1941-2009), seminar leader*

Bible Truth Behind the Quote:
"For those who love God all things work together for good, for those who are called according to his purpose" (Romans 8:28). This recognition helps us to respond positively to our circumstances.

— 22 —

God often comforts us, not by changing the circumstances of our lives, but by changing our attitude toward them.

—*S.H.B. Masterman, Christian leader*

Bible Truth Behind the Quote:
God wants us to understand that He is in control of our circumstances and that He has a purpose in allowing such circumstances (Romans 8:28). We can thus learn to say with Paul: "I have learned in whatever situation I am to be content" (Philippians 4:11).

— 23 —

Live as if Christ died yesterday, rose this morning, and is coming back again tomorrow.

—*Martin Luther (1483-1546), priest, theology professor, reformer*

Bible Truth Behind the Quote:
Our "blessed hope" is "the appearing of the glory of our great God and Savior Jesus Christ" (Titus 2:13). Just contemplating this fact brings encouragement to our daily lives (1 Thessalonians 4:18).

AUTHENTICITY

— 24 —

Be what thou seemest! Live the creed!
—*Horatius Bonar (1808-1889), Scottish churchman, poet*

Bible Truth Behind the Quote:
Don't be hypocritical—clean on the outside but filthy on the inside (Luke 11:39; 16:15).

AUTHORITY

— 25 —

Authority is God-ordained, but authoritarianism
and raw power, in almost all forms, is dangerous.
—*James Dobson (born 1936), founder of Focus on the Family*

Bible Truth Behind the Quote:
God ordained authority in human government (Romans 13:1), the family unit (1 Corinthians 11:3), and the church (Acts 14:23; 1 Timothy 3:1-13; Titus 1:5-9). Authority, however, can be abused, as was the case with the wicked shepherds of Israel (Ezekiel 34:1-7).

AVAILABILITY TO GOD

— 26 —

God does not ask about our ability or our
inability, but our availability.
—*Anonymous*

Bible Truth Behind the Quote:
Jesus gave no written tests to the disciples but simply invited: "Follow me" (Matthew 4:19; 8:22). He invites all: "Come to me" (Matthew 11:28).

AWE AND WONDER

— 27 —

Whenever I am afield or outdoors, there steals over me the acute consciousness that I am confronted on every hand by the superb workmanship of my Father. It is as if every tree, rock, river, flower, mountain, bird, or blade of grass had stamped upon it the indelible label, "Made by God." Is it any wonder that in a simple yet sublime sense of devotion, respect, and reverence for all life, Christ longed for His Father's name to be hallowed throughout the earth?

—*Phillip Keller (1920-1997), author*

Bible Truth Behind the Quote:
God's "invisible attributes, namely, his eternal power and divine nature, have been clearly perceived, ever since the creation of the world, in the things that have been made" (Romans 1:20). In Psalm 104 we find the psalmist meditating on God's wondrous creation.

BACKSLIDING

— 28 —

A stranded ship, an eagle with a broken wing, a garden covered with weeds, a harp without strings, a church in ruins—all these are sad sights, but a backslider is a sadder sight still.

—*J.C. Ryle (1816-1900), Anglican bishop, Liverpool*

Bible Truth Behind the Quote:
David, who had backslidden by sinning with Bathsheba, was indeed a sad sight. He was acutely aware of his transgressions with his sin "ever" before him, he was in dire need of cleansing and renewal, and his "bones" had been "broken" (Psalm 51). We should learn a lesson from his mistake.

— 29 —

Backsliding begins when knee-bending stops!

—*Anonymous*

Bible Truth Behind the Quote: ·
We are exhorted to pray, "Lead us not into temptation, but deliver us from evil" (Matthew 6:13). The failure to pray in this way is a prelude to a fall.

— 30 —

Men fall in private long before they fall in public.

—*J.C. Ryle (1816-1900), Anglican bishop, Liverpool*

Bible Truth Behind the Quote:
Sin has a high price tag, for it can ultimately bring public shame and disgrace even though it began in private (Genesis 3:7; Proverbs 3:35; 13:5).

— 31 —

The best way never to fall is ever to fear.
—*William Jenkyn (1613-1685), English clergyman*

Bible Truth Behind the Quote:
As the apostle Paul put it, "Let anyone who thinks that he stands take heed lest he fall" (1 Corinthians 10:12).

BEARING FRUIT

— 32 —

A tree is shown by its fruits, and in the same way those who profess to belong to Christ will be seen by what they do. For what is needed is not mere present professions, but perseverance to the end in the power of faith.
—*Ignatius of Antioch (35-117), third bishop and patriarch of Antioch*

Bible Truth Behind the Quote:
Jesus urged, "By this my Father is glorified, that you bear much fruit and so prove to be my disciples" (John 15:8; see also Matthew 7:17-19; Luke 6:43-44).

BEAUTY

— 33 —

Beauty is God's handwriting. Welcome it in every fair face, every fair day, every fair flower.
—*Charles Kingsley (1819-1875), Anglican clergyman*

Bible Truth Behind the Quote:
Paul tells us that God's "invisible attributes, namely, his eternal power and divine nature, have been clearly perceived, ever since the creation of the world, in the things that have been made" (Romans 1:20). The psalmist likewise affirmed, "The heavens declare the glory of God, and the sky above proclaims his handiwork. Day to day pours out speech, and night to night reveals knowledge. There is no speech, nor are there words, whose voice is not heard" (Psalm 19:1-3).

BELITTLING

— 34 —

You have to be little to belittle.

—*Anonymous*

Bible Truth Behind the Quote:
We are big in God's eyes if we "encourage one another and build one another up" (1 Thessalonians 5:11), considering others as better than ourselves (Philippians 2:3).

BIBLE

— 35 —

Remember that our Bible is a blood-stained book. The
blood of martyrs is on the Bible, the blood of translators
and confessors. The doctrines which we preach to you are
doctrines that have been baptized in blood—swords have
been drawn to slay the confessors of them. And there is
not a truth which has not been sealed by them at the stake
or the block, where they have been slain by hundreds.

—*Charles Spurgeon (1834-1892), pastor, New Park Street Chapel, London*

Bible Truth Behind the Quote:
Despite countless attacks against the Bible and those who defend it, "the word of the Lord remains forever" (1 Peter 1:25). It is an anchor that will always be there for us.

— 36 —

The Bible is alive, it speaks to me; it has feet, it runs
after me; it has hands, it lays hold on me.

—*Martin Luther (1483-1546), priest, professor of theology, reformer*

Bible Truth Behind the Quote:
"The word of God is living and active" (Hebrews 4:12). There is a dynamic quality to Scripture. It never leaves a person untouched. God affirms that His Word "shall not return to me empty, but it shall accomplish that which I purpose, and shall succeed in the thing for which I sent it" (Isaiah 55:11).

— 37 —

Accustom yourself to a serious meditation every morning. Fresh
airing our souls in heaven will engender in us a purer spirit and
nobler thoughts. A morning seasoning will secure us for all the day.

—*Stephen Charnock (1628-1680), Puritan clergyman*

Bible Truth Behind the Quote:
Let us imitate the psalmist who said, "I will meditate on your precepts and fix my eyes on your ways" (Psalm 119:15). "I will ponder all your work, and meditate on your mighty deeds" (Psalm 77:12).

— 38 —

Nobody can take away from you those texts from
the Bible which you have learned by heart.
—*Corrie ten Boom (1892-1983), Dutch Christian Holocaust survivor*

Bible Truth Behind the Quote:
We ought to imitate the psalmist who said, "I have stored up your word in my heart" (Psalm 119:11) and "your law is within my heart" (Psalm 40:8).

— 39 —

The Bible is the only news book in the world. The newspaper tells
what has taken place, but this book tells us what will take place.
—*Dwight L. Moody (1837-1899), evangelist*

Bible Truth Behind the Quote:
In the Bible, we find God "declaring the end from the beginning and from ancient times things not yet done" (Isaiah 46:10). This proves that the Bible is a God book because only God can tell the future.

— 40 —

I never knew all there was in the Bible until I spent those
years in jail. I was constantly finding new treasures.
—*John Bunyan (1628-1688), English Christian writer, preacher*

Bible Truth Behind the Quote:
"It is good for me that I was afflicted, that I might learn your statutes" (Psalm 119:71). Moreover, "we know that for those who love God all things work together for good, for those who are called according to his purpose" (Romans 8:28). Jail turned out to be a blessing!

— 41 —

I study my Bible as I gather apples. First, I shake the
whole tree that the ripest might fall. Then I shake each
limb, and when I have shaken each limb, I shake each
branch and every twig. Then I look under every leaf.
—*Martin Luther (1483-1546), priest, professor of theology, reformer*

Bible Truth Behind the Quote:
"Do your best to present yourself to God as one approved, a worker who has no need to be ashamed, rightly handling the word of truth" (2 Timothy 2:15).

— 42 —

Leave not off reading the Bible till you find your hearts
warmed…Let it not only inform you, but inflame you.

—Thomas Watson (1620-1686), Puritan preacher, author

Bible Truth Behind the Quote:
After the resurrected Jesus explained the Scriptures to two disciples, they said, "Did not
our hearts burn within us while he talked to us on the road, while he opened to us the
Scriptures?" (Luke 24:32).

— 43 —

The Bible is God's chart for you to steer by, to keep you from
the bottom of the sea, and to show you where the harbor is,
and how to reach it without running on rocks and bars.

—Henry Ward Beecher (1813-1887), Congregationalist clergyman

Bible Truth Behind the Quote:
"Your word is a lamp to my feet and a light to my path" (Psalm 119:105).

— 44 —

The Bible is a letter God has sent to us;
prayer is a letter we send to him.

—Matthew Henry (1662-1714), Bible commentator, Presbyterian minister

Bible Truth Behind the Quote:
The whole of Scripture—Genesis to Revelation—portrays God and His people in constant communication with each other. A tip: We remain closest to God when we "pray
without ceasing" (1 Thessalonians 5:17).

— 45 —

The vigor of our spiritual life will be in exact proportion to the
place held by the Bible in our life and thoughts. I solemnly state
this from the experience of fifty-four years. The first three years
after conversion I neglected the Word of God. Since I began to
search it diligently, the blessing has been wonderful. I have read
the Bible through 100 times, and always with increasing delight.
Each time it seems like a new book to me. Great has been the
blessing from consecutive, diligent, daily study. I look upon it as a
lost day when I have not had a good time over the Word of God.

—George Müller (1805-1898), director of orphanages in Bristol, England

Bible Truth Behind the Quote:
There is great blessing in putting Scripture first in one's life (see Psalm 119). Scripture is
"profitable for teaching, for reproof, for correction, and for training in righteousness"
(2 Timothy 3:16).

— 46 —

The hardest part of a missionary career is to maintain
regular, prayerful Bible study. Satan will always find
you something to do, when you ought to be occupied
about that—if it is only arranging a window blind!

—*J. Hudson Taylor (1832-1905), founder of China Inland Mission*

Bible Truth Behind the Quote:

Scripture warns of "the schemes of the devil" (Ephesians 6:11). One such scheme is to distract people from Scripture (see Luke 8:12). We are thus to be sober-minded and watchful (1 Peter 5:8).

— 47 —

Read the Bible not as a newspaper, but as a letter from home.
If a promise lies on the page as a blank check, cash it. If
prayer is recorded, appropriate it and launch it as a feathered
arrow from the bow of your desire. If an example of holiness
gleams before you, ask God to do as much for you.

—*F.B. Meyer (1847-1929), Baptist pastor, evangelist*

Bible Truth Behind the Quote:

We ought to "be doers of the word, and not hearers only" (James 1:22). Jesus affirmed, "Everyone then who hears these words of mine and does them will be like a wise man who built his house on the rock" (Matthew 7:24).

— 48 —

Disregard the study of God, and you sentence yourself
to stumble and blunder through life blindfolded.

—*J.I. Packer (born 1926), author, theologian*

Bible Truth Behind the Quote:

The person who ignores God's Word is "like a foolish man who built his house on the sand" (Matthew 7:26). How much better it is to follow God's Word, which is a "lamp" to our feet and a "light" to our path (Psalm 119:105; see also Proverbs 6:23).

— 49 —

The first great and primary business to which I ought to attend
every day was, to have my soul happy in the Lord. The first thing
to be concerned about was not, how much I might serve the
Lord, how I might glorify the Lord; but how I might get my soul
into a happy state, and how my inner man may be nourished…I
saw that the most important thing I had to do was to give myself
to the reading of the Word of God and to meditation on it.

—*George Müller (1805-1898), director of orphanages in Bristol, England*

Bible Truth Behind the Quote:
The man who is truly blessed is the one whose "delight is in the law of the LORD, and on his law he meditates day and night" (Psalm 1:1-2).

— 50 —

There are four things that we ought to do with the Word of
God—admit it as the Word of God, commit it to our hearts
and minds, submit to it, and transmit it to the world.
— *William Wilberforce (1759-1833), philanthropist, anti-slave activist*

Bible Truth Behind the Quote:
All this is at the heart of James 1:22, "Be doers of the word, and not hearers only, deceiving yourselves."

— 51 —

He that reads his Bible to find fault with it will soon
discover that the Bible finds fault with him.
— *Charles Spurgeon (1834-1892), pastor, New Park Street Chapel, London*

Bible Truth Behind the Quote:
Paul said, "If it had not been for the law, I would not have known sin" (Romans 7:7). The more we understand God's Word, the more we see that we fall short (Romans 3:20; 4:15).

— 52 —

Remember who your ruler is. Don't forget His daily briefing.
— *Carl F.H. Henry (1913-2003), American evangelical theologian*

Bible Truth Behind the Quote:
Let us meditate on God's Word daily (Psalm 1:1-2; see also Psalm 25:5).

— 53 —

[Meditation is] holding the Word of God in the mind until
it has affected every area of one's life and character.
— *Andrew Murray (1828-1917), South African writer, pastor*

Bible Truth Behind the Quote:
"I will meditate on your precepts and fix my eyes on your ways. I will delight in your statutes; I will not forget your word" (Psalm 119:15-16).

— 54 —

What the Bible says, God says.
— *Anonymous*

Bible Truth Behind the Quote:
"All Scripture is breathed out by God" (2 Timothy 3:16), having been written by men "carried along by the Holy Spirit" (2 Peter 1:21). "The word of the Lord remains forever" (1 Peter 1:25).

— 55 —

There is no substitute for reading the Bible; it throws
a great deal of light on the commentaries!

—Anonymous

Bible Truth Behind the Quote:
Jesus affirmed the Bible's divine inspiration (Matthew 22:43), indestructibility (Matthew 5:17-18), infallibility (John 10:35), final authority (Matthew 4:4,7,10), historicity (Matthew 12:40; 24:37), scientific accuracy (Matthew 19:2-5), and factual inerrancy (Matthew 22:29; John 17:17). No wonder He so often said, "It is written…" (Matthew 4:4-10).

— 56 —

The original documents of the Bible were written by men,
who were, though permitted to exercise their own personalities
and literary talents, yet wrote under the control and guidance
of the Spirit of God, the result being in every word of the
original documents a perfect and errorless recording of
the exact message which God desired to give to man.

—Benjamin B. Warfield (1851-1921), professor at Princeton Seminary

Bible Truth Behind the Quote:
"No prophecy was ever produced by the will of man, but men spoke from God as they were carried along by the Holy Spirit" (2 Peter 1:21). Thus we are told "God spoke by the mouth of his holy prophets" (Acts 3:21).

— 57 —

Bible study is like eating peanuts. The more
you eat, the more you want to eat.

—Paul Little (1928-1975), evangelist, InterVarsity Christian Fellowship

Bible Truth Behind the Quote:
The psalmist said, "I will delight in your statutes" (Psalm 119:16), "Your testimonies are my delight" (verse 24), "Behold, I long for your precepts" (verse 40), and "I find my delight in your commandments" (verse 47).

— 58 —

What greater rebellion, impiety, or insult to God
can there be than not to believe his promises?

—*Martin Luther (1483-1546), priest, professor of theology, reformer*

Bible Truth Behind the Quote:
"He who promised is faithful" (Hebrews 10:23). Indeed, "not one word has failed of all his good promise" (1 Kings 8:56).

Bible Application

— 59 —

Lay hold on the Bible until the Bible lays hold on you.

—*William H. Houghton (1887-1947), evangelist, fourth president of Moody Bible Institute*

Bible Truth Behind the Quote:
"Oh that my ways may be steadfast in keeping your statutes! Then I shall not be put to shame, having my eyes fixed on all your commandments" (Psalm 119:5-6).

Bible Interpretation

— 60 —

In the Old Testament the New lies hidden; in
the New Testament the Old is laid open.

—*Augustine (354-430), bishop of Hippo*

Bible Truth Behind the Quote:
This is illustrated in Matthew's Gospel, where many Old Testament prophecies are interpreted specifically in regard to Jesus the Messiah.

— 61 —

Compare Scripture with Scripture. False doctrines,
like false witnesses, agree not among themselves.

—*William Gurnall (1617-1679), English author*

Bible Truth Behind the Quote:
All Scripture is breathed out by God (2 Timothy 3:16), superintended by the Holy Spirit (2 Peter 1:21). Since the Holy Spirit is the "Spirit of truth" (John 16:13), He does not contradict Himself. Therefore, it makes sense to interpret Scripture by comparing one verse with another.

— 62 —

If we would understand the parts, our wisest
course is to get to know the whole.

—*J.I. Packer (born 1926), author, theologian*

Bible Truth Behind the Quote:

It is in our best interest to understand "the whole counsel of God" (Acts 20:27). This broad understanding of God's Word governs our interpretation of any single verse.

— 63 —

The entire Holy Scripture is the context and guide for
understanding the particular passages of Scripture.

—*Bernard Ramm (1916-1992), Baptist theologian*

Bible Truth Behind the Quote:

Following this interpretive method helps us to avoid the error of those who "twist" the Scriptures "to their own destruction" (2 Peter 3:16).

— 64 —

The Scripture is to be its own interpreter, or rather the
Spirit speaking in it; nothing can cut the diamond but the
diamond; nothing can interpret the Scripture but Scripture.

—*Thomas Watson (1620-1686), Puritan preacher, author*

Bible Truth Behind the Quote:

Scripture instructs us to rightly handle "the word of truth" (2 Timothy 2:15). One means of doing this is to compare Scripture with Scripture.

— 65 —

The infallible rule of interpretation of Scripture is the
Scripture itself; therefore, when there is a question about
the true and full sense of any Scripture, it must be searched
and known by other places that speak more clearly.

—*Westminster Confession*

Bible Truth Behind the Quote:

Peter says of Paul's biblical books, "There are some things in them that are hard to understand" (2 Peter 3:16). But such verses become clear when comparing them with easier verses.

— 66 —

When we claim biblical authority for an idea, we must
be prepared to show from the grammar, the history, the
culture, and the context that the writer in fact taught that
idea. Otherwise the Bible is not used but abused.

—Gordon Lewis, professor, Denver Seminary

Bible Truth Behind the Quote:
By consulting grammar, history, and context, we become equipped to rightly handle "the
word of truth" (2 Timothy 2:15).

— 67 —

Explain the Scriptures by the Scriptures.

—Clement of Alexandria (150 -215), theologian, philosopher

Bible Truth Behind the Quote:
Paul instructed young Timothy, "Do your best to present yourself to God as one approved, a worker who has no need to be ashamed, rightly handling the word of truth"
(2 Timothy 2:15).

BIBLE PROMISES

— 68 —

God is the God of promise. He keeps His word, even when that seems
impossible; even when the circumstances seem to point to the opposite.

—Colin Urquhart (born 1940), Bible teacher, United Kingdom

Bible Truth Behind the Quote:
"Not one word of all the good promises that the LORD had made to the house of Israel
had failed; all came to pass" (Joshua 21:45). Our God is a promise-keeper.

BIBLE STUDY

— 69 —

A readiness to believe every promise implicitly, to obey every
command unhesitatingly, to stand perfect and complete in
all the will of God, is the only true spirit of Bible study.

—Andrew Murray (1828-1917), South African writer, pastor

Bible Truth Behind the Quote:
"In the way of your testimonies I delight as much as in all riches. I will meditate on your
precepts and fix my eyes on your ways. I will delight in your statutes; I will not forget
your word" (Psalm 119:14-16).

BLESSING

— 70 —

God rarely allows a soul to see how great a blessing he is.
—*Oswald Chambers (1874-1917), author,* My Utmost for His Highest

Bible Truth Behind the Quote:
Scripture often warns against the danger of being "puffed up with conceit" (1 Timothy 3:6; 6:4).

— 71 —

God is more anxious to bestow his blessings
on us than we are to receive them.
—*Augustine (354-430), bishop of Hippo*

Bible Truth Behind the Quote:
God seeks to shower blessings on His people (Psalm 144:15). Moreover, God is "able to do far more abundantly than all that we ask or think" (Ephesians 3:20) and stands ready to do so.

BUSYNESS

— 72 —

We hurt people by being too busy. Too busy to notice
their needs. Too busy to drop that note of comfort or
encouragement or assurance of love. Too busy to listen
when someone needs to talk. Too busy to care.
—*Billy Graham (born 1918), evangelist*

Bible Truth Behind the Quote:
Jesus said to a busy Martha, "Martha, Martha, you are anxious and troubled about many things" (Luke 10:41). It is better not to be under the tyranny of the urgent (see Psalm 39:6).

— 73 —

A man can be so busy making a living that he forgets to make a life.
—*William Barclay (1907-1978), professor, University of Glasgow*

Bible Truth Behind the Quote:
We must ever be reminded that "one's life does not consist in the abundance of his possessions" (Luke 12:15).

CHANGE IS COMING

— 74 —

If you're going through difficult times today, hold steady.
It will change soon. If you are experiencing smooth
sailing and easy times now, brace yourself. It will change
soon. The only thing you can be certain of is change.

—James Dobson (born 1936), founder, Focus on the Family

Bible Truth Behind the Quote:
Scripture affirms "You do not know what tomorrow will bring" (James 4:14). We thus ought to say, "If the Lord wills, we will live and do this or that" (verse 15). More broadly, we should learn to say with Paul, "I have learned in whatever situation I am to be content" (Philippians 4:11).

CHARACTER

— 75 —

The two great tests of character are wealth and poverty.

—Anonymous

Bible Truth Behind the Quote:
Whether we are rich or poor, we must not be greedy for money (1 Peter 5:2) or love money (1 Timothy 3:2-3; Hebrews 13:5). There is great danger in greed (1 Peter 5:2-3), and money lovers are never satisfied (Ecclesiastes 5:10).

— 76 —

The test of your character is what you would do
if you knew no one would ever know.

—Bob Jones (1883-1968), American evangelist

Bible Truth Behind the Quote:
Ananias and Sapphira probably thought their private sin of dishonesty regarding land would never become known (Acts 5:1-5). Of course, God knows all. "Nothing is hidden that will not be made manifest, nor is anything secret that will not be known and come to light" (Luke 8:17).

— 77 —

Character is what you are in the dark.

—Dwight L. Moody (1837-1899), evangelist

Bible Truth Behind the Quote:
Job was "blameless and upright, one who feared God and turned away from evil" (Job 1:1). He was a good man even when all alone.

— 78 —

The most important part of us is the part that no one ever sees.

—Erwin Lutzer (born 1941), pastor, Moody Church, Chicago

Bible Truth Behind the Quote:
Paul told the Philippians, "Therefore, my beloved, as you have always obeyed, so now, not only as in my presence but much more in my absence, work out your own salvation with fear and trembling" (Philippians 2:12). We ought to live righteously even when others may not see us do it.

— 79 —

Surely what a man does when he is taken off his guard is
the best evidence for what sort of man he is. If there are
rats in a cellar, you are most likely to see them if you go
in very suddenly. But the suddenness does not create the
rats: it only prevents them from hiding. In the same way
the suddenness of the provocation does not make me ill-
tempered; it only shows me what an ill-tempered man I am.

—C.S. Lewis (1898-1963), author, professor, Oxford University

Bible Truth Behind the Quote:
Scripture reveals that "the Son of Man is coming at an hour you do not expect" (Matthew 24:44). Some will be ready; others will not be ready (Mark 13:33). This event will reveal people's character—both good and bad.

— 80 —

God has a program of character development for each
one of us. He wants others to look at our lives and say,
"He walks with God, for he lives like Christ."

—Erwin Lutzer (born 1941), pastor, Moody Church, Chicago

Bible Truth Behind the Quote:
"Let your light shine before others, so that they may see your good works and give glory to your Father who is in heaven" (Matthew 5:16).

— 81 —

If I take care of my character, my reputation will take care of itself.

—Dwight L. Moody (1837-1899), evangelist

Bible Truth Behind the Quote:
"A good name is better than precious ointment" (Ecclesiastes 7:1). It makes sense, then, to earn a good name by maintaining virtuous behavior (2 Peter 1:5).

CHARITY

— 82 —

You have not lived today until you have done something
for someone who cannot pay you back.

—*John Bunyan (1628-1688), English Christian writer, preacher*

Bible Truth Behind the Quote:
We ought always to do good and share with others (Hebrews 13:16), making a special effort to give to the poor (Matthew 19:21; Luke 11:41; 12:33; 1 John 3:17).

— 83 —

Christian life consists of faith and charity.

—*Martin Luther (1483-1546), priest, professor of theology, reformer*

Bible Truth Behind the Quote:
"If a brother or sister is poorly clothed and lacking in daily food, and one of you says to them, 'Go in peace, be warmed and filled,' without giving them the things needed for the body, what good is that? So also faith by itself, if it does not have works, is dead" (James 2:15-17).

— 84 —

Our prayers and fastings are of less avail,
unless they are aided by almsgiving.

—*Cyprian (d. 258), bishop of Carthage*

Bible Truth Behind the Quote:
What can supercharge our prayers? We ought to do good and share with others (Hebrews 13:16), always help the poor (Matthew 19:21; Luke 11:41; 12:33; 1 John 3:17), give to those who ask (Matthew 5:42), share food with those who are hungry (Isaiah 58:7,10), and share money generously (Romans 12:8).

— 85 —

Lots of people think they are charitable if they give
away their old clothes and things they don't want.

—*Myrtle Reed (1874-1911), American author, poet, and journalist*

Bible Truth Behind the Quote:
We ought always to share our material goods generously (Romans 12:8; Ephesians 4:28).

CHILD OF GOD

— 86 —

Which would you prefer? To be king of the mountain
for a day? Or to be a child of God for eternity?

—*Max Lucado (born 1955), author, minister, Oak Hills Church*

Bible Truth Behind the Quote:
It is better to be a child of God, for as God's children, we have an "inheritance that
is imperishable, undefiled, and unfading, kept in heaven" (1 Peter 1:4). We are "heirs
according to promise" (Galatians 3:29).

CHRIST, DEITY OF

— 87 —

As the print of the seal on the wax is the express
image of the seal itself, so Christ is the express
image—the perfect representation—of God.

—*Ambrose (337-397), bishop of Milan*

Bible Truth Behind the Quote:
Jesus is "the radiance of the glory of God and the exact imprint of his nature" (Hebrews
1:3).

CHRIST, LOVE OF

— 88 —

We are never nearer Christ than when we find ourselves
lost in a holy amazement at His unspeakable love.

—*John Owen (1616-1683), church leader, theologian*

Bible Truth Behind the Quote:
"I am sure that neither death nor life, nor angels nor rulers, nor things present nor things
to come, nor powers, nor height nor depth, nor anything else in all creation, will be able
to separate us from the love of God in Christ Jesus our Lord" (Romans 8:38-39).

CHRISTIANITY

— 89 —

Christianity is not a theory or speculation, but a life;
not a philosophy of life, but a living presence.

—*Samuel Taylor Coleridge (1772-1834), English poet, philosopher*

Bible Truth Behind the Quote:
"Our fellowship is with the Father and with his Son Jesus Christ" (1 John 1:3). We have been "called into the fellowship of his Son, Jesus Christ our Lord" (1 Corinthians 1:9).

— 90 —

Christianity is a kind of love affair with our loving Lord and Savior,
and the more days we turn into spiritual Valentine's Days…
the richer and more joyful the relationship itself will become.

—*J.I. Packer (born 1926), author, theologian*

Bible Truth Behind the Quote:
As Paul put it, "I count everything as loss because of the surpassing worth of knowing Christ Jesus my Lord. For his sake I have suffered the loss of all things and count them as rubbish, in order that I may gain Christ" (Philippians 3:8).

— 91 —

It isn't that Christianity has been tried and found wanting. It
is that it has been found difficult and so never really tried.

—*Gilbert Keith Chesterton (1874-1936), English author, apologist*

Bible Truth Behind the Quote:
Many are exposed to Christianity, but few turn to the Lord. "Enter by the narrow gate. For the gate is wide and the way is easy that leads to destruction, and those who enter by it are many" (Matthew 7:13).

— 92 —

Going to church doesn't make you a Christian any more
than going to a garage makes you an automobile.

—*Billy Sunday (1862-1935), American athlete, evangelist*

Bible Truth Behind the Quote:
"Not everyone who says to me, 'Lord, Lord,' will enter the kingdom of heaven" (Matthew 7:21). "Truly, truly, I say to you, unless one is born again he cannot see the kingdom of God" (John 3:3).

— 93 —

Christianity is not true because it works. It works because it is true.

—*Os Guinness (born 1941), author*

Bible Truth Behind the Quote:
Jesus affirmed, "For this purpose I was born and for this purpose I have come into the world—to bear witness to the truth. Everyone who is of the truth listens to my voice" (John 18:37).

— 94 —

Christianity is the religion of an educated mind.
—*Sir William Ramsay (1852-1916), Scottish chemist*

Bible Truth Behind the Quote:
We are to love God with all our heart, soul, *and mind* (Mark 12:30). Paul said, "Whatever is true…think about these things" (Philippians 4:8). Paul reasoned with the Jews (Acts 17:17).

— 95 —

The Christian philosophy is a philosophy of self-denial, self-control, and self-restraint. The satanic philosophy is a philosophy of "live as you please," "have what you want," "don't let anyone tell you what to do," and "it's your life, you have a right to live it."
—*Bob Jones (1883-1968), American evangelist*

Bible Truth Behind the Quote:
Jesus warned, "Any one of you who does not renounce all that he has cannot be my disciple" (Luke 14:33). "Whoever does not take his cross and follow me is not worthy of me" (Matthew 10:38).

— 96 —

We want gain without pain; we want the resurrection without going through the grave; we want life without experiencing death; we want a crown without going by way of the Cross. But in God's economy, the way up is down.
—*Nancy Leigh DeMoss, author*

Bible Truth Behind the Quote:
Jesus stated, "If anyone would come after me, let him deny himself and take up his cross and follow me" (Matthew 16:24).

— 97 —

Christianity is not devotion to work, or to a cause, or a doctrine, but devotion to a person, the Lord Jesus Christ.
—*Oswald Chambers (1874-1917), author,* My Utmost for His Highest

Bible Truth Behind the Quote:
As Paul put it, "No one can lay a foundation other than that which is laid, which is Jesus Christ" (1 Corinthians 3:11).

— 98 —

Christianity is not the acceptance of certain ideas. It is a personal attitude of trust and devotion to a person.
—*Stephen Neill (1900-1984), Scottish Anglican bishop*

Bible Truth Behind the Quote:
Jesus Himself is the way, the truth, and the life, and no one can have a relationship with God except through Him (John 14:6). "There is one God, and there is one mediator between God and men, the man Christ Jesus" (1 Timothy 2:5).

— 99 —

Christianity is the land of beginning again.
—*W.A. Criswell (1909-2002), pastor, author*

Bible Truth Behind the Quote:
Acts 3:19-20 speaks of repenting, turning "again," having sins blotted out, and then experiencing "times of refreshing." It is an invitation open to all.

— 100 —

Christianity isn't only going to church on Sunday. It is
living twenty-four hours of every day with Jesus Christ.
—*Billy Graham (born 1918), evangelist*

Bible Truth Behind the Quote:
Our daily goal and experience ought to be to know God and Jesus Christ, whom the Father has sent (John 17:3). "There is salvation in no one else, for there is no other name under heaven given among men by which we must be saved" (Acts 4:12).

— 101 —

Religion is humans trying to work their way to God through
good works. Christianity is God coming to men and women
through Jesus Christ, offering them a relationship with himself.
—*Josh McDowell (born 1939), evangelist, author*

Bible Truth Behind the Quote:
Romans 5:8 instructs us that God has concretely demonstrated His love for us in that while we were still sinners, completely unattractive from a moral standpoint, Christ nevertheless came to die for us.

— 102 —

A Christian is, in essence, somebody
personally related to Jesus Christ.
—*John R.W. Stott (born 1921), Anglican clergyman, leader of the worldwide evangelical movement*

Bible Truth Behind the Quote:
Jesus is the very heart of our salvation (John 14:6; Acts 4:12; 1 Timothy 2:5). Without Jesus and His resurrection from the dead, there is no Christianity (see 1 Corinthians 15:17).

— 103 —

I believe in Christianity as I believe that the sun has risen, not
only because I see it, but because by it I see everything else.

—*C.S. Lewis (1898-1963), author, professor, Oxford University*

Bible Truth Behind the Quote:

As Christians, we see the world through renewed minds. "Do not be conformed to this
world, but be transformed by the renewal of your mind" (Romans 12:2).

CHRISTMAS

— 104 —

You can never truly enjoy Christmas until you can look up into
the Father's face and tell him you have received his Christmas gift.

—*John Rice (1895-1980), Baptist evangelist*

Bible Truth Behind the Quote:

The angel instructed Joseph that Mary "will bear a son, and you shall call his name Jesus,
for he will save his people from their sins" (Matthew 1:21). This is the true Christmas story!
Jesus is a gift that keeps on giving.

CHURCH

— 105 —

An isolated Christian is a paralyzed Christian.

—*Fred Babiczuk, Catholic priest*

Bible Truth Behind the Quote:

It is only by fellowshipping with other Christians that we are spiritually built up (Luke
22:32), encouraged (1 Thessalonians 4:18; 5:11), warned (Hebrews 3:13), and loved (John
13:34; Hebrews 13:1; 1 John 4:7).

— 106 —

Christianity is essentially a social religion, and to turn
it into a solitary religion is indeed to destroy it.

—*John Wesley (1703-1791), founder of the Methodist church*

Bible Truth Behind the Quote:

The early believers often "gathered together" for their mutual benefit (Acts 4:31; 12:12;
14:27; 15:6,30; 20:7). Jesus promised, "Where two or three are gathered in my name,
there am I among them" (Matthew 18:20).

— 107 —

An avoidable absence from church is an
infallible evidence of spiritual decay.
—*Frances Ridley Havergal (1836-1879), English poet, hymn writer*

Bible Truth Behind the Quote:
We are not to forsake assembling together at church, but are to regularly meet to encourage one another (Hebrews 10:25).

— 108 —

One of the quickest ways for a pastor to raise needless questions
about his integrity, to become burdened with things unnecessary,
and to be tempted to treat members with partiality is to become
involved in the church's finances. Though the elders are ultimately
responsible, the day-to-day affairs are best left to the deacons.
—*Curtis C. Thomas, pastor, author*

Bible Truth Behind the Quote:
The pastor must never put himself in a situation in which he may be tempted to show partiality, which is offensive to God (see 1 Timothy 5:21; James 2:1,9). The pastor must be "above reproach" (Titus 1:7).

— 109 —

The excellence of the church does not
consist in multitude but in purity.
—*John Calvin (1509-1564), French reformer*

Bible Truth Behind the Quote:
The critical question for the church is not how many, but how holy? The church's ideal is to be without "spot or wrinkle" and "without blemish" (Ephesians 5:27).

— 110 —

The reason why congregations have been so dead is
because they have had dead men preaching to them…
How can dead men beget living children?
—*George Whitefield (1714-1770), itinerant minister, Great Awakening of the 1730s*

Bible Truth Behind the Quote:
A preacher cannot pass on to others that which he does not possess. The biblical pattern is that like produces like (for example, Genesis 1:12). Church leaders must therefore be "trustworthy, above reproach, sober-minded, self-controlled, respectable, hospitable, able to teach, not violent but gentle, not quarrelsome, and not a lover of money" (1 Timothy 3:1-11), so that he can pass these virtues on to the church body.

— 111 —

Depend upon it, as long as the church is living so much like the world, we cannot expect our children to be brought into the fold.
—*Dwight L. Moody (1837-1899), American evangelist*

Bible Truth Behind the Quote:
The resurrected Jesus told one church, "For you say, I am rich, I have prospered, and I need nothing, not realizing that you are wretched, pitiable, poor, blind, and naked" (Revelation 3:17). Such churches will do no spiritual good.

— 112 —

We do not want, as the newspapers say, a church that will move with the world. We want a church that will move the world.
—*Gilbert Keith Chesterton (1874-1936), English author, apologist*

Bible Truth Behind the Quote:
The church is called to witness to the world (Luke 24:45-49; Acts 1:7-8), do good to all people (Galatians 6:10; Titus 3:14), make disciples (Matthew 28:19-20), and preach the Word (Mark 16:15-16; 1 Timothy 4:6,13).

— 113 —

The church's service and mission in the world is absolutely dependent on its being different from the world, being in the world but not of the world.
—*Jim Wallis (born 1948), author, political activist*

Bible Truth Behind the Quote:
Believers are not to be "of the world" (John 17:16). Indeed, "whoever wishes to be a friend of the world makes himself an enemy of God" (James 4:4).

— 114 —

It is right for the Church to be in the world; it is wrong for the world to be in the Church. A boat in water is good; that is what boats are for. However, water inside the boat causes it to sink.
—*Harold Lindsell (1913-1998), author, magazine editor*

Bible Truth Behind the Quote:
Let us not forget that "all that is in the world—the desires of the flesh and the desires of the eyes and pride in possessions—is not from the Father but is from the world" (1 John 2:16). Such things can be a cancer to the church.

— 115 —

The martyrs were bound, imprisoned, scorched, racked, burned, raped, butchered—and they multiplied.
—*Augustine (354-430), bishop of Hippo*

Bible Truth Behind the Quote:
Paul was thrown into prison but affirmed, "What has happened to me has really served to advance the gospel" (Philippians 1:12). "We know that for those who love God all things work together for good, for those who are called according to his purpose" (Romans 8:28).

— 116 —

A look into history will quickly convince any interested person that the true Church has almost always suffered more from prosperity than from poverty. Her times of greatest spiritual power have usually coincided with her periods of indigence and rejection; with wealth came weakness and backsliding.

—*A. W. Tozer (1897-1963), American pastor, author*

Bible Truth Behind the Quote:
Jesus affirmed, "How difficult it is for those who have wealth to enter the kingdom of God" (Luke 18:24).

— 117 —

Churchgoers are like coals in a fire. When they cling together, they keep the flame aglow; when they separate, they die out.

—*Billy Graham (born 1918), evangelist*

Bible Truth Behind the Quote:
The church is the place where we are "mutually encouraged by each other's faith" (Romans 1:12).

— 118 —

Be united with other Christians. A wall with loose bricks is not good. The bricks must be cemented together.

—*Corrie ten Boom (1892-1983), Dutch Christian Holocaust survivor*

Bible Truth Behind the Quote:
Paul exhorts that Christians "agree and that there be no divisions among you, but that you be united in the same mind and the same judgment" (1 Corinthians 1:10).

— 119 —

Biblically the church is an organism not an organization—a movement, not a monument. It is not a part of the community; it is a whole new community. It is not an orderly gathering; it is a new order with new values, often in sharp conflict with the values of the surrounding society.

—*Chuck Colson (born 1931), author, founder of Prison Fellowship*

Bible Truth Behind the Quote:
The church is called a "new man" (Ephesians 2:15), God's household (1 Timothy 3:14-15), and God's temple (1 Corinthians 3:16). It is not "business as usual" in the world.

— 120 —

Nothing will divide the church so much as the love of power.
—*Chrysostom (347-407), early church father*

Bible Truth Behind the Quote:
Third John 1:9 makes reference to "Diotrephes, who likes to put himself first," and who "does not acknowledge our authority." Such an attitude is damaging to churches.

CHURCH ATTENDANCE

— 121 —

Some go to church to take a walk; some go there to laugh and talk.
Some go there to meet a friend; some go there their time to spend.
Some go there to meet a lover; some go there a fault to cover.
Some go there for speculation; some go there for observation.
Some go there to doze and nod; the wise go there to worship God.
—*Charles Spurgeon (1834-1892), pastor, New Park Street Chapel, London*

Bible Truth Behind the Quote:
It is sobering that there are church attendees who "go through the motions" and think they are right with God—but they are not (Matthew 7:21-22). A day of reckoning is coming (2 Corinthians 5:10).

— 122 —

There is nothing more unchristian than a solitary Christian.
—*John Wesley (1703-1791), founder of the Methodist church*

Bible Truth Behind the Quote:
The early Christians "devoted themselves to the apostles' teaching and fellowship" (Acts 2:42).

CHURCH INFLUENCE

— 123 —

I believe that one reason why the church of God at this
present moment has so little influence over the world is
because the world has so much influence over the church.
—*Charles Spurgeon (1834-1892), pastor, New Park Street Chapel, London*

Bible Truth Behind the Quote:
This was a big problem with the church at Corinth. Many of the Christians there were still quite worldly (2 Corinthians 5:1). Scripture reveals that "the world is passing away along with its desires, but whoever does the will of God abides forever" (1 John 2:17). It's one or the other—the world or the will of God.

CHURCH—PERFECT?

— 124 —

If you wait for a perfect church, you must wait until
you get to Heaven; and even if you could find a perfect
assembly on earth, I am sure they would not admit you
to their fellowship, for you are not perfect yourself.

—Anonymous

Bible Truth Behind the Quote:
Even Paul, an apostle and church leader, considered himself the "foremost" among sinners (1 Timothy 1:16; see Romans 7:15-20).

— 125 —

If I had never joined a church till I had found one that was perfect,
I should never have joined one at all. And the moment I did
join it, if I had found one, I should have spoiled it, for it would
not have been a perfect church after I had become a member of
it. Still, imperfect as it is, it is the dearest place on earth to us.

—Charles Spurgeon (1834-1892), pastor, New Park Street Chapel, London

Bible Truth Behind the Quote:
Because of our imperfections, we are to cut each other some slack. Scripture exhorts us to put on "compassion, kindness, humility, meekness, and patience, bearing with one another and, if one has a complaint against another, forgiving each other; as the Lord has forgiven you, so you also must forgive" (Colossians 3:12-13).

CITIZEN OF HEAVEN

— 126 —

If you are a Christian, you are not a citizen of this
world trying to get to heaven; you are a citizen of
heaven making your way through this world.

—Vince Havner (1901-1986), Baptist pastor

Bible Truth Behind the Quote:
The apostle Paul informs us that "our citizenship is in heaven, and from it we await a Savior, the Lord Jesus Christ" (Philippians 3:20). We are on our way to a "better country, that is, a heavenly one" (Hebrews 11:16).

CITIZENSHIP

— 127 —

Whatever makes men good Christians, makes them good citizens.
—Daniel Webster (1782-1852), American statesman

Bible Truth Behind the Quote:
Christians are honest, law-abiding, virtuous people (Romans 13:1; Philippians 4:8; 1 Thessalonians 4:11-12). This makes them good citizens. Our ultimate citizenship is in heaven (Philippians 3:20).

COMFORT

— 128 —

God does not comfort us to make us
comfortable but to make us comforters.
—John Henry Jowett (1864-1923), pastor, Westminster Chapel, London

Bible Truth Behind the Quote:
God "comforts us in all our affliction, so that we may be able to comfort those who are in any affliction, with the comfort with which we ourselves are comforted by God" (2 Corinthians 1:4).

COMMITMENT

— 129 —

The Christian life is not adding Jesus to one's own way of
life but renouncing that personal way of life for His and
being willing to pay whatever cost that may require.
—John MacArthur (born 1939), pastor, Grace Community Church

Bible Truth Behind the Quote:
Jesus warned, "Whoever does not bear his own cross and come after me cannot be my disciple" (Luke 14:27).

— 130 —

God is not moved or impressed with our worship until
our hearts are moved and impressed by Him.

—Kelly Sparks, worship leader

Bible Truth Behind the Quote:
"Oh come, let us worship and bow down; let us kneel before the LORD, our Maker!"
(Psalm 95:6). "Worship the LORD in the splendor of holiness; tremble before him, all the
earth!" (Psalm 96:9).

— 131 —

It is but right that our hearts should be on God,
when the heart of God is so much on us.

—Richard Baxter (1615-1691), English Puritan church leader

Bible Truth Behind the Quote:
God's heart was focused on us even before the world was created (Ephesians 1:4).

— 132 —

Too many of us have a Christian vocabulary
rather than a Christian experience.

—Charles F. Banning

Bible Truth Behind the Quote:
One can even refer to Jesus as "Lord" and yet be unacquainted with Him (Matthew 7:21-
22).

— 133 —

Give me one hundred men who fear nothing but sin and
desire nothing but God, and I care not whether they be
clergymen or laymen, they alone will shake the gates of
Hell and set up the kingdom of Heaven upon the earth.

—John Wesley (1703-1791), founder of the Methodist church

Bible Truth Behind the Quote:
The early apostles were not trained clergy, but under the power of the Holy Spirit, they
were witnesses unto "the end of the earth" (Acts 1:8).

— 134 —

Consume my life, my God, for it is Thine. I seek not
a long life, but a full one, like You, Lord Jesus.

—Jim Elliot (1927-1956), missionary to Ecuador

Bible Truth Behind the Quote:
"Present your bodies as a living sacrifice, holy and acceptable to God" (Romans 12:1).

— 135 —

Lord, I give up all my own plans and purposes, all my own desires
and hopes, and accept Thy will for my life. I give myself, my
life, my all utterly to Thee to be Thine forever. Fill me with Thy
Holy Spirit. Use me as Thou wilt; send me where Thou wilt;
work out Thy whole will in my life at any cost, now and forever.
—*Betty Stam (1907-1934), China Inland mission worker*

Bible Truth Behind the Quote:
This echoes the cry of the psalmist: "I delight to do your will, O my God" (Psalm 40:8).

— 136 —

Christ gave Himself up entirely for you: therefore
must your life be dedicated entirely to Him.
—*Erich Sauer (1898-1959), Wiedenest Bible School, West Germany*

Bible Truth Behind the Quote:
With one foot in the world and one foot in God's kingdom, a partial dedication will not
do (see 1 Kings 3:3; 22:43; Luke 16:13). Our dedication must be total (Luke 9:62).

COMPASSION

— 137 —

Though our Savior's passion is over, his compassion is not.
—*William Penn (1644-1718), English Quaker, founder of Pennsylvania*

Bible Truth Behind the Quote:
Scripture assures us that Jesus understands all our weaknesses, and shows continuous
compassion toward us (see Matthew 9:36; 14:14; 15:32; Mark 6:34). Because of what
Jesus has done for us at the cross, Scripture exhorts, "Let us then with confidence draw
near to the throne of grace, that we may receive mercy and find grace to help in time of
need" (Hebrews 4:16).

CONFESSION

— 138 —

The way to cover our sin is to uncover it by confession.
—*Richard Sibbes (1577-1635), English theologian*

Bible Truth Behind the Quote:
We are promised, "If we confess our sins, he is faithful and just to forgive us our sins and to cleanse us from all unrighteousness" (1 John 1:9).

— 139 —

The confession of evil works is the first beginning of good works.
—*Augustine (354-430), bishop of Hippo*

Bible Truth Behind the Quote:
"I said, 'I will confess my transgressions to the LORD,' and you forgave the iniquity of my sin" (Psalm 32:5).

CONSCIENCE

— 140 —

I would bear any affliction rather than be
burdened with a guilty conscience.
—*Charles Spurgeon (1834-1892), pastor, New Park Street Chapel, London*

Bible Truth Behind the Quote:
Sin can deeply wound the conscience (1 Corinthians 8:12). A clear conscience comes by obedience (Romans 13:5).

— 141 —

Peace of conscience is nothing but the echo of pardoning mercy.
—*William Gurnall (1617-1679), English author*

Bible Truth Behind the Quote:
The merciful work of Christ can cleanse us from an evil conscience (Hebrews 10:22).

— 142 —

Happy is he who can put away from him all that
may defile his conscience or burden it.
—*Thomas à Kempis (1380-1471), author,* The Imitation of Christ

Bible Truth Behind the Quote:
Scripture speaks of the importance of a "good conscience" (1 Peter 3:16) and a "clear conscience" (Hebrews 13:18). Scripture also warns of the danger of a wounded conscience (1 Corinthians 8:12) and a seared conscience (1 Timothy 4:2).

— 143 —

A good conscience and a good confidence go together.
—*Thomas Brooks (1608-1680), minister, London*

Bible Truth Behind the Quote:
Part of Paul's confidence in his ministry work was rooted in a clear conscience (2 Corinthians 1:12).

— 144 —

Count not of great importance who is for you, or against you, but let this be your aim and care, that God be with you in everything you do. Have a good conscience, and God shall defend you.
—*Thomas à Kempis (1380-1471), author,* The Imitation of Christ

Bible Truth Behind the Quote:
Romans 8:31 exhorts, "If God is for us, who can be against us?" Psalm 28:7 likewise exhorts, "The Lord is my strength and my shield."

— 145 —

A good conscience is a mine of wealth. And in truth, of what greater riches can there be, what thing more sweet than a good conscience?
—*Bernard of Clairvaux (1090-1153), Frankish abbot*

Bible Truth Behind the Quote:
We are exhorted to hold on to "faith and a good conscience" (1 Timothy 1:19).

— 146 —

You ought so to order yourself in every act and thought, as if today you were on the point to die. If you had a good conscience you would not greatly fear death.
—*Thomas à Kempis (1380-1471), author,* The Imitation of Christ

Bible Truth Behind the Quote:
Paul affirmed, "We are of good courage, and we would rather be away from the body and at home with the Lord" (2 Corinthians 5:8). Paul was ready!

— 147 —

No torment in the world is comparable to an accusing conscience.
—*William Gurnall (1617-1679), English author*

Bible Truth Behind the Quote:
In Scripture we read of "grief or pangs of conscience" (1 Samuel 25:31). Such can be avoided by obedience to God (Romans 13:5).

— 148 —

My conscience is captive to the Word of God.
—*Martin Luther (1483-1546), priest, professor of theology, reformer*

Bible Truth Behind the Quote:
Paul said, "I always take pains to have a clear conscience toward both God and man" (Acts 24:16).

— 149 —

That man can never have good days that keep an evil conscience.
—*Benjamin Keach (1640-1704), Particular Baptist preacher, London*

Bible Truth Behind the Quote:
Scripture warns of those who, with a damaged conscience, have made a shipwreck of their faith (1 Timothy 1:19).

— 150 —

The best tranquilizer is a clear conscience.
—*Anonymous*

Bible Truth Behind the Quote:
The person who is truly blessed is the one who avoids sin and delights in God's Word (Psalm 1:1-3).

— 151 —

Conscience is God's sergeant He employs to arrest the sinner.
Now the sergeant hath no power to release his prisoner upon
any private composition between him and the prisoner; but
listens, whether the debt be fully paid, or the creditor be fully
satisfied; then, and not till then he is discharged of his prisoner.
—*William Gurnall (1617-1679), English author*

Bible Truth Behind the Quote:
It is only through Jesus that our conscience can be purified (Hebrews 9:14).

— 152 —

The conscience is to our souls what pain sensors are
to our bodies: it inflicts distress, in the form of guilt,
whenever we violate what our hearts tell us is right.
—*John MacArthur (born 1939), pastor, Grace Community Church*

Bible Truth Behind the Quote:
A wounded conscience can cause grief (1 Samuel 25:31). However, as Paul notes, we can be grieved into repenting (2 Corinthians 7:9), which is what we all ought to do.

— 153 —

A good conscience will be found a pleasant
visitor at our bedside in a dying hour.
—*J.C. Ryle (1816-1900), Anglican bishop, Liverpool*

Bible Truth Behind the Quote:
Paul, near death and with a clean conscience, could say, "I have fought the good fight, I
have finished the race, I have kept the faith" (2 Timothy 4:7).

— 154 —

A regular diet of Scripture will strengthen a weak
conscience or restrain an overactive one. Conversely,
error, human wisdom, and wrong moral influences filling
the mind will corrupt or cripple the conscience.
—*John MacArthur (born 1939), pastor, Grace Community Church*

Bible Truth Behind the Quote:
The psalmist said, "I have stored up your word in my heart, that I might not sin against
you" (Psalm 119:11).

CONSEQUENCES

— 155 —

If a man gets drunk and goes out and breaks his leg so that
it must be amputated, God will forgive him if he asks it,
but he will have to hop around on one leg all his life.
—*Dwight L. Moody (1837-1899), evangelist*

Bible Truth Behind the Quote:
David was forgiven of his sin with Bathsheba, but he still paid a heavy price for his disobedience (2 Samuel 12:10).

CONSISTENCY

— 156 —

Consistency:
It's the jewel worth·wearing;
It's the anchor worth weighing;
It's the thread worth weaving;
It's a battle worth winning.
—*Charles Swindoll (born 1934), pastor, Stonebriar Community Church*

Bible Truth Behind the Quote:
"Oh that my ways may be steadfast in keeping your statutes! Then I shall not be put to shame, having my eyes fixed on all your commandments" (Psalm 119:5-6).

CONTAMINATION

— 157 —

Nothing is more dangerous than associating with the ungodly.
—*John Calvin (1509-1564), French reformer*

Bible Truth Behind the Quote:
"Blessed is the man who walks not in the counsel of the wicked, nor stands in the way of sinners, nor sits in the seat of scoffers" (Psalm 1:1).

CONVERSION

— 158 —

Every generation needs a re-generation.
—*Charles Spurgeon (1834-1892), pastor, New Park Street Chapel, London*

Bible Truth Behind the Quote:
Jesus' words to Nicodemus are just as relevant to us as to him. He said, "Truly, truly, I say to you, unless one is born again he cannot see the kingdom of God" (John 3:3).

— 159 —

I felt my heart strangely warmed, I feel I did trust in
Christ, Christ alone, for salvation; an assurance was
given me that he had taken away my sins, even mine,
and saved me from the law of sin and death.
—*John Wesley (1703-1791), founder of the Methodist church*

Bible Truth Behind the Quote:
"Since we have been justified by faith, we have peace with God through our Lord Jesus Christ" (Romans 5:1). Peace with God warms the heart.

— 160 —

He who made us also remade us.
—*Augustine (354-430), bishop of Hippo*

Bible Truth Behind the Quote:
We have become saved "not because of works done by us in righteousness, but according to his own mercy, by the washing of regeneration and renewal of the Holy Spirit" (Titus 3:5).

CONVICTIONS

— 161 —

When principles that run against your deepest convictions begin to win the day, then battle is your calling, and peace has become sin; you must, at the price of dearest peace, lay your convictions bare before friend and enemy, with all the fire of your faith.

—*Abraham Kuyper (1837-1920), Dutch theologian*

Bible Truth Behind the Quote:
Don't back down from doing what is right in the sight of the Lord (Deuteronomy 6:18; 12:25,28; 21:9; 1 Kings 11:38; Psalm 119:121; 2 Corinthians 13:7).

COOPERATION

— 162 —

We must learn to live together as brothers or perish together as fools.

—*Martin Luther King, Jr. (1929-1968), clergyman, activist in the African-American Civil Rights Movement*

Bible Truth Behind the Quote:
Racism is absolutely against the will of God, for God "made from one man every nation of mankind to live on all the face of the earth" (Acts 17:26). Moreover, God's redeemed will come from "every tribe and language and people and nation" (Revelation 5:9).

COVETOUSNESS

— 163 —

One can be covetous when he has little, much, or anything between, for covetousness comes from the heart, not from the circumstances of life.

—*Charles Ryrie (born 1925), theologian, Dallas Theological Seminary*

Bible Truth Behind the Quote:
We must ever be on the watch for greed (Proverbs 21:26; Luke 12:15) and the love of money (1 Timothy 3:3). It is a cancer to one's soul.

CRITICISM

— 164 —

Criticism is often a form of self-boasting.

—*Anonymous*

Bible Truth Behind the Quote:
Jesus urges us to first take the log out of our own eye before trying to take the speck out of someone else's (Luke 6:41-42).

CROSS

— 165 —

The purpose of the cross is to repair the irreparable.

—*Erwin Lutzer (born 1941), pastor, Moody Church, Chicago*

Bible Truth Behind the Quote:
"For our sake he made him to be sin who knew no sin, so that in him we might become the righteousness of God" (2 Corinthians 5:21). We've been repaired!

CRUCIFIED WITH CHRIST

— 166 —

Christ died to save us from hell but not to save us from the cross. He died so that we could be glorified, but not to keep us from being crucified...For the Christian the cross of Christ is not merely a past place of substitution. It is also a present place of daily execution.

—*John Piper (born 1936), Evangelical Calvinist preacher, author*

Bible Truth Behind the Quote:
Paul speaks of "the cross of our Lord Jesus Christ, by which the world has been crucified to me, and I to the world" (Galatians 6:14).

— 167 —

There was a day when I died to George Müller; his opinions and preferences, tastes and will; died to the world, its approval or censure; died to the approval or blame even of my brethren or friends; and since then I have striven only to show myself approved unto God.

—*George Müller (1805-1898), director of orphanages in Bristol, England*

Bible Truth Behind the Quote:
"Those who belong to Christ Jesus have crucified the flesh with its passions and desires" (Galatians 5:24).

DARKNESS TO LIGHT

— 168 —

The Lord has turned all our sunsets into sunrise.

—Clement of Alexandria (150 -215), theologian, philosopher

Bible Truth Behind the Quote:
In reference to the first coming of Christ, Scripture reveals that "the people dwelling in darkness have seen a great light…on them a light has dawned" (Matthew 4:16). Today we are privileged to follow Jesus, the light of the world (John 8:12).

DEATH AND DYING

— 169 —

If anyone cannot set his mind at rest by disregarding
death, that man should know that he has not yet
gone far enough in the faith of Christ.

—John Calvin (1509-1564), French reformer

Bible Truth Behind the Quote:
"O death, where is your victory? O death, where is your sting?" (1 Corinthians 15:55). Paul tells us that death will be swallowed up in victory (verse 54).

— 170 —

The best of all is, God is with us. Farewell! Farewell!

—Upon his deathbed, John Wesley (1703-1791), founder of the Methodist church

Bible Truth Behind the Quote:
"Even though I walk through the valley of the shadow of death, I will fear no evil, for you are with me" (Psalm 23:4).

— 171 —

We may positively state that nobody has made any progress in the
school of Christ, unless he cheerfully looks forward towards the
day of his death, and towards the day of the final resurrection.

—John Calvin (1509-1564), French reformer

Bible Truth Behind the Quote:
Paul said, "For to me to live is Christ, and to die is gain…My desire is to depart and be with Christ, for that is far better" (Philippians 1:21,23).

— 172 —

All death can do to the believer is deliver him to Jesus.
It brings us into the eternal presence of our Savior.

—*John MacArthur (born 1939), pastor, Grace Community Church*

Bible Truth Behind the Quote:
Paul affirmed, "We would rather be away from the body and at home with the Lord" (2 Corinthians 5:8).

— 173 —

There are no U-Hauls behind hearses.

—*John Piper (born 1936), Evangelical Calvinist preacher, author*

Bible Truth Behind the Quote:
"We brought nothing into the world, and we cannot take anything out of the world" (1 Timothy 6:7).

— 174 —

It is remarkable that the Holy Spirit has given us very few deathbed scenes in the book of God. We have very few in the Old Testament, fewer still in the New. And I take it that the reason may be, because the Holy Ghost would have us to take more account of how we live than how we die, for life is the main business. He who learns to die daily while he lives will find it no difficulty to breathe out his soul for the last time into the hands of his faithful Creator.

—*Charles Spurgeon (1834-1892), pastor, New Park Street Chapel, London*

Bible Truth Behind the Quote:
Without fear, Paul—speaking of his death—said, "the time of my departure has come" (2 Timothy 4:6). Paul's attitude is an example to us.

— 175 —

And thou, most kind and gentle death,
waiting to hush our latest breath;
O praise Him—Alleluia!
Thou leadest home the child of God
And Christ our Lord the way hath trod.

—*St. Francis of Assisi (1181-1226), founder of Franciscans*

Bible Truth Behind the Quote:
Jesus is "the firstborn from the dead" (Colossians 1:18), leading the way for us.

— 176 —

Men have been helped to live by remembering that they must die.

Charles Spurgeon (1834-1892), pastor, New Park Street Chapel, London

Bible Truth Behind the Quote:
Psalm 90:12 informs us that by numbering our days, we gain a heart of wisdom. The psalmist prayed, "O LORD, make me know my end and what is the measure of my days; let me know how fleeting I am!" (Psalm 39:4).

— 177 —

Death is God's delightful way of giving us life.
—*Oswald Chambers (1874-1917), author,* My Utmost for His Highest

Bible Truth Behind the Quote:
"This is the promise that he made to us—eternal life" (1 John 2:25).

— 178 —

Eighty-six years I have served him, and he has done me no wrong. How can I blaspheme my King who has saved me?
—*To his executioners, who were telling him to recant or die,*
St. Polycarp (69-155), second century Christian bishop of Smyrna

Bible Truth Behind the Quote:
"Be faithful unto death, and I will give you the crown of life" (Revelation 2:10).

— 179 —

A saint was once dying, and another who sat
by him said, "Farewell, brother, I shall never
see you again in the land of the living."
"Oh," said the dying man, "I shall see you
again in the land of the living, where I am
going. This is the land of the dying."
—*Charles Spurgeon (1834-1892), pastor, New Park Street Chapel, London*

Bible Truth Behind the Quote:
Speaking of believers in heaven, Jesus said to some Jewish leaders that God "is not God of the dead, but of the living" (Matthew 22:32). Heaven is the land of the living.

— 180 —

All the care in the world will not make us continue a
minute beyond the time God has appointed.
—*J.C. Ryle (1816-1900), Anglican bishop, Liverpool*

Bible Truth Behind the Quote:
"In your book were written, every one of them, the days that were formed for me, when as yet there was none of them" (Psalm 139:16). "My times are in your hand" (Psalm 31:15).

— 181 —

Your last breath here will instantaneously give place to
deathless life, complete healing, and exquisite joy there.
The last earthly shadow will melt in the cloudless glory-
light of a better world. What we call "the valley of the
shadow" here on this side is so bright with light from the
other side, that as soon as we enter it, darkness vanishes.

—*J. Sidlow Baxter (1903-1999), pastor, theologian*

Bible Truth Behind the Quote:
Jesus has delivered us from the fear and the sting of death (1 Corinthians 15:55; Hebrews
2:15).

— 182 —

Death should not be viewed as a terminus but as a tunnel leading
into an ampler and incredibly more wonderful and beautiful
world. The death of a believer is a transition, not a final condition.

—*J. Oswald Sanders (1902-1992), director, Overseas Missionary Fellowship*

Bible Truth Behind the Quote:
"He will wipe away every tear from their eyes, and death shall be no more, neither shall
there be mourning, nor crying, nor pain anymore, for the former things have passed
away" (Revelation 21:4).

— 183 —

Never fear dying, beloved. Dying is the last, but the
least matter that a Christian has to be anxious about.
Fear living—that is a hard battle to fight, a stern
discipline to endure, a rough voyage to undergo.

—*Charles Spurgeon (1834-1892), pastor, New Park Street Chapel, London*

Bible Truth Behind the Quote:
Life on earth involves a constant battle with three enemies: the world, the flesh, and the
devil (see 1 John 2:16). Death releases us from all this (Revelation 21:4).

— 184 —

For Christians, death on its earthward side is simply that
the tired mortal body falls temporarily to sleep, while
on the heavenward side we suddenly find ourselves
with our dear Savior-King and with other Christian
loved ones in the heavenly home. Why fear that?

—*J. Sidlow Baxter (1903-1999), pastor, theologian*

Bible Truth Behind the Quote:
We look forward to both a resurrection (1 Corinthians 15:50-55) and a reunion with Christian loved ones (1 Thessalonians 4:13-17). Nothing to fear there!

— 185 —

Let dissolution come when it will, it can do the Christian no harm, for it will be but a passage out of her prison into a palace; out of a sea of troubles into a haven of rest; out of a crowd of enemies into an innumerable company of true, loving and faithful friends; out of shame, reproach and contempt, into exceeding great and eternal glory.

—*John Bunyan (1628-1688), English Christian writer, preacher*

Bible Truth Behind the Quote:
We will one day have a grand and glorious reunion with all our Christian loved ones and friends who have passed on (1 Thessalonians 4:13-17).

— 186 —

For those who trust Jesus Christ, death is not a sheriff dragging us off to court, but a servant ushering us into the presence of a loving Lord.

—*Haddon Robinson, professor, Gordon-Conwell Theological Seminary*

Bible Truth Behind the Quote:
To be away from the body at the moment of death is to instantly be at home with the Lord (and Christian loved ones) in heaven (2 Corinthians 5:8).

— 187 —

It's not so much I'm afraid of death as dying.

—*Joni Eareckson Tada (born 1949), founder, Joni and Friends*

Bible Truth Behind the Quote:
Though the process of dying may seem frightening, once we pass through that door, we will be able to experientially say that truly the Lord has taken the stinger out of death (1 Corinthians 15:55).

— 188 —

Heaven and hell are not places far away. You may be in heaven before the clock ticks again, it is so near. Oh, that we, instead of trifling about such things because they seem so far away, would solemnly realize them, since they are so very near! This very day, before the sun goes down, some hearer now sitting in this place may see the realities of heaven or hell.

—*Charles Spurgeon (1834-1892), pastor, New Park Street Chapel, London*

Bible Truth Behind the Quote:
Ecclesiastes 7:2 tells us, "Death is the destiny of every man; the living should take this to heart" (NIV). James 4:14 affirms, "You do not know what tomorrow will bring. What is your life? For you are a mist that appears for a little time and then vanishes."

— 189 —

Death is a mighty leveler.
—*J.C. Ryle (1816-1900), Anglican bishop, Liverpool*

Bible Truth Behind the Quote:
"Death is the destiny of every man" (Ecclesiastes 7:2 NIV). Whether one is rich or poor, black or white, fat or thin, death encroaches upon all.

— 190 —

Nothing is so certain as death, and nothing
is so uncertain as the hour of death.
—*Augustine (354-430), bishop of Hippo*

Bible Truth Behind the Quote:
While death is the "destiny of every man" (Ecclesiastes 7:2 NIV), we do not know when the specific day will come (James 4:14). Thus, we must always be ready (Psalm 39:4)!

— 191 —

The very happiest persons I have ever met with have been
departing believers. The only people for whom I have felt any
envy have been dying members of this very church, whose
hands I have grasped in their passing away. Almost without
exception I have seen in them holy delight and triumph.
—*Charles Spurgeon (1834-1892), pastor, New Park Street Chapel, London*

Bible Truth Behind the Quote:
Scripture affirms, "*We are of good courage*, and we would rather be away from the body and at home with the Lord" (2 Corinthians 5:8).

— 192 —

Weep not for me but for yourselves.
—*John Bunyan (1628-1688), English Christian writer, preacher*

Bible Truth Behind the Quote:
As Christians, we do not "grieve as others do who have no hope" (1 Thessalonians 4:13). Weep for unbelievers!

— 193 —

The best moment of a Christian's life is his last one,
because it is the one that is nearest heaven.

—Anonymous

Bible Truth Behind the Quote:
Paul said it best, "My desire is to depart and be with Christ, for that is far better" (Philippians 1:23).

— 194 —

The foolish fear death as the greatest of evils, the wise
desire it as a rest after labors and the end of ills.

—Ambrose (337-397), bishop of Milan

Bible Truth Behind the Quote:
Christians who die will indeed "rest from their labors" (Revelation 14:13)

— 195 —

Death is only a grim porter to let us into a stately palace.

—Richard Sibbes (1577-1635), English theologian

Bible Truth Behind the Quote:
Death is the last enemy to be conquered (1 Corinthians 15:26), but it is an enemy that has been disarmed (verse 55).

— 196 —

How pleasantly does the good man speak of dying;
as if it were but undressing and going to bed!

—Matthew Henry (1662-1714), Bible commentator, Presbyterian minister

Bible Truth Behind the Quote:
We see this attitude reflected in both Paul (Philippians 1:21) and Peter (2 Peter 1:15).

— 197 —

The moment you come into this world
you are beginning to go out of it.

—Anonymous

Bible Truth Behind the Quote:
Scripture reveals that "death spread to all men because all sinned" (Romans 5:12). Following birth, the gradual process of death begins.

— 198 —

A Christian knows that death shall be the funeral of all
his sins, his sorrows, his afflictions, his temptations, his
vexations, his oppressions, his persecutions. He knows
that death shall be the resurrection of all his hopes, his
joys, his delights, his comforts, his contentments.

—*Thomas Brooks (1608-1680), minister, London*

Bible Truth Behind the Quote:
Following death, we will be tearless, deathless, and pain-free (Revelation 21:4).

DEATH, MOMENT OF

— 199 —

I am going into eternity, and it is sweet for me to think of eternity.

—*Upon his deathbed, David Brainerd (1718-1747), missionary to Native Americans*

Bible Truth Behind the Quote:
God "has put eternity into man's heart" (Ecclesiastes 3:11). Believers will spend all eternity in heaven. "In your presence there is fullness of joy; at your right hand are pleasures forevermore" (Psalm 16:11).

— 200 —

Children, when I am gone, sing a song of praise to God.

—*Upon her deathbed, Susanna Wesley (1669-1742),*
mother of John and Charles Wesley

Bible Truth Behind the Quote:
No matter what the circumstances are, "let us continually offer up a sacrifice of praise to God" (Hebrews 13:15).

— 201 —

If this is dying, it is the pleasantest thing imaginable.

—*Upon her deathbed, Lady Glenorchy (1741-1786), patroness of missionary work, Scotland*

Bible Truth Behind the Quote:
Glenorchy knew well the words of Christ: "Where I am, there will my servant be also" (John 12:26). She departed the body and was instantly at home with her Lord (2 Corinthians 5:8).

— 202 —

I know I am dying, but my deathbed is a bed of roses. I have no
thorns planted upon my dying pillow. Heaven is already begun.

—*Upon his deathbed, John Pawson, Eighteenth-century Christian leader*

Bible Truth Behind the Quote:
Christ has taken the stinger out of death (1 Corinthians 15:55).

— 203 —

This is glorious! Earth recedes, Heaven
is opening, God is calling me.
—*Upon his deathbed, Dwight L. Moody (1837-1899), evangelist*

Bible Truth Behind the Quote:
"No eye has seen, no ear has heard, no mind has conceived what God has prepared for those who love him" (1 Corinthians 2:9 NIV).

DEFEAT

— 204 —

Collapse in the Christian life is seldom a
blowout; it is usually a slow leak.
—*Paul Little (1928-1975), evangelist, InterVarsity Christian Fellowship*

Bible Truth Behind the Quote:
David experienced a slow moral leak. He first committed fornication in his heart when he watched Bathsheba from the rooftop. Then he committed physical adultery. Then he tried to deceive Bathsheba's husband into sleeping with her. Then he sent her husband to the front line of a battle so he'd surely die (2 Samuel 11).

DEPENDABILITY

— 205 —

The greatest ability is dependability.
—*Bob Jones (1883-1968), American evangelist*

Bible Truth Behind the Quote:
We ought to be faithful to the end (Hebrews 3:14), even in small matters (Luke 16:10). We must always stand true to what we believe (1 Corinthians 16:13).

DEPENDENCE ON GOD

— 206 —

We become independent of our fear of social judgment and the
disapproval of men in proportion to our dependence on God.
—*Paul Tournier (1898-1986), Swiss physician, author*

Bible Truth Behind the Quote:
Paul asked, "Am I now seeking the approval of man, or of God? Or am I trying to please man? If I were still trying to please man, I would not be a servant of Christ" (Galatians 1:10).

Dependence on the Spirit

— 207 —

Before Christ sent the church into the world, he sent the Spirit into the church. The same order must be observed today.

—*John Stott (born 1921), Anglican clergyman*

Bible Truth Behind the Quote:
Before the mighty ministry that began in Acts 2, Jesus promised His followers: "You will receive power when the Holy Spirit has come upon you, and you will be my witnesses in Jerusalem and in all Judea and Samaria, and to the end of the earth" (Acts 1:8).

Devil

— 208 —

If you do not submit to God, you never will resist the devil. And you will remain constantly under his tyrannical power. Which shall be your master, God or devil? One of these must. No man is without a master.

—*Charles Spurgeon (1834-1892), pastor, New Park Street Chapel, London*

Bible Truth Behind the Quote:
James 4:7 exhorts, "Submit yourselves therefore to God. Resist the devil, and he will flee from you."

— 209 —

The best means of resisting the devil is to destroy whatever of the world remains in us, in order to raise for God, upon its ruins, a building all of love. Then shall we begin, in this fleeting life, to love God as we shall love him in eternity.

—*John Wesley (1703-1791), founder of the Methodist church*

Bible Truth Behind the Quote:
We are exhorted, "You shall love the Lord your God with all your heart and with all your soul and with all your mind" (Matthew 22:37).

— 210 —

There are two equal and opposite errors into which our race can
fall about the devils. One is to disbelieve in their existence. The
other is to believe, and to feel an excessive and unhealthy interest
in them. They themselves are equally pleased by both errors.

—*C.S. Lewis (1898-1963), author, professor, Oxford University*

Bible Truth Behind the Quote:
Beware the "schemes of the devil" (Ephesians 6:11). He is the father of lies and is a master deceiver (John 8:44).

— 211 —

As the most dangerous winds may enter at little openings,
so the devil never enters more dangerously than by little
unobserved incidents, which seem to be nothing, yet
insensibly open the heart to great temptations.

—*John Wesley (1703-1791), founder of the Methodist church*

Bible Truth Behind the Quote:
Never forget the catastrophic chain of events that followed David's initial peek at Bathsheba from the rooftop (2 Samuel 11:2).

— 212 —

It is Satan's custom by small sins to draw us to
greater, as the little sticks set the great ones on fire,
and a wisp of straw kindles a block of wood.

—*Thomas Manton (1620-1667), English Puritan clergyman*

Bible Truth Behind the Quote:
We should be careful to "not be outwitted by Satan; for we are not ignorant of his designs" (2 Corinthians 2:11).

— 213 —

An unbridled tongue is the chariot of the
devil, wherein he rides in triumph.

—*Edward Reyner (1600-1660), English clergyman, devotional writer*

Bible Truth Behind the Quote:
The tongue, though small, can cause a world of trouble (James 3:5-8).

— 214 —

The devil does most when men are doing least.

—*Anonymous*

Bible Truth Behind the Quote:
The Bible clearly warns against idle lives (2 Thessalonians 3:11; see also Proverbs 21:25; Ecclesiastes 4:5).

— 215 —

I am a great enemy to flies. When I have a good book,
they flock upon it and parade up and down upon it
and soil it. Tis just the same with the devil. When
our hearts are purest, he comes and soils them.
—*Martin Luther (1483-1546), priest, professor of theology, reformer*

Bible Truth Behind the Quote:
Satan accuses and slanders (Job 1:6-11; Revelation 12:10), fosters spiritual pride (1 Timothy 3:6), instigates jealousy (James 3:13-16), plants doubt in minds (Genesis 3:1-5), and tempts to immorality (1 Corinthians 7:5).

— 216 —

Satan fails to speak of the remorse, the futility, the loneliness, and
the spiritual devastation which go hand in hand with immorality.
—*Billy Graham (born 1918), evangelist*

Bible Truth Behind the Quote:
The unrighteous have many sorrows (Psalm 32:10; Luke 6:25). Godly sorrow experienced by Christians, however, can bring repentance (2 Corinthians 7:10).

— 217 —

The devil loves to fish in troubled waters.
—*John Trapp (1601-1669), English Anglican Bible commentator*

Bible Truth Behind the Quote:
A situation where anger is present, for example, constitutes "troubled waters" in which the devil loves to fish (Ephesians 4:26-27).

— 218 —

It is an old policy the devil hath, to jostle
out a greater good by a less.
—*Nehemiah Rogers, pastor, Essex*

Bible Truth Behind the Quote:
We must constantly be alert to the devil's schemes (Ephesians 6:11). We should be careful to "not be outwitted by Satan; for we are not ignorant of his designs" (2 Corinthians 2:11).

— 219 —

Till we sin, Satan is a parasite; but when once we
are in the devil's hands, he turns tyrant.

—*Thomas Manton (1620-1667), English Puritan clergyman*

Bible Truth Behind the Quote:

The devil is like a lion seeking to devour Christians (1 Peter 5:8). This lion finds it easiest to attack weak prey (Christians who have sinned).

— 220 —

The devil does not tempt unbelievers and
sinners who are already his own.

—*Thomas à Kempis (1380-1471), author,* The Imitation of Christ

Bible Truth Behind the Quote:

The two references to "tempter" in the Bible are in reference to Christ (Matthew 4:3) and to Christians (1 Thessalonians 3:5).

— 221 —

When the devil is called the god of this world, it is not because
he made it, but because we serve him with our worldliness.

—*Thomas Aquinas (1225-1274), Italian philosopher, theologian*

Bible Truth Behind the Quote:

The devil is "the ruler of this world" (John 12:31) and the "god of this world" (2 Corinthians 4:4) by virtue of his global evil influence and control.

— 222 —

If you give the devil an inch, he will try to become your ruler.

—*Anonymous*

Bible Truth Behind the Quote:

Scripture speaks of those who have succumbed to "the snare of the devil, after being captured by him to do his will" (2 Timothy 2:26). Resist him (James 4:7).

— 223 —

I know well that when Christ is nearest, Satan is also busiest.

—*Robert Murray M'Cheyne (1813-1843), minister, Church of Scotland*

Bible Truth Behind the Quote:

The church at Smyrna stood strong for Christ, and Christ subsequently warned the church, "The devil is about to throw some of you into prison, that you may be tested...Be faithful unto death, and I will give you the crown of life" (Revelation 2:10).

DEVIL'S LIES

— 224 —

Whom the devil cannot deceive, he tries to destroy, and
whom he cannot destroy, he attempts to deceive.

—*Ray Stedman (1917-1992), pastor, Peninsula Bible Church*

Bible Truth Behind the Quote:
The devil "was a murderer from the beginning, and has nothing to do with the truth, because there is no truth in him. When he lies, he speaks out of his own character, for he is a liar and the father of lies" (John 8:44).

DIFFICULTIES

— 225 —

Difficulties provide a platform on which
the Lord can display His power.

—*J. Hudson Taylor (1832-1905), founder, China Inland Mission*

Bible Truth Behind the Quote:
"The Lord knows how to rescue the godly from trials" (2 Peter 2:9). "Call upon me in the day of trouble; I will deliver you, and you shall glorify me" (Psalm 50:15).

— 226 —

Many men owe the grandeur of their lives
to their tremendous difficulties.

—*Charles Spurgeon (1834-1892), pastor, New Park Street Chapel, London*

Bible Truth Behind the Quote:
We can count it joy when we encounter difficulties, for such difficulties can be used by God to build endurance in our lives (James 1:2-4).

DILIGENCE

— 227 —

The leading rule for a man of every calling is diligence;
never put off until tomorrow what you can do today.

—*Abraham Lincoln (1809-1865); sixteenth President of the United States*

Bible Truth Behind the Quote:
We are to be strong and steady (1 Corinthians 15:58) and never tire of doing good (Galatians 6:9). And whatever we do, we are to do well (Ecclesiastes 9:10).

Disappointments

— 228 —

I read of a Christian who said, "I used to have many
disappointments, until I changed one letter of the word
and chopped it in two, so that instead of 'disappointments,'
I read it, 'his appointments.' That was a wonderful
change, for 'disappointments' break your heart, but
'his appointments' you accept cheerfully."

—*Charles Spurgeon (1834-1892), pastor, New Park Street Chapel, London*

Bible Truth Behind the Quote:
For those who love God, all things work together for good under His sovereign providential control (Romans 8:28).

Discernment

— 229 —

He that knows nothing will believe anything.

—*Thomas Fuller (1608-1661), English churchman, historian*

Bible Truth Behind the Quote:
We all ought to pray for a discerning heart (1 Kings 3:9; Psalm 119:125).

— 230 —

Our scientific power has outrun our spiritual power.
We have guided missiles and misguided men.

—*Martin Luther King, Jr. (1929-1968), clergyman,
activist in the African-American Civil Rights Movement*

Bible Truth Behind the Quote:
Tragically, many people "have neither knowledge nor understanding, they walk about in darkness" (Psalm 82:5). Wicked rulers are extremely dangerous (Proverbs 28:15). We ought to resolve to pray for our government leaders (1 Timothy 2:1-2).

Discipline, God's

— 231 —

We often learn more of God under the rod that
strikes us, than under the staff that comforts us.

—*Stephen Charnock (1628-1680), Puritan clergyman*

Bible Truth Behind the Quote:
It was after God physically disciplined David for his sin with Bathsheba (Psalm 51:8) that David finally turned back to God. The psalmist prayed, "It is good for me that I was afflicted, that I might learn your statutes" (Psalm 119:71).

— 232 —

When we are chastened we must pray to be taught, and
look into the law as the best expositor of providence. It is
not the chastening itself that does good, but the teaching
that goes along with it and is the exposition of it.
—*Matthew Henry (1662-1714), Bible commentator, Presbyterian minister*

Bible Truth Behind the Quote:
Blessed are those God corrects (Job 5:17; Psalm 94:12) and those who submit to His Word (John 8:51; 1 John 2:17).

— 233 —

You will either respond to God's light or
you will respond to His heat.
—*Anonymous*

Bible Truth Behind the Quote:
"The Lord disciplines the one he loves, and chastises every son whom he receives" (Hebrews 12:6). If we do not respond in obedience to the light in God's Word, then God—because He loves us—may apply a little disciplinary heat.

— 234 —

We ought as much to pray for a blessing upon
our daily rod as upon our daily bread.
—*John Owen (1616-1683), church leader, theologian*

Bible Truth Behind the Quote:
The Lord disciplines us only because we need it (Psalm 119:75).

— 235 —

By chastening, the Lord separates the sin that
he hates from the sinner whom he loves.
—*Anonymous*

Bible Truth Behind the Quote:
By disciplining us, God is treating us as His own children (Hebrews 12:7).

— 236 —

God's corrections are instructions, His lashes our lessons, His
scourges our schoolmasters, His chastisements our admonitions!

—*Thomas Brooks (1608-1680), minister, London*

Bible Truth Behind the Quote:
"He disciplines us for our good, that we may share his holiness" (Hebrews 12:10).

— 237 —

Sometimes God has to put us flat on our back
before we are looking up to Him.

—*Jack Graham (born 1950), Baptist pastor*

Bible Truth Behind the Quote:
The psalmist's physical discipline from God (Psalm 32:3-4) led to his repentance and confession of sin (verse 5).

— 238 —

God warns before he wounds.

—*Matthew Henry (1662-1714), Bible commentator, Presbyterian minister*

Bible Truth Behind the Quote:
God provides His Word to show us what He expects from us (for example, 1 Corinthians 11:23-26). If we shun His instructions, He responds accordingly in discipline (for example, 1 Corinthians 11:27-32).

DISCOURAGEMENT

— 239 —

Disappointments are inevitable; discouragement is a choice.

—*Charles Stanley (born 1932), senior pastor, First Baptist Church of Atlanta*

Bible Truth Behind the Quote:
Hand your disappointments over to God in prayer, and His peace will guard your heart (Philippians 4:7).

— 240 —

The Christian's chief occupational hazards
are depression and discouragement.

—*John Stott (born 1921), Anglican clergyman*

Bible Truth Behind the Quote:
God's people can suffer from a broken heart (Psalm 34:18; Proverbs 17:22). Yet God promises: "Fear not, for I am with you; be not dismayed, for I am your God; I will strengthen you, I will help you, I will uphold you with my righteous right hand" (Isaiah 41:10).

— 241 —

You cannot prevent the birds of sorrow from flying over your
head, but you can prevent them from building nests in your hair.

—Anonymous

Bible Truth Behind the Quote:
We ought daily to cast all our anxieties upon God, for He cares for us (1 Peter 5:7).

DISGRACING OTHERS

— 242 —

A desire to disgrace others never sprang from grace.

—George Swinnock (1627-1673), English Puritan pastor

Bible Truth Behind the Quote:
Scripture exhorts us to speak encouraging words to each other (Ephesians 4:29), remembering that gentle words bring life and health (Proverbs 15:4) but harsh words stir up anger (Proverbs 15:1; Ephesians 4:31). We will be held accountable for the words that come out of our mouths (Matthew 12:36-37).

DISHONESTY

— 243 —

Lies and false reports are among Satan's choicest weapons.

—J.C. Ryle (1816-1900), Anglican bishop, Liverpool

Bible Truth Behind the Quote:
Satan is "a liar and the father of lies" and "has nothing to do with the truth" (John 8:44).

DISILLUSIONMENT WITH CHRISTIANS

— 244 —

A large measure of disappointment with God stems
from disillusionment with other Christians.

—Philip Yancey (born 1949), Christian author

Bible Truth Behind the Quote:
Paul may have experienced some disappointments when his companions in ministry virtually deserted him, but he apparently instantly forgave them (2 Timothy 4:10,16).

DOCTRINE

— 245 —

If God consistently sent lightning bolts in response to bad doctrine, our planet would sparkle nightly like a Christmas tree.
—*Philip Yancey (born 1949), Christian author*

Bible Truth Behind the Quote:
Scripture refers to "teachings of demons" (1 Timothy 4:1) and people who "will not endure sound teaching" (2 Timothy 4:3). Scripture also refers to a different gospel (Galatians 1:8), a different Jesus, and a different spirit (2 Corinthians 11:4). Christians beware!

DOERS OF THE WORD

— 246 —

If you were arrested for being a Christian, would there be enough evidence to convict you?
—*David Otis Fuller (1903–1988), Baptist pastor*

Bible Truth Behind the Quote:
We are to be "be doers of the word, and not hearers only, deceiving yourselves" (James 1:22). Jesus exhorted, "Let your light shine before others, so that they may see your good works and give glory to your Father who is in heaven" (Matthew 5:16).

— 247 —

You can judge the quality of their faith from the way they behave. Discipline is an index to doctrine.
—*Tertullian (160-220), early Christian apologist*

Bible Truth Behind the Quote:
As James puts it, "What good is it, my brothers, if someone says he has faith but does not have works?" (James 2:14). He warns, "As the body apart from the spirit is dead, so also faith apart from works is dead" (verse 26).

EARTH

— 248 —

Our tiny earth acquires significance for the whole universe.
Upon this small planet will be fought the decisive battle between
God and the Devil. Although a mere atom in comparison
with the colossal stars of universal space, it is, though not as
regards size and matter, but as regards the history of salvation,
the center of the universe. On it the Highest presents Himself
in solemn covenants and Divine appearances; on it the Son of
God became man; on it stood the cross of the Redeemer of the
world; and on it—though indeed on the new earth, yet still on
the earth—will be at last the throne of God and the Lamb.

—*Erich Sauer (1898-1959), Wiedenest Bible School, West Germany*

Bible Truth Behind the Quote:
Just as God uses humble, insignificant human beings to accomplish His purposes (1 Corinthians 1:27), so He has used a humble planet for the same (Genesis 1:1-2).

ENCOURAGEMENT

— 249 —

If I had my life to live over, I would spend
more time encouraging others.

—*F.B. Meyer (1847-1929), Baptist pastor, evangelist*

Bible Truth Behind the Quote:
Christians are often exhorted to encourage one another (Ephesians 6:22; Colossians 4:8;
1 Thessalonians 4:18; 5:11,14; 1 Timothy 5:1).

— 250 —

If you wish to be disappointed, look to others. If you
wish to be downhearted, look to yourself. If you wish
to be encouraged...look upon Jesus Christ.

—*Erich Sauer (1898-1959), Wiedenest Bible School, West Germany*

Bible Truth Behind the Quote:
We ought to continually look to Jesus, "the founder and perfecter of our faith" (Hebrews 12:2).

— 251 —

One of the highest human duties is the duty of encouragement…
It is easy to discourage others. The world is full of discouragers.
We have a Christian duty to encourage one another.

—*William Barclay (1907-1978), professor, University of Glasgow*

Bible Truth Behind the Quote:
"Encourage one another and build one another up" (1 Thessalonians 5:11).

ENDURANCE

— 252 —

Endurance is the queen of all virtues.

—*Chrysostom (347-407), early church father*

Bible Truth Behind the Quote:
We are exhorted to run with endurance (Hebrews 12:1), especially during times of testing (James 1:12).

ENTHUSIASM ABOUT FAITH

— 253 —

Catch on fire with enthusiasm and people will
come for miles to watch you burn.

—*John Wesley (1703-1791), founder of the Methodist church*

Bible Truth Behind the Quote:
On the day of Pentecost, people got so excited that when Peter preached, he had to tell the crowd, "these people are not drunk, as you suppose, since it is only the third hour of the day" (Acts 2:15). When you walk in the Spirit and manifest such things as love, peace, and joy (Galatians 5:22), people will notice you too!

ENVY

— 254 —

Envy is a coal that comes hissing hot from hell.

—*Philip James Baily (1816-1902), English poet*

Bible Truth Behind the Quote:
Envy leads to evil (James 3:14-16), is harmful (Ecclesiastes 4:4), is rooted in the sin nature (Galatians 5:19-21), and rots bones (Proverbs 14:30).

Epitaph

— 255 —

Epitaph in a graveyard in England:
I have sinned;
I have repented;
I have trusted;
I have loved;
I rest;
I shall rise;
I shall reign.

—Anonymous

Bible Truth Behind the Quote:
We can all be assured of our salvation. In John's Gospel, we read, "Jesus did many other signs in the presence of the disciples, which are not written in this book; but these are written so that you may believe that Jesus is the Christ, the Son of God, and that by believing you may have life in his name" (John 20:30-31).

Eternal Life

— 256 —

For a small reward, a man will hurry away on a long journey;
while for eternal life, many will hardly take a single step.

—Thomas à Kempis (1380-1471), author, The Imitation of Christ

Bible Truth Behind the Quote:
Jesus "came to his own, and his own people did not receive him" (John 1:11).

Eternal Perspective

— 257 —

Not only is it certain that this life will end, but it is certain
that from the perspective of eternity it will be seen to have
passed in a flash. The toils which seem so endless will be seen
to have been quite transitory and abundantly worthwhile.

—John Wenham (1913-1996), Anglican Bible scholar

Bible Truth Behind the Quote:
"The sufferings of this present time are not worth comparing with the glory that is to be revealed to us" (Romans 8:18).

— 258 —

Time is short. Eternity is long. It is only reasonable
that this short life be lived in the light of eternity.

—*Charles Spurgeon (1834-1892), pastor, New Park Street Chapel, London*

Bible Truth Behind the Quote:
"Set your minds on things that are above, not on things that are on earth" (Colossians 3:2).

— 259 —

The lack of long, strong thinking about our promised hope of
glory is a major cause of our plodding, lack-luster lifestyle...
It is the heavenly Christian that is the lively Christian.

—*J.I. Packer (born 1926), author, theologian*

Bible Truth Behind the Quote:
We should seek that which is above, where Christ Himself is (Colossians 3:1).

— 260 —

We are refugees from the sinking ship of this present world order,
so soon to disappear; our hope is fixed in the eternal order, where
the promises of God are made good to his people in perpetuity.

—*F.F. Bruce (1910-1990), Bible scholar*

Bible Truth Behind the Quote:
We are en route to a place of no tears, no death, no mourning, no crying, no pain, and where all things are new (Revelation 21:4-5).

— 261 —

Eternity to the godly is a day that has no sunset; eternity
to the wicked is a night that has no sunrise.

—*Thomas Watson (1620-1686), Puritan preacher, author*

Bible Truth Behind the Quote:
We can praise the Lord that we have been delivered from the kingdom of darkness into the kingdom of light, the kingdom of Jesus Christ (Colossians 1:13).

— 262 —

The more of heaven we cherish, the less of earth we covet.

—*Anonymous*

Bible Truth Behind the Quote:
Our present earthly reality will one day burn in preparation for the new heavens and earth (2 Peter 3:12-13). This keeps things in perspective.

— 263 —

In our sad condition, our only consolation is the expectancy
of another life. Here below all is incomprehensible.

—Martin Luther (1483-1546), priest, professor of theology, reformer

Bible Truth Behind the Quote:
"Now we see in a mirror dimly, but then face to face" (1 Corinthians 13:12).

— 264 —

Take courage. We walk in the wilderness today
and in the Promised Land tomorrow.

—Dwight L. Moody (1837-1899), evangelist

Bible Truth Behind the Quote:
While we are earth citizens, our ultimate and true citizenship is in heaven (Philippians 3:20).

— 265 —

God hath given to man a short time here upon earth,
and yet upon this short time eternity depends.

—Jeremy Taylor (1613-1667), clergyman, Church of England

Bible Truth Behind the Quote:
Don't wait! "Now is the favorable time; behold, now is the day of salvation" (2 Corinthians 6:2).

— 266 —

However big and pressing the questions related to our
present short life on earth may seem, they shrink into
littleness compared with this timeless, measureless concern
of death and the vast hereafter. How long earthly life looks
to questing youth! How quickly fled it seems to the aged!

—J. Sidlow Baxter (1903-1999), pastor, theologian

Bible Truth Behind the Quote:
"I trust in you, O Lord; I say, 'You are my God.' My times are in your hand" (Psalm 31:14-15).

— 267 —

Our duty as Christians is always to keep
heaven in our eyes and earth under our feet.

—Matthew Henry (1662-1714), Bible commentator, Presbyterian minister

Bible Truth Behind the Quote:
Let's keep our eyes perpetually and intensely focused on heaven (Colossians 3:1-3).

— 268 —

I am immortal until the will of God for me is accomplished.

—David Livingstone (1813-1873), medical missionary

Bible Truth Behind the Quote:

God is absolutely sovereign over all our earthly days. "In your book were written, every one of them, the days that were formed for me, when as yet there were none of them" (Psalm 139:16).

— 269 —

It ought to be the business of every day to prepare for our last day.

—Matthew Henry (1662-1714), Bible commentator, Presbyterian minister

Bible Truth Behind the Quote:

How awful it will be for the unprepared fool to whom the Lord suddenly says: "This night your soul is required of you" (Luke 12:20).

— 270 —

O spend your time as you would hear of it in the Judgment!

—Richard Baxter (1615-1691), English Puritan church leader

Bible Truth Behind the Quote:

There's no escaping that we all will give an account for our actions, thoughts, and words at the judgment seat of Christ (2 Corinthians 5:10).

— 271 —

This world is the land of the dying;
the next is the land of the living.

—Tryon Edwards (1809-1894), theologian

Bible Truth Behind the Quote:

Heaven is the land of no-death (Matthew 22:32; Revelation 21:4-5).

— 272 —

He is a happy man who so lives that death at
all times may find him at leisure to die.

—Owen Feltham (1602-1668), English writer

Bible Truth Behind the Quote:

People are wisest who "discern their latter end" (Deuteronomy 32:29), and who pray, "O Lord, make me know my end and what is the measure of my days; let me know how fleeting I am!" (Psalm 39:4).

— 273 —

We are strangers here. Don't make yourself at home.

—*Anonymous*

Bible Truth Behind the Quote:
Our true destiny is a "better country, that is, a heavenly one" (Hebrews 11:16).

— 274 —

How do you know, O man, but the next step you take may be into
Hell? Death may seize you, judgment find you, and then the great
gulf will be fixed between you and endless glory forever and ever.

—*George Whitefield (1714-1770), itinerant minister, Great Awakening*

Bible Truth Behind the Quote:
No one knows the day of his or her death (Luke 12:20). For this reason, he or she should immediately prepare for what lies beyond death by trusting in Christ today (2 Corinthians 6:2).

— 275 —

Eternity is primary. Heaven must become our first and
ultimate point of reference. We are built for it, redeemed
for it, and on our way to it. Success demands that we see
and respond to now in the light of then. All that we have,
are, and accumulate must be seen as resources by which
we can influence and impact the world beyond. Even our
tragedies are viewed as events that can bring eternal gain.

—*Joseph Stowell, president, Cornerstone University*

Bible Truth Behind the Quote:
The psalmist expressed it best, "Whom have I in heaven but you? And there is nothing on earth that I desire besides you" (Psalm 73:25).

— 276 —

As the fairest flower lies packed away within the little
shriveled seed, and wants but time and sun to develop
all its beauty, so perfection, glory, immortality and bliss
unspeakable lie slumbering and hidden away with the
grace, which God has given to all His people.

—*Charles Spurgeon (1834-1892), pastor, New Park Street Chapel, London*

Bible Truth Behind the Quote:
Redeemed human beings simply have no capacity to grasp the resplendent glory of what lies beyond the grave (1 Corinthians 2:9).

— 277 —

Let thy hope of heaven master thy fear of death. Why
shouldst thou be afraid to die, who hopest to live by dying!
—*William Gurnall (1617-1679), English author*

Bible Truth Behind the Quote:
Anchor yourself on the "hope laid up for you in heaven" (Colossians 1:5).

— 278 —

No two Christians will ever meet for the last time.
—*Anonymous*

Bible Truth Behind the Quote:
There will be a grand reunion of Christians in heaven (1 Thessalonians 4:13-17).

— 279 —

Nothing is more contrary to a heavenly hope than an earthly heart.
—*William Gurnall (1617-1679), English author*

Bible Truth Behind the Quote:
A heart focused on earthly things does not make sense, for at death we cannot take any earthly things with us (1 Timothy 6:7). How much better it is to await our glorious inheritance in heaven (1 Peter 1:4).

— 280 —

People will not learn to live who have not learned to die.
—*Jim Elliot (1927-1956), missionary to Ecuador*

Bible Truth Behind the Quote:
Paul affirmed, "I have been crucified with Christ. It is no longer I who live, but Christ who lives in me. And the life I now live in the flesh I live by faith in the Son of God, who loved me and gave himself for me" (Galatians 2:20).

— 281 —

To be familiar with the grave is prudence.
—*Charles Spurgeon (1834-1892), pastor, New Park Street Chapel, London*

Bible Truth Behind the Quote:
To never give thought to death and what lies beyond is sheer folly (Psalm 90:12).

— 282 —

In all things look to the end, and how you
will stand before that just Judge.
—*Thomas à Kempis (1380-1471), author, The Imitation of Christ*

Bible Truth Behind the Quote:
Each of us will render an account to God for our actions (Romans 14:12).

— 283 —

One of the old martyrs said to his persecutors as they were
leading him to his death, "You take a life from me that I
cannot keep, and bestow a life upon me that I cannot lose."
—*Dwight L. Moody (1837-1899), evangelist*

Bible Truth Behind the Quote:
Stephen felt the same way. At the moment of his execution, he prayed: "Lord Jesus, receive
my spirit" (Acts 7:59), having just witnessed the heavens open where he witnessed Jesus
in heaven (verse 55).

— 284 —

Heavenly-mindedness is sanity. It is the best regimen
for keeping our hearts whole, our minds clear…It
allows us to endure life's agonies without despair.
—*Mark Buchanan, Christian author*

Bible Truth Behind the Quote:
Paul himself was temporarily caught up to heaven (2 Corinthians 12:1-7). What he witnessed there no doubt kept him "heavenly-minded" for the duration of his ministry.

— 285 —

Lord, make me to know that I am so frail that I may die at any
time—early morning, noon, night, midnight, cockcrow. I may die
in any place. If I am in the house of sin, I may die there. If I am in
the place of worship, I may die there. I may die in the street. I may
die while undressing tonight. I may die in my sleep, die before I
get to my work tomorrow morning. I may die in any occupation.
—*Charles Spurgeon (1834-1892), pastor, New Park Street Chapel, London*

Bible Truth Behind the Quote:
Because none of us knows the day we will die, is it not the height of folly to put off turning to Christ for salvation today (Luke 12:20; 2 Corinthians 6:2).

— 286 —

Our pleasant communion with our kind Christian friends is only
broken off for a small moment, and is soon to be eternally resumed.
These eyes of ours shall once more look upon their faces, and these
ears of ours shall once more hear them speak…Blessed and happy
indeed will that meeting be—better a thousand times than the

parting! We parted in sorrow, and we shall meet in joy; we parted
in stormy weather, and we shall meet in a calm harbor; we parted
amidst pains and aches, and groans and infirmities: we shall meet with
glorious bodies, able to serve our Lord forever without distraction.

—*J.C. Ryle (1816-1900), Anglican bishop, Liverpool*

Bible Truth Behind the Quote:
After informing the Thessalonian Christians of the coming reunion of all Christians
in heaven, Paul instructed them, "Therefore encourage one another with these words"
(1 Thessalonians 4:18).

— 287 —

It is vanity to wish to live long, and to be careless to
live well. It is vanity to mind only this present life, and
not to foresee those things which are to come.

—*Thomas à Kempis (1380-1471), author,* The Imitation of Christ

Bible Truth Behind the Quote:
Scripture urges, "Remember also your Creator in the days of your youth, before the evil
days come and the years draw near of which you will say, 'I have no pleasure in them'"
(Ecclesiastes 12:1).

— 288 —

We are immortal till our work is done.

—*George Whitefield (1714-1770), itinerant minister, Great Awakening*

Bible Truth Behind the Quote:
In God's providence, we simply will not die until God's assigned purpose for our lives is
complete (Job 14:5; Psalm 139:16).

— 289 —

It is vanity to set your love on that which speedily passes
away, and not to hasten to where everlasting joy abides.

—*Thomas à Kempis (1380-1471), author,* The Imitation of Christ

Bible Truth Behind the Quote:
Earthly things do not satisfy. "All things are full of weariness; a man cannot utter it; the
eye is not satisfied with seeing, nor the ear filled with hearing" (Ecclesiastes 1:8). It is better
to seek heaven, where there is "fullness of joy" in the presence of the Lord (Psalm 16:11).

— 290 —

People will never set their faces decidedly towards heaven, and live
like pilgrims, until they really feel that they are in danger of hell.

—*J.C. Ryle (1816-1900), Anglican bishop, Liverpool*

Bible Truth Behind the Quote:
The repentant tax collector would not even lift up his eyes to heaven, but beat his breast in remorse, saying, "God, be merciful to me, a sinner" (Luke 18:13).

— 291 —

Those who have cultivated a genuine heavenly-mindedness—
who have named and nurtured the human longing for Elsewhere
and Otherwise—have been people who have worked and
prayed the most passionately, courageously, tirelessly, and
unswervingly for the kingdom to come on earth as it is in heaven.
—*Mark Buchanan, Christian author*

Bible Truth Behind the Quote:
"Your kingdom come, your will be done, on earth as it is in heaven" (The Lord's Prayer, Matthew 6:10).

— 292 —

Anticipating heaven doesn't eliminate pain, but it lessens it and
puts it in perspective. Meditating on heaven is a great pain reliever.
It reminds us that suffering and death are temporary conditions.
—*Randy Alcorn, director, Eternal Perspective Ministries*

Bible Truth Behind the Quote:
Our momentary affliction, while painful at the moment, is preparing us for unimaginable glory (2 Corinthians 4:17).

— 293 —

In the Christian scheme of things, this world and the time spent
here are not all there is. Earth is a proving ground, a dot in eternity.
—*Philip Yancey (born 1949), Christian author*

Bible Truth Behind the Quote:
Notice the constant refrain "and he died" in the Genesis genealogy (Genesis 5:5,8, 11,14,17,20,27,31). We all have only a comparatively tiny dot of time on this earth.

— 294 —

He is no fool who gives what he cannot
keep to gain what he cannot lose.
—*Jim Elliot (1927-1956), missionary to Ecuador*

Bible Truth Behind the Quote:
"Whoever would save his life will lose it, but whoever loses his life for my sake will find it" (Matthew 16:25).

ETERNAL SECURITY

— 295 —

In God's faithfulness lies eternal security.

—*Corrie ten Boom (1892-1983), Dutch Christian Holocaust survivor*

Bible Truth Behind the Quote:
God is "faithful and just" to forgive us of our sins and to cleanse us of all unrighteousness (1 John 1:9).

EVANGELISM

— 296 —

I look upon all the world as my parish.

—*John Wesley (1703-1791), founder of the Methodist church*

Bible Truth Behind the Quote:
We are to make disciples "of all nations" (Matthew 28:19).

— 297 —

Our task is to live our personal communion with Christ
with such intensity as to make it contagious.

—*Paul Tournier (1898-1986), Swiss physician, author*

Bible Truth Behind the Quote:
Each of us ought to shine as sparkling lights in the world (Matthew 5:14-16).

— 298 —

The church is under orders. Evangelistic inactivity is disobedience.

—*John Stott (born 1921), Anglican clergyman*

Bible Truth Behind the Quote:
We are called to be God's witnesses to the uttermost parts of the earth (Acts 1:8).

— 299 —

You are in one of two groups: Either you are a
Christian, or God is now calling you to be one.

—*John Piper (born 1936), Evangelical Calvinist preacher, author*

Bible Truth Behind the Quote:
There are two groups of people, the saved and the unsaved (John 3:18). God does not desire that any perish (2 Peter 3:9).

— 300 —

You are a Christian because somebody cared. Now it's your turn.
—*Warren Wiersbe (born 1929), pastor, author*

Bible Truth Behind the Quote:
We each ought to "do the work of an evangelist" (2 Timothy 4:5).

— 301 —

Personal ambition and empire-building are
hindering the spread of the gospel.
—*John Stott (born 1921), Anglican clergyman*

Bible Truth Behind the Quote:
John made reference to Diotrephes, "who likes to put himself first" (3 John 1:9). Personal ambition thwarts ministry.

— 302 —

Just as no one can go to hell or heaven for me, so no one can
believe for me and so no one can open or close heaven or hell
for me, and no one can drive me either to believe or disbelieve.
—*Martin Luther (1483-1546), priest, professor of theology, reformer*

Bible Truth Behind the Quote:
Scripture is clear. "Whoever believes in the Son has eternal life" (John 3:36). "Whoever" means you and me. Whoever does not believe is condemned (verse 18).

— 303 —

Oh Lord, give me souls, or take my soul!
—*George Whitefield (1714-1770), Anglican itinerant minister*

Bible Truth Behind the Quote:
Pray for more harvesters (Luke 10:2)!

EVIL

— 304 —

God himself would not permit evil in this
world if good did not come of it.
—*Thomas Aquinas (1225-1274), Italian philosopher, theologian*

Bible Truth Behind the Quote:
"For those who love God all things work together for good, for those who are called according to his purpose" (Romans 8:28).

— 305 —

God judged it better to bring good out of
evil than to suffer no evil to exist.

—*Augustine (354-430), bishop of Hippo*

Bible Truth Behind the Quote:
God's plans alone stand (Psalm 33:8-11; Isaiah 46:10), and His plan is based on His unfathomable wisdom (Romans 16:27).

— 306 —

He who passively accepts evil is as much involved in it as
he who helps to perpetrate it. He who accepts evil without
protesting against it is really cooperating with it.

—*Martin Luther King, Jr. (1929-1968), clergyman,*
activist in the African-American Civil Rights Movement

Bible Truth Behind the Quote:
"Whoever knows the right thing to do and fails to do it, for him it is sin" (James 4:17).

— 307 —

Only when God hath brought to light all the hidden things
of darkness, whosoever were the actors therein, will it be seen
that wise and good were all His ways, that He saw through
the thick cloud, and governed all things by the wise counsel of
His own will, that nothing was left to chance, or the caprice of
men, but God disposed all strongly and sweetly, and wrought
all into one connected chain of justice, mercy, and truth.

—*John Wesley (1703-1791), founder of the Methodist church*

Bible Truth Behind the Quote:
God declares the end from the beginning (Isaiah 46:10) and works out His sovereign purpose in earth history (Ephesians 1:11).

— 308 —

We poor blind creatures, here today and gone tomorrow, born
in sin, surrounded by sinners, living in a constant atmosphere
of weakness, infirmity, and imperfection—can form none but
the most inadequate conceptions of the hideousness of evil.

—*J.C. Ryle (1816-1900), Anglican bishop, Liverpool*

Bible Truth Behind the Quote:
Our blindness to sin is itself a manifestation of sin (see 1 John 2:11; Revelation 3:17).

— 309 —

A good end cannot sanctify evil means; nor must
we ever do evil that good may come of it.

—*William Penn (1644-1718), English Quaker, founder of Pennsylvania*

Bible Truth Behind the Quote:
Paul exhorts us, "Abstain from every form of evil" (1 Thessalonians 5:22).

EVOLUTION

— 310 —

The evolutionists seem to know everything about the
missing link except the fact that it is missing.

—*Gilbert Keith Chesterton (1874-1936), English author, apologist*

Bible Truth Behind the Quote:
"All things were made through him [Christ], and without him was not any thing made
that was made" (John 1:3, insertion added for clarification).

— 311 —

It is absurd for the evolutionists to complain that it's
unthinkable for an admittedly unthinkable God to make
everything out of nothing and then pretend it is more
thinkable that nothing should turn itself into anything.

—*Gilbert Keith Chesterton (1874-1936), English author, apologist*

Bible Truth Behind the Quote:
"Every house is built by someone, but the builder of all things is God" (Hebrews 3:4). "In
the beginning, God created the heavens and the earth" (Genesis 1:1).

FAILURE

— 312 —

Often the doorway to success is entered
through the hallway of failure.

—*Erwin Lutzer (born 1941), pastor, Moody Church, Chicago*

Bible Truth Behind the Quote:
Peter denied Jesus three times (Matthew 26:34,75), yet was restored (John 21:15-17) and
went on to become one of the great leaders of the first-century church (Acts 2–10).

FAITH

— 313 —

Attempt great things for God and expect great things from God.
—*William Carey (1761-1834), English Baptist missionary*

Bible Truth Behind the Quote:
God is "able to do far more abundantly than all that we ask or think" (Ephesians 3:20) and stands ready to do so.

— 314 —

Faith does not operate in the realm of the possible.
There is no glory for God in that which is humanly
possible. Faith begins where man's power ends.
—*George Müller (1805-1898), director of orphanages in Bristol, England*

Bible Truth Behind the Quote:
"What is impossible with men is possible with God" (Luke 18:27).

— 315 —

True Christian faith fulfills man's desires to perceive the eternal. It
gives him a more extensive knowledge of all things invisible. Living
faith introduces him to what the eye has not seen, nor the ear
heard, nor the heart conceived in the clearest light, with the fullest
certainty and evidence. Knowing these benefits, who would not
wish for such a faith? With faith comes not only this awareness,
but also the fulfillment of the promise of holiness and happiness.
—*John Wesley (1703-1791), founder of the Methodist church*

Bible Truth Behind the Quote:
"We walk by faith, not by sight" (2 Corinthians 5:7).

— 316 —

A little faith will bring your soul to heaven; a
great faith will bring heaven to your soul.
—*Charles Spurgeon (1834-1892), pastor, New Park Street Chapel, London*

Bible Truth Behind the Quote:
A great faith recognizes that "to die is gain" and seeks "to depart and be with Christ, for that is far better" (Philippians 1:21-23).

— 317 —

You don't have to see the whole staircase; just take the first step.

—*Martin Luther King, Jr. (1929-1968), clergyman,*
activist in the African-American Civil Rights Movement

Bible Truth Behind the Quote:
When Abraham left Ur to head to the promised land, he did not yet see the promised land. He took one faith-step at a time (Genesis 15:7).

— 318 —

Faith is to believe what we do not see. The reward
of this faith is to see what we believe.

—*Augustine (354-430), bishop of Hippo*

Bible Truth Behind the Quote:
While today we "walk by faith, not by sight" (2 Corinthians 5:7), one day we will walk by sight, being in the direct presence of God in heaven (Revelation 21:3).

— 319 —

It is the office of faith to believe what we do not see, and it
shall be the reward of faith to see what we do believe.

—*Thomas Adams (1583-1652), English clergyman, preacher*

Bible Truth Behind the Quote:
"Now we see in a mirror dimly, but then face to face" (1 Corinthians 13:12).

— 320 —

Believing God means getting down on your knees.

—*Martin Luther (1483-1546), priest, professor of theology, reformer*

Bible Truth Behind the Quote:
"Whatever you ask in prayer, you will receive, if you have faith" (Matthew 21:22).

— 321 —

I believe that the happiest of all Christians and the truest of
Christians are those who never dare to doubt God, but take His
Word simply as it stands, and believe it, and ask no questions,
just feeling assured that if God has said it, it will be so.

—*Charles Spurgeon (1834-1892), pastor, New Park Street Chapel, London*

Bible Truth Behind the Quote:
"Your testimonies are my delight; they are my counselors" (Psalm 119:24).

— 322 —

Your God is too small.

—*J. B. Phillips (1906-1982), Bible translator, author, clergyman*

Bible Truth Behind the Quote:
"Who is like you, O LORD, among the gods? Who is like you, majestic in holiness, awesome in glorious deeds, doing wonders?" (Exodus 15:11).

— 323 —

Faith and good conscience are hope's two wings.

—*William Gurnall (1617-1679), English author*

Bible Truth Behind the Quote:
"I will hope continually and will praise you yet more and more" (Psalm 71:14).

— 324 —

Faith expects from God what is beyond all expectation.

—*Andrew Murray (1828-1917), South African writer, pastor*

Bible Truth Behind the Quote:
"I will trust, and will not be afraid; for the LORD GOD is my strength and my song, and he has become my salvation" (Isaiah 12:2). God is "able to do far more abundantly than all that we ask or think" (Ephesians 3:20).

— 325 —

Faith sees the invisible, believes the unbelievable,
and receives the impossible.

—*Corrie ten Boom (1892-1983), Dutch Christian Holocaust survivor*

Bible Truth Behind the Quote:
Despite how unbelievable and seemingly impossible it was for Abraham and Sarah to have a child in old age, God accomplished the impossible (Genesis 21:2)! He can accomplish impossible things for us too (Luke 18:27).

— 326 —

Faith is the sight of the inward eye.

—*Alexander Maclaren (1826-1910), English minister*

Bible Truth Behind the Quote:
"My eyes are ever toward the LORD" (Psalm 25:15).

— 327 —

Never be afraid to entrust an unknown
future to an all-knowing God.

—*Anonymous*

Bible Truth Behind the Quote:
"In your book were written, every one of them, the days that were formed for me, when as yet there were none of them" (Psalm 139:16). "My times are in your hand" (Psalm 31:15).

— 328 —

Faith helps us when we are down; but unbelief
throws us down when we are up.
—*John Bunyan (1628-1688), English Christian writer, preacher*

Bible Truth Behind the Quote:
We ought always to cling tightly to our faith (1 Timothy 1:19).

— 329 —

We have a God who delights in impossibilities.
—*Andrew Murray (1828-1917), South African writer, pastor*

Bible Truth Behind the Quote:
Nothing is too difficult for God (Genesis 18:14; Jeremiah 32:17,27).

— 330 —

You do not test the resources of God until you try the impossible.
—*F.B. Meyer (1847-1929), Baptist pastor, evangelist*

Bible Truth Behind the Quote:
God has incomparably great power (Ephesians 1:19-20).

— 331 —

Faith gives us living joy and dying rest.
—*Dwight L. Moody (1837-1899), evangelist*

Bible Truth Behind the Quote:
"For to me to live is Christ, and to die is gain" (Philippians 1:21).

— 332 —

Faith is a Declaration of Dependence in opposition to
sin which is man's Declaration of Independence.
—*Bernard Ramm (1916-1992), Baptist theologian*

Bible Truth Behind the Quote:
"Whatever does not proceed from faith is sin" (Romans 14:23).

— 333 —

Since true faith is anchored upon scriptural facts, we
are certainly not to be influenced by impressions.
—*Miles Stanford (1914-1999), American author*

Bible Truth Behind the Quote:
"Faith comes from hearing, and hearing through the word of Christ" (Romans 10:17).

— 334 —

Faith enables the believing soul to treat the future
as present and the invisible as seen.
—*J. Oswald Sanders (1902-1992), director, Overseas Missionary Fellowship*

Bible Truth Behind the Quote:
"I know the plans I have for you, declares the LORD, plans for wholeness and not for evil,
to give you a future and a hope" (Jeremiah 29:11).

— 335 —

Probabilities are the big temptation when
it comes to exercising faith.
—*Miles Stanford (1914-1999), American author*

Bible Truth Behind the Quote:
"Trust in the LORD with all your heart, and do not lean on your own understanding"
(Proverbs 3:5).

— 336 —

Trusting God means looking beyond what
we can see to what God sees.
—*Charles Stanley (born 1932), senior pastor, First Baptist Church of Atlanta*

Bible Truth Behind the Quote:
We are to walk by faith (trusting in what God sees) and not by sight (trusting in what we
see) (2 Corinthians 5:7).

— 337 —

Many people are willing to believe regarding those things that
seem probable to them. Faith has nothing to do with probabilities.
The province of faith begins where probabilities cease and sight
and sense fail. Appearances are not to be taken into account.
The question is—whether God has spoken it in His Word.
—*George Müller (1805-1898), director of orphanages in Bristol, England*

Bible Truth Behind the Quote:
"Do not judge by appearances" (John 7:24).

— 338 —

A faith that hasn't been tested can't be trusted.
—*Adrian Rogers (1931-2005), Baptist pastor, author*

Bible Truth Behind the Quote:
"The testing of your faith produces steadfastness" (James 1:3).

— 339 —

Faith means believing in what will only make sense in reverse.
—*Philip Yancey (born 1949), Christian author*

Bible Truth Behind the Quote:
"By faith Noah, being warned by God concerning events as yet unseen, in reverent fear constructed an ark for the saving of his household" (Hebrews 11:7).

— 340 —

Faith, mighty faith, the promise sees,
and looks to that alone;
laughs at impossibilities,
and cries it shall be done.
—*Charles Wesley (1707-1788), leader of Methodist Movement, hymn writer*

Bible Truth Behind the Quote:
"He who promised is faithful" (Hebrews 10:23). Indeed, "not one word has failed of all his good promise" (1 Kings 8:56).

— 341 —

Our faith grows by expression. If we want to keep
our faith, we must share it. We must act.
—*Billy Graham (born 1918), evangelist*

Bible Truth Behind the Quote:
"You will be my witnesses in Jerusalem and in all Judea and Samaria, and to the end of the earth" (Acts 1:8).

— 342 —

God does not expect us to submit our faith to Him without
reason, but the very limits of reason make faith a necessity.
—*Augustine (354-430), bishop of Hippo*

Bible Truth Behind the Quote:
"Trust in the Lord with all your heart, and do not lean on your own understanding" (Proverbs 3:5).

— 343 —

Faith and sight are set in opposition to each other in Scripture, but
not faith and reason…True faith is essentially reasonable because
it trusts in the character and the promises of God. A believing
Christian is one whose mind reflects and rests on these certitudes.

—John Stott (born 1921), Anglican clergyman

Bible Truth Behind the Quote:
God has "granted to us his precious and very great promises" (2 Peter 1:4).

— 344 —

I do not want merely to possess faith; I
want a faith that possesses me.

—Charles Kingsley (1819-1875), Anglican clergyman

Bible Truth Behind the Quote:
Hebrews 11:1 tells us that "faith is the assurance of things hoped for, the conviction of
things not seen." The operative word is "assurance." The kind of faith that can possess us
is one that has no doubts.

FAITH, THE

— 345 —

The church, though scattered throughout the whole world to the
ends of the earth, has received from the apostles and their disciples
this faith; in one God, the Father Almighty, maker of heaven and
earth and the sea and all things in them; and in one Christ Jesus,
the Son of God, who was made flesh for our salvation; and in the
Holy Spirit, who through the prophets proclaimed God's saving
dealings with man in the coming, virgin birth, passion, resurrection
from the dead, and bodily ascension into heaven of our beloved
Lord Jesus Christ and his second coming from heaven in the
glory of the Father to sum up all things and to raise up all human
flesh so that…he should execute just judgment upon all men.

—Irenaeus (died 202), early church father

Bible Truth Behind the Quote:
We are to "contend for *the faith* that was once for all delivered to the saints" (Jude 3). "The
faith" is that apostolic body of truth handed down to the early church.

FAITH AND WORKS

— 346 —

It is faith alone that justifies, but the faith that justifies is not alone.
—*John Calvin (1509-1564), French reformer*

Bible Truth Behind the Quote:
"Faith by itself, if it does not have works, is dead" (James 2:17).

FAITHFULNESS

— 347 —

How can there be great faith where there is little faithfulness?
—*William Gurnall (1617-1679), English author*

Bible Truth Behind the Quote:
"I know your works: you are neither cold nor hot. Would that you were either cold or hot!" (Revelation 3:15). No strong faith here! No strong faithfulness here!

— 348 —

Faithfulness in little things is a big thing.
—*Chrysostom (347–407), early church father*

Bible Truth Behind the Quote:
Jesus teaches that those who show themselves faithful in small matters will be entrusted with much more important matters (Luke 19:11-27).

FALLING AWAY

— 349 —

If thou wilt fly from God, the devil will
lend thee both spurs and a horse.
—*Thomas Adams (1583-1652), English clergyman, preacher*

Bible Truth Behind the Quote:
Satan seeks your fall. Satan tempts believers to sin (Ephesians 2:1-3; 1 Thessalonians 3:5), to lie (Acts 5:3), and to commit sexually immoral acts (1 Corinthians 7:5). He hinders their work in any way he can (1 Thessalonians 2:18), sows tares among them (Matthew 13:38-39), and incites persecutions against them (Revelation 2:10).

FALLING SHORT

— 350 —

The best of God's people have abhorred themselves.

—*Thomas Manton (1620-1667), English Puritan clergyman*

Bible Truth Behind the Quote:
Paul considered himself the "foremost" among sinners (1 Timothy 1:16; see Romans 7:15-20).

— 351 —

There is no progress possible to the man who
does not see and mourn over his defects.

—*Anonymous*

Bible Truth Behind the Quote:
"I believe; help my unbelief" (Mark 9:24).

— 352 —

You cannot put straight in others what is warped in yourself.

—*Athanasius (293-373), theologian, bishop of Alexandria, church father*

Bible Truth Behind the Quote:
"How can you say to your brother, 'Let me take the speck out of your eye,' when there is the log in your own eye?" (Matthew 7:4).

FAMILY

— 353 —

Some parents, like Eli, bring up their
children to bring down their house.

—*George Swinnock (1627-1673), Puritan minister*

Bible Truth Behind the Quote:
"Train up a child in the way he should go; even when he is old he will not depart from it" (Proverbs 22:6).

— 354 —

If you neglect to instruct children in the way of holiness, will
the devil neglect to instruct them in the way of wickedness?
No; if you will not teach them to pray, he will to curse, swear,
and lie; if ground be uncultivated, weeds will spring.

—*John Flavel (1627-1691), English Presbyterian clergyman*

Bible Truth Behind the Quote:
Bring children up "in the discipline and instruction of the Lord" (Ephesians 6:4).

— 355 —

The family is the most basic unit of government. As
the first community to which a person is attached and
the first authority under which a person learns to live,
the family establishes society's most basic values.
—*Charles Caleb Colton (1780-1832), Brittish writer*

Bible Truth Behind the Quote:
Good parents exercise a good and long-lasting influence over their children (1 Kings 9:4;
2 Chronicles 17:3; 2 Timothy 1:5).

— 356 —

I learned more about Christianity from my mother
than from all the theologians of England.
—*John Wesley (1703-1791), founder of the Methodist church*

Bible Truth Behind the Quote:
Children ought to listen to what their parents teach them (Proverbs 1:8; 6:20; 23:22).

— 357 —

The easiest place in which to be spiritual is in
public; the most difficult is at home.
—*Charles Ryrie (born 1925), theologian, Dallas Theological Seminary*

Bible Truth Behind the Quote:
Problems can easily develop between husbands and wives (Matthew 5:32) or between
parents and their children (Ephesians 6:4; Colossians 3:21).

FASTING

— 358 —

When the stomach is full it is easy to talk of fasting.
—*Jerome (374-420), apologist, translator*

Bible Truth Behind the Quote:
People ought to count the cost before making a commitment (Matthew 8:19-20).

— 359 —

Fasting is calculated to bring a note of urgency and
importance into our praying, and to give force to our

pleading in the court of heaven. The man who prays with fasting is giving heaven notice that he is truly in earnest.

—*Arthur Wallis (1922-1988), Bible teacher, author*

Bible Truth Behind the Quote:
Fasting can be combined with prayer (Luke 2:37) or worship (Acts 13:2).

FATHERHOOD

— 360 —

A father's holy life is a rich legacy for his sons.

—*Charles Spurgeon (1834-1892), pastor, New Park Street Chapel, London*

Bible Truth Behind the Quote:
Parents set an example for their children. "The LORD was with Jehoshaphat, because he walked in the earlier ways of his father David. He did not seek the Baals" (2 Chronicles 17:3).

FATHERS AND SONS

— 361 —

The best gift a father can give to his son is the gift of himself—his time. For material things mean little, if there is not someone to share them with.

—*Neil C. Strait (1934-2003), Church of the Nazarene pastor*

Bible Truth Behind the Quote:
A father ought to seek to be a good influence on his son (see 1 Kings 9:4; 2 Chronicles 17:3; 2 Timothy 1:5), and that requires spending time with him. A father should seek to "bring them up in the discipline and instruction of the Lord" (Ephesians 6:4), and that requires time.

FEAR

— 362 —

Of whom shall I be afraid? One with God is a majority.

—*Martin Luther (1483-1546), priest, professor of theology, reformer*

Bible Truth Behind the Quote:
The psalmist affirmed, "I will not be afraid of many thousands of people who have set themselves against me all around" (3:6). "The LORD is my light and my salvation; whom shall I fear?" (27:1). "In God I trust; I shall not be afraid. What can man do to me?" (56:11).

— 363 —

Fear. His modus operandi is to manipulate you with the
mysterious, to taunt you with the unknown. Fear of death,
fear of failure, fear of God, fear of tomorrow—his arsenal
is vast. His goal? To create cowardly, joyless Christians. He
doesn't want you to make that journey to the mountain. He
figures if he can rattle you enough, you will take your eyes off
the peaks and settle for a dull existence in the flat lands.

—Max Lucado (born 1955), author, minister, Oak Hills Church

Bible Truth Behind the Quote:
Fear not, for God is with you (Psalm 23:4).

— 364 —

Only he who can say, "The LORD is the strength of my life,"
can say, "Of whom shall I be afraid?" (Psalm 27:1 KJV).

—Alexander Maclaren (1826-1910), English minister

Bible Truth Behind the Quote:
If God is for us, who can be against us? (Romans 8:31).

FEAR OF THE LORD

— 365 —

We fear men so much, because we fear God
so little. One fear cures another.

—William Gurnall (1617-1679), English author

Bible Truth Behind the Quote:
We are to fear the Lord and obey His commands (Deuteronomy 5:29; Ecclesiastes 12:13).

— 366 —

Tis sweet to grow old in the fear of the Lord,
As life's shadows longer creep.
Till our steps grow slow, and our sun swings low—
He gives his beloved sleep.

—John Wesley (1703-1791), founder of the Methodist church

Bible Truth Behind the Quote:
Do not fear anything except the Lord (Isaiah 8:13).

— 367 —

Fear God and work hard.

—*David Livingstone (1813-1873), medical missionary*

Bible Truth Behind the Quote:
Always act in the fear of the Lord (2 Chronicles 19:9).

— 368 —

The fear of God is both a virtue and a keeper of other virtues.

—*Anonymous*

Bible Truth Behind the Quote:
Fear of the Lord is the beginning of wisdom (Psalm 111:10; Proverbs 1:7; 9:10).

— 369 —

He who fears God has nothing else to fear.

—*Charles Spurgeon (1834-1892), pastor, New Park Street Chapel, London*

Bible Truth Behind the Quote:
"The angel of the LORD encamps around those who fear him, and delivers them" (Psalm 34:7).

FEELINGS

— 370 —

A Christian life based on feeling is headed for a gigantic collapse.

—*Erwin Lutzer (born 1941), pastor, Moody Church, Chicago*

Bible Truth Behind the Quote:
Emotions can be positive (Psalm 45:7; 112:1; Proverbs 15:30) or negative (Leviticus 19:18; Psalm 37:8; Proverbs 27:4; Ecclesiastes 7:9). They can fluctuate.

FELLOWSHIP

— 371 —

Satan watches for those vessels that sail without a convoy.

—*George Swinnock (1627-1673), English Puritan pastor*

Bible Truth Behind the Quote:
Christians, for their own good, are exhorted to attend church, "not neglecting to meet together, as is the habit of some, but encouraging one another, and all the more as you see the Day drawing near" (Hebrews 10:25).

First Impressions

— 372 —

First impressions never have a second chance.

—Charles Swindoll (born 1934), pastor, Stonebriar Community Church

Bible Truth Behind the Quote:
We ought *always* to be kind (1 Thessalonians 5:15) and be clothed with mercy and love (Colossians 3:12-14).

Forgiveness

— 373 —

No talebearer can inform on us, no enemy can make an accusation stick; no forgotten skeleton can come tumbling out of some hidden closet to abash us and expose our past; no unsuspected weakness in our characters can come to light to turn God away from us, since He knew us utterly before we knew Him and called us to Himself in the full knowledge of everything that was against us.

—A. W. Tozer (1897-1963), American pastor, author

Bible Truth Behind the Quote:
God utterly and completely knows all about us; nothing is hidden from His sight (Psalm 139:1-4).

— 374 —

Forgiveness brings great joy, not only to the forgiven, but especially to the forgiver. The Greek term for "forgiveness" (*aphiemi*) comes from a word that means "to let go." Forgiveness is a release, a letting go of self-destructive feelings such as anger, bitterness, and revenge. Those attitudes poison intimacy with God and harmony with human beings.

—Philip Graham Ryken, pastor, Tenth Presbyterian Church

Bible Truth Behind the Quote:
We are always to forgive one another (Matthew 6:12,14; Ephesians 4:32; Colossians 3:13). We should forgive as we have been forgiven (Ephesians 4:32).

— 375 —

Every man should keep a fair-sized cemetery in which to bury the faults of his friends.

—Henry Ward Beecher (1813-1887), Congregationalist clergyman

Bible Truth Behind the Quote:
We ought to forgive without measure (Matthew 18:21-22).

— 376 —

There is no torment like the inner torment of an unforgiving spirit.
It refuses to be soothed, it refuses to be healed, it refuses to forget.
—*Charles Swindoll (born 1934), pastor, Stonebriar Community Church*

Bible Truth Behind the Quote:
"If you do not forgive others their trespasses, neither will your Father forgive your trespasses" (Matthew 6:15).

— 377 —

Forgiveness is not an occasional act, it is a permanent attitude.
—*Martin Luther King, Jr. (1929-1968), clergyman,
activist in the African-American Civil Rights Movement*

Bible Truth Behind the Quote:
We should forgive, forgive, and keep on forgiving (Matthew 18:21-22).

— 378 —

The voice of sin is loud, but the voice of forgiveness is louder.
—*Dwight L. Moody (1837-1899), evangelist*

Bible Truth Behind the Quote:
There is blessedness and joy in being forgiven (Psalm 32:1-2).

— 379 —

I believe that as often as I transgress, God is more
ready to forgive me than I am ready to offend.
—*Charles Spurgeon (1834-1892), pastor, New Park Street Chapel, London*

Bible Truth Behind the Quote:
Psalm 103:12 promises, "As far as the east is from the west, so far does he remove our transgressions from us."

— 380 —

When God pardons, he consigns the offense
to everlasting forgetfulness.
—*Merv Rosell, evangelist, Youth for Christ*

Bible Truth Behind the Quote:
God's forgiveness is total and complete: "As far as the east is from the west, so far does he remove our transgressions from us" (Psalm 103:12).

FRIENDS

— 381 —

It brings comfort to have companions in whatever happens.

—*Chrysostom (347-407), early church father*

Bible Truth Behind the Quote:
A friend can be closer than a brother (Proverbs 18:24).

FUTURE

— 382 —

We know not what the future holds, but we
do know who holds the future.

—*Willie J. Ray (1896-1992), Baptist pastor*

Bible Truth Behind the Quote:
God Himself affirms, "I am God, and there is no other; I am God, and there is none like me, declaring the end from the beginning and from ancient times things not yet done, saying, 'My counsel shall stand, and I will accomplish all my purpose'" (Isaiah 46:9-10).

GAINING CHRIST

— 383 —

They lose nothing who gain Christ.

—*Samuel Rutherford (c. 1600-1661), Scottish Presbyterian theologian*

Bible Truth Behind the Quote:
As the apostle Paul put it, "I count everything as loss because of the surpassing worth of knowing Christ Jesus my Lord. For his sake I have suffered the loss of all things and count them as rubbish, in order that I may gain Christ" (Philippians 3:8).

GIVING

— 384 —

God does not need our money. But you and
I need the experience of giving it.

—*James Dobson (born 1936), founder, Focus on the Family*

Bible Truth Behind the Quote:
We ought always to give to those in need (Luke 11:41; 12:33; Hebrews 13:16).

— 385 —

He who bestows his goods upon the poor,
shall have as much again,
and ten times more.

—John Bunyan (1628-1688), English Christian writer, preacher

Bible Truth Behind the Quote:
"It is more blessed to give than to receive" (Acts 20:35).

— 386 —

The man who gives little with a smile gives more
than the man who gives much with a frown.

—Anonymous

Bible Truth Behind the Quote:
"God loves a cheerful giver" (2 Corinthians 9:7).

— 387 —

The bread that is spoiling in your house belongs to the
hungry. The shoes that are mildewing under your bed
belong to those who have none. The clothes stored
away in your trunk belong to those who are naked.

—Basil the Great (330-379), bishop of Caesarea Mazaca, theologian

Bible Truth Behind the Quote:
"I was hungry and you gave me food...I was naked and you clothed me...When?...The
King will answer them, 'Truly, I say to you, as you did it to one of the least of these my
brothers, you did it to me'" (Matthew 25:35-40).

— 388 —

If we fail to feed the needy, we do not have God's love,
no matter what we say. Regardless of what we do or
say at 11 AM on a Sunday morn, affluent people who
neglect the poor are not the people of God.

—Ronald Sider (born 1939), theologian, Christian activist

Bible Truth Behind the Quote:
A kind act done to the poor is likened to a kind act done to Christ (Matthew 25:35,40).

GOD, AWESOME

— 389 —

The world appears very little to a soul that
contemplates the greatness of God.

—*Brother Lawrence (1614-1691), author,* The Practice of the Presence of God

Bible Truth Behind the Quote:
"O LORD, our Lord, how majestic is your name in all the earth! You have set your glory above the heavens" (Psalm 8:1).

— 390 —

Then alone do we know God truly, when they believe that
God is far beyond all that we can possibly think of God.

—*Thomas Aquinas (1225-1274), Italian philosopher, theologian*

Bible Truth Behind the Quote:
"Who is like you, O LORD, among the gods? Who is like you, majestic in holiness, awesome in glorious deeds, doing wonders?" (Exodus 15:11).

— 391 —

How should finite comprehend infinite? We shall
apprehend him, but not comprehend him.

—*Richard Sibbes (1577-1635), English theologian*

Bible Truth Behind the Quote:
God affirms, "As the heavens are higher than the earth, so are my ways higher than your ways and my thoughts than your thoughts" (Isaiah 55:9).

GOD, BEAUTY OF

— 392 —

God is beauty.

—*St. Francis of Assisi (1181-1226), founder of Franciscans*

Bible Truth Behind the Quote:
With the psalmist, let us yearn to "dwell in the house of the LORD all the days of my life, to gaze upon the beauty of the LORD" (Psalm 27:4).

God, Blessing of

— 393 —

God always gives His best to those who leave the choice with Him.
—*Warren Wiersbe (born 1929), pastor, author*

Bible Truth Behind the Quote:
Father knows best (Psalm 139:1-4; Matthew 11:21; 1 John 3:20).

God, Dependability of

— 394 —

The more we depend on God, the more dependable we find He is.
—*Cliff Richards (born 1940), recording artist*

Bible Truth Behind the Quote:
God is always utterly and completely dependable in times of trouble (Psalm 50:15).

God, False Concept of

— 395 —

Some people think that God peers over the balcony of heaven
trying to find anybody who is enjoying life. And when He spots
a happy person, He yells, "Now cut that out!" That concept
of God should make us shudder because it's blasphemous!
—*Paul Little (1928-1975), evangelist, InterVarsity Christian Fellowship*

Bible Truth Behind the Quote:
God seeks to bring incredible blessing to us, not take it away (see, for example, 2 Chronicles 1:11-12).

God, Glory of

— 396 —

We were made to be prisms refracting the
light of God's glory into all of life.
—*John Piper (born 1936), Evangelical Calvinist preacher, author*

Bible Truth Behind the Quote:
Let your light shine (Matthew 5:16).

— 397 —

Glory be to thee, O God, the Father, the Maker of
the world: glory be to thee, O God, the Son, the
Redeemer of mankind: glory be to thee, O God,
the Holy Ghost, the Sanctifier of thy people.

—*B.F. Westcott (1825-1901), English churchman, theologian*

Bible Truth Behind the Quote:
Our triune God is an awesome God! "The grace of the Lord Jesus Christ and the love of
God and the fellowship of the Holy Spirit be with you all" (2 Corinthians 13:14).

— 398 —

A sight of God's glory humbles. The stars
vanish when the sun appears.

—*Thomas Watson (1620-1686), Puritan preacher, author*

Bible Truth Behind the Quote:
Just as Isaiah was humbled when he beheld the glory of God (Isaiah 6:1-5), so was John
humbled when he witnessed the glory of the resurrected and ascended Jesus (Revelation
1:17). God "dwells in unapproachable light" (1 Timothy 6:16).

GOD, GOOD

— 399 —

Times are bad, God is good.

—*Richard Sibbes (1577-1635), English theologian*

Bible Truth Behind the Quote:
Give thanks for God is always good (1 Chronicles 16:34; Psalm 118:29; 136:1).

GOD HELPS HIS CHILDREN

— 400 —

I used to ask God to help me. Then I asked if I might help
Him. I ended up by asking Him to do His work through me.

—*J. Hudson Taylor (1832-1905), founder, China Inland Mission*

Bible Truth Behind the Quote:
"I can do all things through him who strengthens me" (Philippians 4:13).

— 401 —

God is a specialist at making something useful and
beautiful out of something broken and confused.
—*Charles Swindoll (born 1934), pastor, Stonebriar Community Church*

Bible Truth Behind the Quote:
Consider how God mightily used Paul, the former persecutor of the church (Acts 22:4).

— 402 —

Whatsoever God takes away from His children, He either replaces
it with a much greater favor or else gives strength to bear it.
—*Richard Sibbes (1577-1635), English theologian*

Bible Truth Behind the Quote:
God can always be trusted to provide strength when you need it (Isaiah 40:29).

— 403 —

The weaker we feel, the harder we lean on God. And
the harder we lean, the stronger we grow.
—*Joni Eareckson Tada (born 1949), founder, Joni and Friends*

Bible Truth Behind the Quote:
God's strength more than compensates for our weakness (2 Corinthians 12:9).

— 404 —

I can look back at my darkest periods and realize that these
were the times when the Lord was holding me closest. But I
couldn't see his face because my face was in his breast—crying.
—*John Michael Talbot (born 1954), founder, Brothers and Sisters of Charity*

Bible Truth Behind the Quote:
"You have delivered my soul from death, my eyes from tears, my feet from stumbling"
(Psalm 116:8).

— 405 —

God helps those who cannot help themselves.
—*Charles Spurgeon (1834-1892), pastor, New Park Street Chapel, London*

Bible Truth Behind the Quote:
"When he saw the crowds, he had compassion for them, because they were harassed and
helpless, like sheep without a shepherd" (Matthew 9:36).

— 406 —

God comes in where my helplessness begins.

—Oswald Chambers (1874-1917), author, My Utmost for His Highest

Bible Truth Behind the Quote:
"Fear not, for I am with you; be not dismayed, for I am your God; I will strengthen you, I will help you, I will uphold you with my righteous right hand" (Isaiah 41:10).

— 407 —

It is when we are out of options that we are
most ready for God's surprises.

—Max Lucado (born 1955), author, minister, Oak Hills Church

Bible Truth Behind the Quote:
"Oh, taste and see that the LORD is good! Blessed is the man who takes refuge in him!" (Psalm 34:8).

— 408 —

It is not my ability, but my response to God's ability, that counts.

—Corrie ten Boom (1892-1983), Dutch Christian Holocaust survivor

Bible Truth Behind the Quote:
Moses was acutely aware of this at the parting of the Red Sea (Exodus 14:21).

— 409 —

You are without power; the enemy is a strong power, but
God has all power. Therefore come with your utter lack of
power to Him who as the Almighty has eternal abundance
of power, and you will be able to conquer the enemy's
strong power. God's omnipotence is able to make your
impotence triumph over all the energy of the adversary.

—Erich Sauer (1898-1959), Wiedenest Bible School, West Germany

Bible Truth Behind the Quote:
As Paul put it, God's power "is made perfect in weakness" (2 Corinthians 12:9).

— 410 —

If all things are possible with God, then all things
are possible to him who believes in Him.

—Corrie ten Boom (1892-1983), Dutch Christian Holocaust survivor

Bible Truth Behind the Quote:
"What is impossible with men is possible with God" (Luke 18:27).

God, Holiness of

— 411 —

Men compare themselves with men, and readily with the worst,
and flatter themselves with that comparative betterness…Consider
the infinite holiness of God, and this will humble us to the dust.

—*Robert Leighton (1611-1684), Scottish minister, bishop of Dunblane, archbishop of Glasgow*

Bible Truth Behind the Quote:
When Isaiah, an upright man, beheld God in His holiness, he cried out, "Woe is me! For I am lost; for I am a man of unclean lips" (Isaiah 6:5).

— 412 —

A true love to God must begin with a delight in his holiness.

—*Jonathan Edwards (1703-1758), American theologian*

Bible Truth Behind the Quote:
Our God is majestic in holiness (Exodus 15:11).

God, Immanence of

— 413 —

You need not cry very loud; he is nearer to us than we think.

—*Brother Lawrence (c. 1614-1691), author,* The Practice of the Presence of God

Bible Truth Behind the Quote:
"The LORD is near to the brokenhearted and saves the crushed in spirit" (Psalm 34:18).

— 414 —

God has never promised to solve our problems.
He has not promised to answer our questions…
He has promised to go with us.

—*Elisabeth Elliot (born 1926), author, wife of Jim Elliot*

Bible Truth Behind the Quote:
God once promised Joshua, "Be strong and courageous. Do not be frightened, and do not be dismayed, for the LORD your God is with you wherever you go" (Joshua 1:9). The same God who was with Joshua is with us!

God, Infinite in Perfections

— 415 —

As well might a gnat seek to drink in the ocean, as a
finite creature to comprehend the Eternal God.

—*Charles Spurgeon (1834-1892), pastor, New Park Street Chapel, London*

Bible Truth Behind the Quote:
God affirms, "As the heavens are higher than the earth, so are my ways higher than your ways and my thoughts than your thoughts" (Isaiah 55:9).

God, Loving

— 416 —

God loves each one of us as if there were only one of us to love.

—*Augustine (354-430), bishop of Hippo*

Bible Truth Behind the Quote:
Paul speaks of "the great love with which he loved us" (Ephesians 2:4).

God, Merciful

— 417 —

As God's mercies are new every morning toward his people,
so his anger is new every morning against the wicked.

—*Matthew Henry (1662-1714), Bible commentator, Presbyterian minister*

Bible Truth Behind the Quote:
"The steadfast love of the Lord never ceases; his mercies never come to an end; they are new every morning; great is your faithfulness" (Lamentations 3:22-23). The wicked experience His anger (Jeremiah 44:3).

— 418 —

God's mercy is so great that you may sooner drain the sea
of its water, or deprive the sun of its light, or make space
too narrow, than diminish the great mercy of God.

—*Charles Spurgeon (1834-1892), pastor, New Park Street Chapel, London*

Bible Truth Behind the Quote:
God is "the Father of mercies" (2 Corinthians 1:3).

God, Omnipotent

— 419 —

How often do we attempt work for God to the limit of our
incompetency, rather than the limit of God's omnipotence?

—*J. Hudson Taylor (1832-1905), founder, China Inland Mission*

Bible Truth Behind the Quote:
God opens doors that no one can shut (Revelation 3:7).

— 420 —

God is so powerful that he can direct any evil to a good end.

—*St. Thomas Aquinas (1225-1274), Italian philosopher, theologian*

Bible Truth Behind the Quote:
Paul affirmed, "We know that for those who love God all things work together for good,
for those who are called according to his purpose" (Romans 8:28).

God, Omnipresent

— 421 —

As no place can be without God, so no place
can compass and contain him.

—*Stephen Charnock (1628-1680), Puritan clergyman*

Bible Truth Behind the Quote:
The highest heaven cannot contain our everywhere-present God (1 Kings 8:27; 2 Chronicles 2:6).

— 422 —

We may ignore, but we can nowhere evade, the presence of God.
The world is crowded with Him. He walks everywhere incognito.

—*C.S. Lewis (1898-1963), author, professor, Oxford University*

Bible Truth Behind the Quote:
God is everywhere, in both heaven and earth (Psalm 113:4-6; Isaiah 66:1; Jeremiah 23:23-24).

God, Patience of

— 423 —

O sinner, the fact that you are alive proves that God
is not dealing with you according to strict justice,

but in patient forbearance; every moment you live is
another instance of omnipotent long-suffering.
—*Charles Spurgeon (1834-1892), pastor, New Park Street Chapel, London*

Bible Truth Behind the Quote:
God is slow to anger (Exodus 34:6; Numbers 14:18; Psalm 86:15; 103:8; Nahum 1:3),
does not want any to perish (2 Peter 3:9), and waits patiently for people to be saved
(2 Peter 3:15).

GOD, PROOF OF

— 424 —

Men cannot open their eyes without being compelled
to see God. Upon his individual works he has engraved
unmistakable marks of his glory. This skillful ordering
of the universe is for us a sort of mirror in which we
can contemplate God, who is otherwise invisible.
—*John Calvin (1509-1564), French reformer*

Bible Truth Behind the Quote:
God's "invisible attributes, namely, his eternal power and divine nature, have been
clearly perceived, ever since the creation of the world, in the things that have been made"
(Romans 1:20).

GOD, PROVIDENTIAL

— 425 —

As children of a sovereign God, we are never
victims of our circumstances.
—*Charles Stanley (born 1932), senior pastor, First Baptist Church of Atlanta*

Bible Truth Behind the Quote:
"For those who love God all things work together for good, for those who are called
according to his purpose" (Romans 8:28).

— 426 —

If God maintains sun and planets in bright
and ordered beauty, He can keep us.
—*F.B. Meyer (1847-1929), Baptist pastor, evangelist*

Bible Truth Behind the Quote:
God sovereignly rules over all (Psalm 103:19) and sustains all by the power of His Word
(Colossians 1:17; Hebrews 1:3).

— 427 —

From our limited vantage point, our lives are marked by an endless series of contingencies. We frequently find ourselves, instead of acting as we planned, reacting to an unexpected turn of events. We make plans but are often forced to change those plans. But there are no contingencies with God. Our unexpected, forced change of plans is a part of His plan. God is never surprised; never caught off guard; never frustrated by unexpected developments. God does as He pleases and that which pleases Him is always for His glory and our good.

—*Jerry Bridges (born 1929), author, affiliated with The Navigators*

Bible Truth Behind the Quote:
"Many are the plans in the mind of a man, but it is the purpose of the LORD that will stand" (Proverbs 19:21).

— 428 —

The work of Satan is overruled so that it assists in bringing to pass the divine purpose, though Satan on his part uses his utmost powers to thwart that purpose.

—*Anonymous*

Bible Truth Behind the Quote:
God sovereignly and omnipotently reigns over all lesser powers (Ephesians 1:20-22).

— 429 —

Everything the devil does, God overreaches to serve His own purpose.

—*Oswald Chambers (1874-1917), author,* My Utmost for His Highest

Bible Truth Behind the Quote:
God affirms, "My counsel shall stand, and I will accomplish all my purpose" (Isaiah 46:10).

— 430 —

Every experience God gives us, every person He puts in our lives, is a perfect preparation for the future that only He can see.

—*Corrie ten Boom (1892-1983), Dutch Christian Holocaust survivor*

Bible Truth Behind the Quote:
This is illustrated in Joseph, whose betrayal by his brothers was used by God to bring about a great good (Genesis 45:8; 50:20).

— 431 —

Our heavenly father never takes anything from his children
unless he means to give them something better.
—George Müller (1805-1898), director of orphanages in Bristol, England

Bible Truth Behind the Quote:
We should always heed this instruction, "Trust in the LORD with all your heart, and do
not lean on your own understanding" (Proverbs 3:5).

GOD, SILENCES OF

— 432 —

The Christian must trust in a withdrawing God.
—William Gurnall (1617-1679), English author

Bible Truth Behind the Quote:
"How long, O LORD? Will you forget me forever? How long will you hide your face from
me?" (Psalm 13:1).

— 433 —

I believe in the sun even if it isn't shining. I believe in love even
when I am alone. I believe in God even when He is silent.
—Anonymous

Bible Truth Behind the Quote:
"Blessed are those who have not seen and yet have believed" (John 20:29).

— 434 —

When Christ leaves His spouse, He forsakes her not altogether
but leaves something in the heart that makes her long after Him.
He absents Himself only that He may enlarge and raise the
desires of the soul, and after the soul has Him again it will not
let Him go. He comes for our good and leaves us for our good.
—Richard Sibbes (1577-1635), English theologian

Bible Truth Behind the Quote:
"Wait for the LORD; be strong, and let your heart take courage; wait for the LORD!"
(Psalm 27:14).

— 435 —

We dare not think that God is absent or daydreaming. The
do-nothing God. He's not tucked away in some far corner of

the universe, uncaring, unfeeling, unthinking…uninvolved.
Count on it—God intrudes in glorious and myriad ways.

—*Joni Eareckson Tada (born 1949), founder, Joni and Friends*

Bible Truth Behind the Quote:
"I waited patiently for the LORD; he inclined to me and heard my cry" (Psalm 40:1).

GOD, SOVEREIGN

— 436 —

Nothing whatever, whether great or small, can happen to a
believer, without God's ordering and permission…There is no
such thing as "chance," "luck" or "accident" in the Christian's
journey through this world. All is arranged and appointed by God.
And all things are "working together" for the believer's good.

—*J.C. Ryle (1816-1900), Anglican bishop, Liverpool*

Bible Truth Behind the Quote:
"We know that for those who love God all things work together for good, for those who
are called according to his purpose" (Romans 8:28).

— 437 —

If God lights the candle, none can blow it out.

—*Charles Spurgeon (1834-1892), pastor, New Park Street Chapel, London*

Bible Truth Behind the Quote:
Christ is the one "who opens and no one will shut, who shuts and no one opens" (Revelation 3:7).

GOD, WILL OF

— 438 —

To walk with God you must walk in the
direction in which God goes.

—*Anonymous*

Bible Truth Behind the Quote:
Christ's sheep follow Him (John 10:27).

— 439 —

The whole duty of man is summed up in obedience to God's will.

—*George Washington (1732-1799), first president of the United States*

Bible Truth Behind the Quote:
Jesus affirmed, "Whoever does the will of God, he is my brother and sister and mother" (Mark 3:35).

— 440 —

A man's heart is right when he wills what God wills.
—*Thomas Aquinas (1225-1274), Italian philosopher, theologian*

Bible Truth Behind the Quote:
"Do not be foolish, but understand what the will of the Lord is" (Ephesians 5:17).

— 441 —

The safest place to be is in the center of God's will.
—*Corrie ten Boom (1892-1983), Dutch Christian Holocaust survivor*

Bible Truth Behind the Quote:
"Whoever does the will of God abides forever" (1 John 2:17).

— 442 —

All my requests are lost in one, "Father, thy will be done!"
—*Charles Wesley (1707-1788), leader of Methodist Movement, hymn writer*

Bible Truth Behind the Quote:
We ought to daily pray, "Your kingdom come, your will be done, on earth as it is in heaven" (Matthew 6:10).

GODLINESS

— 443 —

Godliness is the child of truth, and it must
be nursed by its own mother.
—*William Gurnall (1617-1679), English author*

Bible Truth Behind the Quote:
"Long for the pure spiritual milk, that by it you may grow up to salvation" (1 Peter 2:2).

GOOD AND EVIL

— 444 —

Life eternal is the supreme good, death eternal the supreme evil.
—*Augustine (354-430), bishop of Hippo*

Bible Truth Behind the Quote:
The wicked "will go away into eternal punishment, but the righteous into eternal life" (Matthew 25:46).

GOOD IDEAS

— 445 —

Not to be fortified with good ideas is to be victimized by bad ones.
—*Carl F.H. Henry (1913-2003), American evangelical theologian*

Bible Truth Behind the Quote:
"Whatever is true, whatever is honorable, whatever is just, whatever is pure, whatever is lovely, whatever is commendable, if there is any excellence, if there is anything worthy of praise, think about these things" (Philippians 4:8).

GOOD WORKS, DOING

— 446 —

Wherever you are, be all there. Live to the hilt every
situation you believe to be the will of God.
—*Jim Elliot (1927-1956), missionary to Ecuador*

Bible Truth Behind the Quote:
We ought always to do the will of God with our whole heart (Ephesians 6:6).

— 447 —

Throw your soul into the work as if your
one employer were the Lord!
—*R.C.H. Lenski (1864-1936), Lutheran commentator*

Bible Truth Behind the Quote:
"Whatever you do, work heartily, as for the Lord and not for men" (Colossians 3:23).

— 448 —

Whatever your life's work, do it well. A man should do his job so
well that the living, the dead, and the unborn could do it no better.
—*Martin Luther King, Jr. (1929-1968), clergyman,
activist in the African-American Civil Rights Movement*

Bible Truth Behind the Quote:
Whatever you do, do it well (Ecclesiastes 9:10).

— 449 —

Even if I knew the world would be destroyed
tomorrow I would plant a tree today.

—*Martin Luther (1483-1546), priest, professor of theology, reformer*

Bible Truth Behind the Quote:
"Do not grow weary in doing good" (2 Thessalonians 3:13).

— 450 —

Had I a hundred hands, I could employ them all.
The harvest is very great. I am ashamed I can do no
more for him who has done so much for me.

—*George Whitefield (1714-1770), Anglican itinerant minister*

Bible Truth Behind the Quote:
"Whatever you do, work heartily, as for the Lord and not for men" (Colossians 3:23).

— 451 —

Do all the good you can,
By all the means you can,
In all the ways you can,
In all the places you can,
At all the times you can,
To all the people you can,
As long as ever you can.

—*John Wesley (1703-1791), founder of the Methodist church*

Bible Truth Behind the Quote:
"Let our people learn to devote themselves to good works" (Titus 3:14).

GOSPEL

— 452 —

The gospel reminds all men of an inescapable personal
destiny in eternity, based on a conclusive decision in time.

—*Carl F.H. Henry (1913-2003), American evangelical theologian*

Bible Truth Behind the Quote:
The gospel "is the power of God for salvation to everyone who believes" (Romans 1:16).

— 453 —

I reckon him a Christian indeed that is neither
ashamed of the Gospel nor a shame to it.

—*Matthew Henry (1662-1714), Bible commentator, Presbyterian minister*

Bible Truth Behind the Quote:
Paul affirmed, "I am not ashamed, for I know whom I have believed" (2 Timothy 1:12).

— 454 —

There are two things to do about the
Gospel—believe it and behave it.
—Susanna Wesley (1669-1742), mother of John and Charles Wesley

Bible Truth Behind the Quote:
In James 2:14, James asks, "What good is it, my brothers, if someone says he has faith but does not have works?" While it is faith in the Gospel that saves us (Acts 16:31), that faith ought to show itself in the way we live!

GOSPEL, URGENCY OF THE

— 455 —

I would freely give my eyes if you might but see Christ, and I
would willingly give my hands if you might but lay hold on Him.
—Charles Spurgeon (1834-1892), pastor, New Park Street Chapel, London

Bible Truth Behind the Quote:
Paul said of the unsaved Jews, "I could wish that I myself were accursed and cut off from Christ for the sake of my brothers, my kinsmen according to the flesh" (Romans 9:3).

GOSSIP

— 456 —

Gossip is the art of confessing other people's sins.
—Anonymous

Bible Truth Behind the Quote:
We are not to spread slanderous gossip (Leviticus 19:16). A gossiper betrays a confidence (Proverbs 11:13), separates close friends (Proverbs 16:28), and causes anger (Proverbs 25:23).

GOVERNMENT

— 457 —

It is impossible to rightly govern the world
without God and the Bible.
—George Washington (1732-1799), first president of the United States

Bible Truth Behind the Quote:
Solomon prayed, "Give your servant therefore an understanding mind to govern your people, that I may discern between good and evil, for who is able to govern this your great people?" (1 Kings 3:9).

GRACE

— 458 —

For grace is given not because we have done good works,
but in order that we may be able to do them.
—Augustine (354-430), bishop of Hippo

Bible Truth Behind the Quote:
After Paul asserted that we are saved solely by grace and apart from works (Ephesians 2:8-9), he then said that good works follow. "For we are his workmanship, created in Christ Jesus for good works" (verse 10).

— 459 —

Grace is love that cares and stoops and rescues.
—John Stott (born 1921), Anglican clergyman

Bible Truth Behind the Quote:
"God is able to make all grace abound to you, so that having all sufficiency in all things at all times, you may abound in every good work" (2 Corinthians 9:8).

— 460 —

The law detects, grace alone conquers sin.
—Augustine (354-430), bishop of Hippo

Bible Truth Behind the Quote:
"The law was given through Moses; grace and truth came through Jesus Christ" (John 1:17). "You are not under law but under grace" (Romans 6:14).

— 461 —

The law tells me how crooked I am. Grace
comes along and straightens me out.
—Dwight L. Moody (1837-1899), evangelist

Bible Truth Behind the Quote:
"Be strengthened by the grace that is in Christ Jesus" (2 Timothy 2:1).

— 462 —

The ocean will hold a boat or a battleship, and God's
grace will stand any weight you put on it.

—*Anonymous*

Bible Truth Behind the Quote:
"May grace and peace be multiplied to you" (1 Peter 1:2).

GRACE, GROWING IN

— 463 —

When I speak of a person growing in grace, I mean
simply this—that his sense of sin is becoming deeper, his
faith stronger, his hope brighter, his love more extensive,
and his spiritual mindedness more marked.

—*J.C. Ryle (1816-1900), Anglican bishop, Liverpool*

Bible Truth Behind the Quote:
"Grow in the grace and knowledge of our Lord and Savior Jesus Christ" (2 Peter 3:18).

GRACE, PERCEIVED NEED FOR

— 464 —

No man can ever enter heaven until he is
first convinced he deserves hell.

—*John W. Everett, Christian leader*

Bible Truth Behind the Quote:
The repentant tax collector realized this truth: Standing far off, he "would not even lift up his eyes to heaven, but beat his breast, saying, God, be merciful to me, a sinner!" (Luke 18:13).

GRATITUDE

— 465 —

When it comes to life, the critical thing is whether you
take things for granted or take them with gratitude.

—*Gilbert Keith Chesterton (1874-1936), English author, apologist*

Bible Truth Behind the Quote:
No matter what, we ought always to be thankful (1 Thessalonians 5:18).

GREAT OPPORTUNITIES

— 466 —

We are faced with great opportunities brilliantly
disguised as impossible situations.

—*Charles Swindoll (born 1934), pastor, Stonebriar Community Church*

Bible Truth Behind the Quote:
"What is impossible with men is possible with God" (Luke 18:27).

GREATNESS

— 467 —

Greatness lies, not in being strong, but in the right use of strength.

—*Henry Ward Beecher (1813-1887), Congregationalist clergyman*

Bible Truth Behind the Quote:
Joseph, empowered in Egypt, could have used his strength to crush his treacherous brothers, but instead he used his strength to bless them (Genesis 45).

GRIEF

— 468 —

He that conceals his grief finds no remedy for it.

—*Anonymous*

Bible Truth Behind the Quote:
Our Lord is sympathetic with us in our grief, for He Himself was a "man of sorrows, and acquainted with grief" (Isaiah 53:3).

GUILT

— 469 —

The act of sin may pass, and yet the guilt remains.

—*Thomas Aquinas (1225-1274), Italian philosopher, theologian*

Bible Truth Behind the Quote:
Guilt that remains can move us to repentance. "Godly grief produces a repentance that leads to salvation" (2 Corinthians 7:10).

HABITS

— 470 —

One of these days you may be unable to get rid of those habits which you are now forming. At first the net of habit is made of cobweb; you can soon break it through. Before long it is made of twine. Soon it will be made of rope. And last of all it will be strong as steel, and then you will be fatally ensnared.

—Charles Spurgeon (1834-1892), pastor, New Park Street Chapel, London

Bible Truth Behind the Quote:
"An evil man is ensnared in his transgression" (Proverbs 29:6).

HAPPINESS

— 471 —

Pleasure-seeking is a barren business; happiness is never found till we have the grace to stop looking for it, and to give our attention to persons and matters external to ourselves.

—J.I. Packer (born 1926), author, theologian

Bible Truth Behind the Quote:
"The righteous shall be glad; they shall exult before God; they shall be jubilant with joy!" (Psalm 68:3).

— 472 —

They alone are truly happy who are seeking to be righteous. Put happiness in the place of righteousness and you will never get it.

—D. Martyn Lloyd-Jones (1899-1981), Welsh Protestant minister

Bible Truth Behind the Quote:
"Be glad in the LORD, and rejoice, O righteous, and shout for joy, all you upright in heart!" (Psalm 32:11).

— 473 —

Where your pleasure is, there is your treasure. Where your treasure is, there is your heart. Where your heart is, there is your happiness.

—Augustine (354-430), bishop of Hippo

Bible Truth Behind the Quote:
"Lay up for yourselves treasures in heaven" (Matthew 6:20).

— 474 —

Happy is he who has learned to make Christ his "all."
—*J.C. Ryle (1816-1900), Anglican bishop, Liverpool*

Bible Truth Behind the Quote:
We should seek to be like Paul. "I have been crucified with Christ. It is no longer I who live, but Christ who lives in me. And the life I now live in the flesh I live by faith in the Son of God, who loved me and gave himself for me" (Galatians 2:20).

— 475 —

Only entirely devoted Christians are entirely happy Christians.
—*Erich Sauer (1898-1959), Wiedenest Bible School, West Germany*

Bible Truth Behind the Quote:
"Rejoice in the LORD, O you righteous" (Psalm 97:12).

— 476 —

People who think that once they are converted
all will be happy, have forgotten Satan.
—*D. Martyn Lloyd-Jones (1899-1981), Welsh Protestant minister*

Bible Truth Behind the Quote:
Satan is the "accuser" (Revelation 12:10) and often accuses the consciences of Christians.

— 477 —

Our loving God wills that we eat, drink, and be merry.
—*Martin Luther (1483-1546), priest, professor of theology, reformer*

Bible Truth Behind the Quote:
"There is nothing better for a person than that he should eat and drink and find enjoyment in his toil" (Ecclesiastes 2:24).

— 478 —

God has linked together holiness and happiness; and what
God has joined together we must not think to put asunder.
—*J.C. Ryle (1816-1900), Anglican bishop, Liverpool*

Bible Truth Behind the Quote:
The holy man has a clear conscience (2 Corinthians 1:12; 1 Timothy 1:5,19; Hebrews 13:18)—a key component of happiness.

— 479 —

My true happiness is to go and sin no more.
—*Robert Murray M'Cheyne (1813-1843), minister, Church of Scotland*

Bible Truth Behind the Quote:
"Sin no more" are words spoken by the Savior Himself (John 5:14; 8:11).

— 480 —

Those that look to be happy must first look to be holy.
—Richard Sibbes (1577-1635), English theologian

Bible Truth Behind the Quote:
God affirms, "You shall be holy, for I am holy" (1 Peter 1:16).

— 481 —

Happiness is the practice of the virtues.
—Clement of Alexandria (150-215), theologian, philosopher

Bible Truth Behind the Quote:
The one who lives God's way experiences true blessing in life. "Blessed is the man who walks not in the counsel of the wicked, nor stands in the way of sinners, nor sits in the seat of scoffers" (Psalm 1:1).

HEALTH AND WEALTH

— 482 —

Health and wealth wean us of our need for Christ.
—Calvin Miller, author, artist

Bible Truth Behind the Quote:
"Only with difficulty will a rich person enter the kingdom of heaven" (Matthew 19:23).

HEALTH FOR THE SOUL

— 483 —

We take excellent care of our bodies, which we have for only a lifetime; yet we let our souls shrivel which we will have for eternity.
—Billy Graham (born 1918), evangelist

Bible Truth Behind the Quote:
"Beloved, I pray that all may go well with you and that you may be in good health, as it goes well with your soul" (3 John 1:2).

HEAVEN

— 484 —

The heavenly country is full of light and glory; having the delightful breezes of divine love, and the comfortable gales of the blessed Spirit; here is no heat of persecution, nor coldness, nor chills of affection; here is plenty of most delicious fruits, no hunger nor thirst; and here are riches, which are solid, satisfying, durable, safe and sure: many are the liberties and privileges here enjoyed; here is a freedom from a body subject to diseases and death, from a body of sin and death, from Satan's temptations, from all doubts, fears, and unbelief, and from all sorrows and afflictions.

—John Gill (1697-1771), English Baptist, biblical scholar

Bible Truth Behind the Quote:
"He will wipe away every tear from their eyes, and death shall be no more, neither shall there be mourning, nor crying, nor pain anymore, for the former things have passed away" (Revelation 21:4).

— 485 —

Images suggesting immense size or brilliant light depict heaven as a place of unimaginable splendor, greatness, excellence, and beauty…It is likely that while John's vision employs as metaphors those items which we think of as being most valuable and beautiful, the actual splendor of heaven far exceeds anything that we have yet experienced.

—Millard Erickson (born 1932), theologian

Bible Truth Behind the Quote:
The heavenly city manifests "the glory of God, its radiance like a most rare jewel, like a jasper, clear as crystal" (Revelation 21:11).

— 486 —

We shall then have joy without sorrow, and rest without weariness…Be of good cheer, Christian, the time is near, when God and thou shalt be near, and as near as thou canst well desire. Thou shalt dwell in his family.

—Richard Baxter (1615-1691), English Puritan church leader

Bible Truth Behind the Quote:
"God himself will be with them as their God" (Revelation 21:3).

— 487 —

When we get to Heaven, the joy of seeing our loved ones once again is immeasurably increased when we realize that all of us will indeed be perfect! There will be no more disagreements or cross words, hurt feelings or misunderstandings, neglect or busyness, interruptions or rivalry, jealousy or pride, selfishness or sin of any kind!

—*Anne Graham Lotz (born 1948), evangelist, daughter of Billy Graham*

Bible Truth Behind the Quote:
A grand reunion with Christian loved ones and friends is coming (1 Thessalonians 4:13-17).

— 488 —

There is a land of pure delight,
Where saints immortal reign;
Infinite day excludes the night,
And pleasures banish pain.

—*Isaac Watts (1674-1748), hymn writer, "There Is a Land of Pure Delight"*

Bible Truth Behind the Quote:
We will live forever in a "better country, that is, a heavenly one" (Hebrews 11:16).

— 489 —

There shall be no more curse—perfect restoration. The throne of God and of the Lamb shall be in it—perfect administration. His servants shall serve him—perfect subordination. And they shall see his face—perfect transformation. And his name shall be on their foreheads—perfect identification. And there shall be no night there; and they need no candle, neither light of the sun; for the Lord giveth them light—perfect illumination. And they shall reign forever and ever—perfect exultation.

—*A. T. Pierson (1837-1911), Presbyterian pastor*

Bible Truth Behind the Quote:
"What no eye has seen, nor ear heard, nor the heart of man imagined, what God has prepared for those who love him" (1 Corinthians 2:9).

— 490 —

Heavenly worship will not be confining or manipulated, but spontaneous and genuine...We will lose ourselves in the sheer joy of expressing with our lips the adoration and love we feel for God in our hearts...You won't find quiet, solemn worship clothed in hushed tones and organ music either. Instead you will hear shouts and loud voices and trumpets.

—*Douglas Connelly, pastor, author*

Bible Truth Behind the Quote:
"Worthy are you, our Lord and God, to receive glory and honor and power, for you created all things, and by your will they existed and were created" (Revelation 4:11).

— 491 —

We will never sin, never make mistakes, never need to
confess, never have to repair or replace things (no leaky
faucets, no changing lightbulbs, no car repairs). We will
never have to...defend ourselves, apologize, experience
guilt, battle with Satan or demons...or experience...
rehabilitation, loneliness, depression, or fatigue.
—*Mark Hitchcock, pastor, author*

Bible Truth Behind the Quote:
"Nothing unclean will ever enter it [heaven], nor anyone who does what is detestable or false, but only those who are written in the Lamb's book of life" (Revelation 21:27, insert added for clarification).

— 492 —

Let us not be afraid to meditate often on the subject of heaven,
and to rejoice in the prospect of good things to come...Let
us take comfort in the remembrance of the other side.
—*J.C. Ryle (1816-1900), Anglican bishop, Liverpool*

Bible Truth Behind the Quote:
Let us often ponder how heaven is inconceivably wonderful (1 Corinthians 2:9; 2 Corinthians 4:17; Colossians 3:2).

— 493 —

Whatever pleasures we have known here on earth
while living under the curse of sin are trivial, paltry
diversions compared to the pure delights of heaven.
—*John MacArthur (born 1939), pastor, Grace Community Church*

Bible Truth Behind the Quote:
"In your presence there is fullness of joy; at your right hand are pleasures forevermore" (Psalm 16:11).

— 494 —

Heaven is a perfectly ordered and harmonious
enjoyment of God and of one another in God.
—*Augustine (354-430), bishop of Hippo*

Bible Truth Behind the Quote:
Heaven is the paradise of God (2 Corinthians 12:2-4; Revelation 2:7;).

— 495 —

Everyone in heaven will be fully blessed, but not everyone will be
equally blessed. Every believer's cup will be full and running over,
but not everyone's cup will be the same size. We determine in
time what our capacity for appreciating God will be in eternity.

—*Norman Geisler (born 1932), Christian apologist*

Bible Truth Behind the Quote:
"We must all appear before the judgment seat of Christ, so that each one may receive
what is due for what he has done in the body, whether good or evil" (2 Corinthians 5:10).

— 496 —

The light in which He dwells is superior to all things visible; it
is something other than the radiance of all suns and stars. It is
not to be beheld by earthly eyes; it is "unapproachable" (1 Tim.
6:16), far removed from all things this side (2 Cor. 12:4). Only the
angels in heaven can behold it (Matt. 18:10); only the spirits of the
perfected in the eternal light (Matt. 5:8; 1 John 3:2; Rev. 22:4);
only the pure and holy, even as He Himself is pure (1 John 3:2-3).

—*Erich Sauer (1898-1959), Wiedenest Bible School, West Germany*

Bible Truth Behind the Quote:
God "dwells in unapproachable light" (1 Timothy 6:16). "The [heavenly] city has no need
of sun or moon to shine on it, for the glory of God gives it light, and its lamp is the Lamb"
(Revelation 21:23, insert added for clarification).

— 497 —

Even as in heaven there will be most perfect charity,
so in hell there will be the most perfect hate.

—*Thomas Aquinas (1225-1274), Italian philosopher, theologian*

Bible Truth Behind the Quote:
In heaven there will be perpetual praise and worship (Revelation 19:6), while in hell there
will be perpetual "weeping and gnashing of teeth" (Matthew 13:50).

— 498 —

It's ironic. In heaven, where I will be able once
again to wipe my own tears, I won't have to.

—*A quadriplegic perspective by Joni Eareckson Tada (born 1949), founder, Joni and Friends*

Bible Truth Behind the Quote:
"He will wipe away every tear from their eyes" (Revelation 21:4).

— 499 —

The king of terrors, the last enemy, will never be able to breach the
pearly gates and disturb the bliss of heaven! No more deathbed
vigils or funerals. The hearse will have made its last journey.

—*J. Oswald Sanders (1902-1992), director, Overseas Missionary Fellowship*

Bible Truth Behind the Quote:
"Death and Hades were thrown into the lake of fire" (Revelation 20:14).

— 500 —

I want to know one thing:
the way to heaven—
how to land safe on that happy shore.
God Himself has condescended to teach the way;
for this very end He came from heaven.
He has written it down in a book.
Oh, give me that book!
At any price give me that book!
I have it—here is knowledge enough for me.
Let me be a man of one book.
Here, then, I am, far from the busy ways of men.
I sit down alone; only God is here.
In His presence I open and read His book
that I may find the way to heaven.

—*John Wesley (1703-1791), founder of the Methodist church*

Bible Truth Behind the Quote:
Wesley's motivation was that heaven is a place of intimate fellowship and enjoyment with
God and Christ (Isaiah 60:19-20; John 12:26; 14:3; 17:24; 2 Corinthians 5:6-7; Philippi-
ans 1:23; 1 Thessalonians 4:17; Revelation 3:4-5,12; 19:6-9).

— 501 —

Heaven will chiefly consist in the enjoyment of God.

—*William S. Plummer (1802-1880), Christian author, commentator*

Bible Truth Behind the Quote:
Scripture promises, "In your presence there is fullness of joy; at your right hand are pleasures forevermore" (Psalm 16:11).

HEAVEN AND HELL

— 502 —

There are only two kinds of people in the end: those
who say to God, "Thy will be done," and those to
whom God says in the end, "Thy will be done."

—*C.S. Lewis (1898-1963), author, professor, Oxford University*

Bible Truth Behind the Quote:
The wicked "will go away into eternal punishment, but the righteous into eternal life"
(Matthew 25:46).

— 503 —

The wicked have a never-dying worm and
the godly a never-fading crown.

—*Thomas Watson (1620-1686), Puritan preacher, author*

Bible Truth Behind the Quote:
In the end, all—believers and unbelievers—will have been perfectly judged (2 Corinthians 5:10; Revelation 21:11-15).

— 504 —

Those who will not deliver themselves into the hand of God's
mercy cannot be delivered out of the hand of His justice.

—*Matthew Henry (1662-1714), Bible commentator, Presbyterian minister*

Bible Truth Behind the Quote:
God is not willing that any should perish (2 Peter 3:9), but those who do not avail themselves of the gift of salvation in Jesus Christ will be justly condemned (John 3:18; Revelation 20:11-12).

— 505 —

Would you know what makes heaven heaven? It is
communion with God. And would you know what
makes hell hell? It is to be forsaken of God.

—*Anonymous*

Bible Truth Behind the Quote:
In heaven, God will dwell with His people face to face (1 Corinthians 13:12; Revelation
21:3).

Hell

— 506 —

Hell is the highest reward that the devil can
offer you for being a servant of his.

—*Billy Sunday (1862-1935), American athlete, evangelist*

Bible Truth Behind the Quote:
The devil himself will be cast into hell (Revelation 20:10).

— 507 —

There are no agnostics in hell.

—*Anonymous*

Bible Truth Behind the Quote:
Scripture reveals that "at the name of Jesus every knee should bow, in heaven and on earth
and under the earth" (Philippians 2:10).

History

— 508 —

When viewed from the perspective of Scripture, history is
more than the recording of the events of the past. Rather,
what has happened in the past, what is happening now, and
what will happen in the future is all evidence of the unfolding
of the purposeful plan devised by the personal God of the
Bible. All the circumstances of life—past, present, and
future—fit into the sovereign plan like pieces of a puzzle.

—*Robert Lightner, theologian, Dallas Theological Seminary*

Bible Truth Behind the Quote:
God affirms, "My counsel shall stand, and I will accomplish all my purpose" (Isaiah
46:10).

Holiness

— 509 —

I believe the holier a man becomes, the more he mourns
over the unholiness which remains in him.

—*Charles Spurgeon (1834-1892), pastor, New Park Street Chapel, London*

Bible Truth Behind the Quote:
Paul considered himself the foremost among sinners (1 Timothy 1:15).

— 510 —

A holy clumsiness is better than a sinful eloquence.

—*Jerome (374-420), apologist, translator*

Bible Truth Behind the Quote:

"As he who called you is holy, you also be holy in all your conduct" (1 Peter 1:15).

— 511 —

A Christian is never in a state of completion
but always in the process of becoming.

—*Martin Luther (1483-1546), priest, professor of theology, reformer*

Bible Truth Behind the Quote:

While Christians have been positionally sanctified (Hebrews 10:10,29), they are also experientially in a daily, on-going process of progressive sanctification (2 Peter 1:3-11).

— 512 —

A holy man is a mighty weapon in the hands of God.

—*Robert Murray M'Cheyne (1813-1843), minister, Church of Scotland*

Bible Truth Behind the Quote:

"The prayer of a righteous person has great power as it is working" (James 5:16).

— 513 —

Holiness is not freedom from temptation,
but power to overcome temptation.

—*G. Campbell Morgan (1863-1945), pastor, Westminster Chapel, London*

Bible Truth Behind the Quote:

"No temptation has overtaken you that is not common to man. God is faithful, and he will not let you be tempted beyond your ability, but with the temptation he will also provide the way of escape, that you may be able to endure it" (1 Corinthians 10:13).

— 514 —

The task of the church is not to make men and
women happy; it is to make them holy.

—*Chuck Colson (born 1931), founder, Prison Fellowship*

Bible Truth Behind the Quote:

Christians in the church are called to "be holy and blameless before him" (Ephesians 1:4). The Lord has "called us to a holy calling" (2 Timothy 1:9).

— 515 —

It's not great talent that God blesses so much as likeness to Jesus.

—*Robert Murray M'Cheyne (1813-1843), minister, Church of Scotland*

Bible Truth Behind the Quote:
"You bless the righteous, O Lord; you cover him with favor as with a shield" (Psalm 5:12).

— 516 —

God is more concerned about our character than our comfort. His goal is not to pamper us physically but to perfect us spiritually.

—*Paul W. Powell (born 1933), retired dean, George W. Truett Theological Seminary*

Bible Truth Behind the Quote:
"It is for discipline that you have to endure. God is treating you as sons. For what son is there whom his father does not discipline?...He disciplines us for our good, that we may share his holiness" (Hebrews 12:7,10).

HOLY SPIRIT

— 517 —

You might as well expect to raise the dead by whispering in their ears, as hope to save souls by preaching to them, if it were not for the agency of the Spirit.

—*Charles Spurgeon (1834-1892), pastor, New Park Street Chapel, London*

Bible Truth Behind the Quote:
It is the Holy Spirit who convicts the world of sin, righteousness, and judgment (John 16:8) and bestows new life at the moment of conversion (Titus 3:5).

— 518 —

If the Holy Spirit guides us at all, he will do it according to the Scriptures, and never contrary to them.

—*George Müller (1805-1898), director of orphanages in Bristol, England*

Bible Truth Behind the Quote:
The Holy Spirit—Himself the ultimate author of Scripture (2 Timothy 3:16)—illumines our minds so we can understand Scripture (1 Corinthians 2:9–3:2).

— 519 —

The Holy Spirit is God the evangelist.

—*J.I. Packer (born 1926), author, theologian*

Bible Truth Behind the Quote:
"You will receive power when the Holy Spirit has come upon you, and you will be my witnesses in Jerusalem and in all Judea and Samaria, and to the end of the earth" (Acts 1:8).

— 520 —

Though every believer has the Holy Spirit, the
Holy Spirit does not have every believer.

—*A. W. Tozer (1897-1963), American pastor, author*

Bible Truth Behind the Quote:
"Do not grieve the Holy Spirit of God, by whom you were sealed for the day of redemption" (Ephesians 4:30).

— 521 —

You might as well try to hear without ears, or
breathe without lungs, as try to live a Christian
life without the Spirit of God in your heart.

—*Dwight L. Moody (1837-1899), evangelist*

Bible Truth Behind the Quote:
"Walk by the Spirit, and you will not gratify the desires of the flesh" (Galatians 5:16).

— 522 —

We do not use the Holy Spirit; He uses us.

—*Warren Wiersbe (born 1929), pastor, author*

Bible Truth Behind the Quote:
"While they were worshiping the Lord and fasting, the Holy Spirit said, 'Set apart for me Barnabas and Saul for the work to which I have called them'" (Acts 13:2).

HOPE

— 523 —

Hope refreshes faith, that it may not become weary. It sustains
faith to the final goal, that it may not fail in midcourse, or even
at the starting gate. In short, by unremitting renewing and
restoring, it invigorates faith again and again with perseverance.

—*John Calvin (1509-1564), French reformer*

Bible Truth Behind the Quote:
"For God alone, O my soul, wait in silence, for my hope is from him" (Psalm 62:5).

— 524 —

Hope is never ill when faith is well.

—*John Bunyan (1628-1688), English Christian writer, preacher*

Bible Truth Behind the Quote:
"So now faith, hope, and love abide" (1 Corinthians 13:13).

— 525 —

The world hopes for the best; but the Lord offers the best hope.
—*John Wesley White, evangelist*

Bible Truth Behind the Quote:
"I wait for the LORD, my soul waits, and in his word I hope" (Psalm 130:5).

— 526 —

There is one thing which gives radiance to everything.
It is the idea of something around the corner.
—*Gilbert Keith Chesterton (1874-1936), English author, apologist*

Bible Truth Behind the Quote:
"Set your hope fully on the grace that will be brought to you at the revelation of Jesus Christ" (1 Peter 1:13).

— 527 —

We must accept finite disappointment, but
we must never lose infinite hope.
—*Martin Luther King, Jr. (1929-1968), clergyman,*
activist in the African-American Civil Rights Movement

Bible Truth Behind the Quote:
"Let us hold fast the confession of our hope without wavering, for he who promised is faithful" (Hebrews 10:23).

— 528 —

Hope thinks nothing is difficult; despair tells
us that difficulty is insurmountable.
—*Isaac Watts (1674-1748), hymn writer*

Bible Truth Behind the Quote:
"I can do all things through him who strengthens me" (Philippians 4:13).

HUMILITY

— 529 —

Nothing sets a person so much out of the devil's reach as humility.
—*Jonathan Edwards (1703–1758), American theologian*

Bible Truth Behind the Quote:
"Humble yourselves, therefore, under the mighty hand of God so that at the proper time he may exalt you…Be sober-minded; be watchful. Your adversary the devil prowls around like a roaring lion, seeking someone to devour" (1 Peter 5:6-8).

— 530 —

A holy man will follow after humility…He will see
more evil in his own heart than in any other in the
world. He will understand something of Abraham's
feeling, when he says, "I am dust and ashes."

—*J.C. Ryle (1816-1900), Anglican bishop, Liverpool*

Bible Truth Behind the Quote:

Isaiah said, "Woe is me! For I am lost; for I am a man of unclean lips" (Isaiah 6:5).

— 531 —

Continual peace is with the humble, but in the heart
of the proud is envy and frequent indignation.

—*Thomas à Kempis (1380-1471), author,* The Imitation of Christ

Bible Truth Behind the Quote:

A humble David said, "In peace I will both lie down and sleep; for you alone, O LORD, make me dwell in safety" (Psalm 4:8).

— 532 —

Let the name of Whitefield perish, but Christ be glorified. Let
my name die everywhere, let even my friends forget me, if by
that means the cause of the blessed Jesus may be promoted.

—*George Whitefield (1714-1770), Anglican itinerant minister*

Bible Truth Behind the Quote:

John the Baptist asserted, "He must increase, but I must decrease" (John 3:30).

— 533 —

I am persuaded the more light we have, the more we
see our own sinfulness: the nearer we get to heaven,
the more we are clothed with humility.

—*J.C. Ryle (1816-1900), Anglican bishop, Liverpool*

Bible Truth Behind the Quote:

A humble Paul said, "Wretched man that I am! Who will deliver me from this body of death?" (Romans 7:24). The answer, of course, is Jesus Christ (verse 25).

— 534 —

The right manner of growth is to grow less in one's own eyes.

—*Thomas Watson (1620-1686), Puritan preacher, author*

Bible Truth Behind the Quote:

"Walk humbly with your God" (Micah 6:8).

— 535 —

He is genuinely great who considers himself small
and cares nothing about high honors.

—*Thomas à Kempis (1380-1471), author,* The Imitation of Christ

Bible Truth Behind the Quote:
Paul affirmed, "Am I now seeking the approval of man, or of God? Or am I trying to please man? If I were still trying to please man, I would not be a servant of Christ" (Galatians 1:10).

— 536 —

It is very difficult to be humble if you are always
successful, so God chastises us with failure at times in
order to humble us, to keep us in a state of humility.

—*D. Martyn Lloyd-Jones (1899-1981), Welsh Protestant minister*

Bible Truth Behind the Quote:
"The Lord disciplines the one he loves, and chastises every son whom he receives" (Hebrews 12:6).

— 537 —

Moses spent forty years thinking he was somebody; then
he spent forty years on the backside of the desert realizing
he was nobody; finally, he spent the last forty years of
his life learning what God can do with a nobody!

—*Dwight L. Moody (1837-1899), evangelist*

Bible Truth Behind the Quote:
"God chose what is foolish in the world to shame the wise; God chose what is weak in the world to shame the strong" (1 Corinthians 1:27).

— 538 —

Humility is the mother, root, nurse, foundation,
and center of all other virtues.

—*Chrysostom (347-407), early church father*

Bible Truth Behind the Quote:
We ought to be clothed with humility (Colossians 3:12; 1 Peter 5:5-6).

— 539 —

God has two thrones, one in the highest
heavens, the other in the lowliest heart.

—*Dwight L. Moody (1837-1899), evangelist*

Bible Truth Behind the Quote:
"I dwell in the high and holy place, and also with him who is of a contrite and lowly spirit, to revive the spirit of the lowly, and to revive the heart of the contrite" (Isaiah 57:15).

— 540 —

The humble man feels no jealousy or envy. He can praise
God when others are preferred before him. He can bear to
hear others praised while he is forgotten because…he has
received the Spirit of Jesus, who pleased not Himself, and
who sought not His own honor. Therefore, in putting on
the Lord Jesus Christ he has put on the heart of compassion,
kindness, meekness, long-suffering, and humility.

—*Andrew Murray (1828-1917), South African writer, pastor*

Bible Truth Behind the Quote:
"Have this mind among yourselves, which is yours in Christ Jesus, who, though he was in the form of God, did not count equality with God a thing to be grasped" (Philippians 2:5-6).

— 541 —

The honors of this world: What are they but
puff, and emptiness, and peril of falling?

—*Augustine (354-430), bishop of Hippo*

Bible Truth Behind the Quote:
Paradoxically, it is the humble who will be truly honored (Proverbs 15:33; 18:12; 29:23; Luke 14:11; 18:14).

— 542 —

Hate and despise all human glory, for it is nothing else
but human folly. It is the greatest snare and the greatest
betrayer that you can possibly admit into your heart.

—*William Law (1686-1761), English cleric, author*

Bible Truth Behind the Quote:
Pride goes before a destruction (Proverbs 16:18; 18:12).

HUSBAND AND WIFE

— 543 —

Let the wife make the husband glad to come home,
and let him make her sorry to see him leave.

—*Martin Luther (1483-1546), priest, professor of theology, reformer*

Bible Truth Behind the Quote:
Husbands, live happily with the woman you love (Ecclesiastes 9:9) and express true love to her (Colossians 3:19). The wife is her husband's joy (Proverbs 12:4).

— 544 —

You'll never see perfection in your mates,
nor will he or she find it in you.

—James Dobson (born 1936), founder, Focus on the Family

Bible Truth Behind the Quote:
We ought continuously to be "bearing with one another and, if one has a complaint against another, forgiving each other; as the Lord has forgiven you, so you also must forgive" (Colossians 3:13).

HYPOCRISY

— 545 —

It is no fault of Christianity if a hypocrite falls into sin.

—Jerome (374-420), apologist, translator

Bible Truth Behind the Quote:
The Bible itself warns us about hypocrites (Matthew 6:5,16; 7:5; James 4:8; 1 Peter 2:1). Hypocrisy proves one of the primary planks of Christianity—human sinfulness (Romans 3:23).

— 546 —

Don't hunt through the church for a hypocrite.
Go home and look in the glass. Hypocrites? Yes.
See that you make the number one less.

—Billy Sunday (1862-1935), American athlete, evangelist

Bible Truth Behind the Quote:
"Be doers of the word, and not hearers only" (James 1:22).

IDLENESS

— 547 —

Idleness tempts the devil to tempt.

—Thomas Watson (1620-1686), Puritan preacher, author

Bible Truth Behind the Quote:
"Give no opportunity to the devil" (Ephesians 4:27).

— 548 —

Find some work for your hands to do, so
that Satan may never find you idle.

—Jerome (374-420), apologist, translator

Bible Truth Behind the Quote:
Avoid falling into the "snare of the devil" (1 Timothy 3:7).

IDOLATRY

— 549 —

A man's god is that for which he lives, for which he is
prepared to give his time, his energy, his money, that which
stimulates him and rouses him, excites, and enthuses him.

—D. Martyn Lloyd-Jones (1899-1981), Welsh Protestant minister

Bible Truth Behind the Quote:
Flee from the worship of idols (1 Corinthians 10:14).

IGNORANCE

— 550 —

The more we know, the more we see of our own ignorance.

—Matthew Henry (1662-1714), Bible commentator, Presbyterian minister

Bible Truth Behind the Quote:
"Trust in the LORD with all your heart, and *do not lean on your own understanding*" (Proverbs 3:5).

— 551 —

It is worse still to be ignorant of your ignorance.

—Jerome (374-420), apologist, translator

Bible Truth Behind the Quote:
To the church in Laodicea, Jesus warned, "For you say, I am rich, I have prospered, and I need nothing, not realizing that you are wretched, pitiable, poor, blind, and naked" (Revelation 3:17). These folks were truly ignorant of their ignorance—a pitiable state.

Imitate the Lord

— 552 —

The most deeply felt obligation on earth is that which
the Christian feels to imitate the Redeemer.

—*Albert Barnes (1798-1870), theologian, commentator*

Bible Truth Behind the Quote:
Christians are called to follow the example of Christ (1 Peter 2:21).

Immature Christians

— 553 —

Christians are like old-fashioned photographs—
over-exposed and underdeveloped.

—*Howard Hendricks (born 1924), professor, Dallas Theological Seminary*

Bible Truth Behind the Quote:
"Let us…go on to maturity" (Hebrews 6:1).

Injustice

— 554 —

Injustice anywhere is a threat to justice everywhere.

—*Martin Luther King, Jr. (1929-1968), clergyman,*
activist in the African-American Civil Rights Movement

Bible Truth Behind the Quote:
Cursed is anyone who is unjust (Deuteronomy 27:19).

Intentions, Important

— 555 —

You are not a better person because you are praised; neither are
you any worse if somebody denigrates you. God knows what
you are. People consider actions, but God evaluates intentions.

—*Thomas à Kempis (1380-1471), author,* The Imitation of Christ

Bible Truth Behind the Quote:
God knows every heart (1 Kings 8:39; Jeremiah 12:3; Acts 1:24; 15:8; Romans 8:27) and
examines people's motives (Proverbs 16:2; Jeremiah 17:10).

JEALOUSY

— 556 —

The mature man is not threatened by other people's ministries.

—Anonymous

Bible Truth Behind the Quote:
Jealousy is an ugly mark of the flesh (Galatians 5:19-20).

— 557 —

Jealousy is the dominating temptation of the ministry.

—Anonymous

Bible Truth Behind the Quote:
The Sadducees expressed jealousy in their religious work (Acts 5:17), something grossly unappealing.

— 558 —

The jealous are troublesome to others; a torment to themselves.

—William Penn (1644-1718), English Quaker, founder of Pennsylvania

Bible Truth Behind the Quote:
Scripture warns that jealousy is destructive (Proverbs 27:4) and is a mark of the flesh (Galatians 5:19-20). Christians ought to strongly resist such urges.

JESUS

— 559 —

He began His ministry by being hungry, yet He is the Bread of Life. Jesus ended His earthly ministry by being thirsty, yet He is the Living Water. Jesus was weary, yet He is our rest. Jesus paid tribute, yet He is the King. Jesus was accused of having a demon, yet He cast out demons. Jesus wept, yet He wipes away our tears. Jesus was sold for thirty pieces of silver, yet He redeemed the world. Jesus was brought as a lamb to the slaughter, yet He is the Good Shepherd. Jesus died, yet by His death He destroyed the power of death.

—Gregory of Nazianzus (329-390), fourth-century archbishop of Constantinople

Bible Truth Behind the Quote:
"There are also many other things that Jesus did. Were every one of them to be written, I suppose that the world itself could not contain the books that would be written" (John 21:25).

— 560 —

It is, in my experience, the people who have never troubled
seriously to study the four gospels who are loudest in
their protest that there was no such person as Jesus.

—*J.B. Phillips (1906-1982), Bible translator, author, clergyman*

Bible Truth Behind the Quote:
"We did not follow cleverly devised myths when we made known to you the power and
coming of our Lord Jesus Christ, but we were eyewitnesses of his majesty" (2 Peter 1:16).

Jesus, Claims of

— 561 —

A man who was merely a man and said the sort of things
Jesus said would not be a great moral teacher. He would
either be a lunatic—on the level with the man who says he
is a poached egg—or else he would be the Devil of Hell.
You must make your choice. Either this man was, and is,
the son of God: or else a madman or something worse.

—*C.S. Lewis (1898-1963), author, professor, Oxford University*

Bible Truth Behind the Quote:
Jesus asserted, "I am the way, and the truth, and the life. No one comes to the Father
except through me" (John 14:6).

Jesus, God-Man

— 562 —

In the miracle of creation, God made man. In the miracle
of the Incarnation, He gave man the God-man.

—*Kenneth O. Gangle (1935-2009), professor, Dallas Theological Seminary*

Bible Truth Behind the Quote:
Jesus is the God-man. "For in him the whole fullness of deity dwells bodily" (Colossians 2:9).

JESUS OUR INTERCESSOR

— 563 —

If I can hear Christ praying for me in the next room,
I would not fear a million enemies. Yet the distance
makes no difference; He is praying for me.

—*Robert Murray M'Cheyne (1813-1843), minister, Church of Scotland*

Bible Truth Behind the Quote:
Jesus "always lives to make intercession" for believers (Hebrews 7:25).

JESUS, LOOKING TO

— 564 —

Looking unto Jesus is at the same time a
looking away from everything else.

—*Erich Sauer (1898-1959), Wiedenest Bible School, West Germany*

Bible Truth Behind the Quote:
We should keep "looking to Jesus, the founder and perfecter of our faith" (Hebrews 12:2)!

JESUS, SUFFICIENCY OF

— 565 —

"Christ liveth in me." And how great the difference!
—instead of bondage, liberty; instead of failure,
quiet victories within; instead of fear and weakness,
a restful sense of sufficiency in Another.

—*Hudson Taylor (1832-1905), missionary, China Inland Mission*

Bible Truth Behind the Quote:
"It is no longer I who live, but Christ who lives in me. And the life I now live in the flesh I live by faith in the Son of God, who loved me and gave himself for me" (Galatians 2:20).

— 566 —

Man can be restored to God by Christ, can know God
through Christ, and can become like God in Christ.

—*G. Campbell Morgan (1863-1945), pastor, Westminster Chapel, London*

Bible Truth Behind the Quote:
We "rejoice in God through our Lord Jesus Christ, through whom we have now received reconciliation" (Romans 5:11).

— 567 —

Jesus Christ is for all the New Testament writers the living
and only panacea for all illness, weakness, and distress.

—*Erich Sauer (1898-1959), Wiedenest Bible School, West Germany*

Bible Truth Behind the Quote:
"They brought him all the sick, those afflicted with various diseases and pains, those oppressed by demons, epileptics, and paralytics, and he healed them" (Matthew 4:24).

— 568 —

Were it not for the consciousness of Christ in my life, hour
by hour, I could not go on. But He is teaching me the
glorious lessons of His sufficiency, and each day I am carried
onward with no feeling of strain or fear of collapse.

—*J. Hudson Taylor (1832-1905), founder, China Inland Mission*

Bible Truth Behind the Quote:
"I can do all things through him who strengthens me" (Philippians 4:13).

— 569 —

The lawyer can deliver his client but from strife, the physician can
deliver his patient but from sickness, the master can deliver his
servant but from bondage, but the Lord delivereth us from all.

—*Henry Smith (1560-1591), English Puritan preacher*

Bible Truth Behind the Quote:
Jesus has "delivered us from the domain of darkness and transferred us to the kingdom of his beloved Son" (Colossians 1:13).

Jesus Died for You and Me

— 570 —

Lord Jesus, you are my righteousness, I am your sin.
You have taken upon yourself what is mine and given
me what is yours. You have become what You were
not so that I might become what I was not.

—*Martin Luther (1483-1546), priest, professor of theology, reformer*

Bible Truth Behind the Quote:
"For our sake he made him to be sin who knew no sin, so that in him we might become the righteousness of God" (2 Corinthians 5:21).

— 571 —

The innocent was punished voluntarily as if guilty, that the
guilty might be gratuitously rewarded as if innocent.
—*Robert Jamieson, Andrew Robert Fausset, David Brown, Bible commentators*

Bible Truth Behind the Quote:
The guilty are "declared righteous" (justified) through redemption in the sinless Christ (Romans 3:24).

— 572 —

Jesus was always without sin actually, but he was made to
be sin for us judicially...While Jesus never committed a sin
personally, he was made to be sin for us substitutionally.
—*Norman Geisler (born 1932), Christian apologist*

Bible Truth Behind the Quote:
"He committed no sin, neither was deceit found in his mouth" (1 Peter 2:22), and yet He judicially took our sin upon Himself (2 Corinthians 5:21).

JOY

— 573 —

No one can live without delight, and that is why a man
deprived of spiritual joy goes over to carnal pleasure.
—*Thomas Aquinas (1225-1274), Italian philosopher, theologian*

Bible Truth Behind the Quote:
"The joy of the LORD is your strength" (Nehemiah 8:10).

JUDGING OTHERS

— 574 —

Oh, how horrible our sins look when they
are committed by someone else.
—*Charles Swindoll (born 1934), pastor, Stonebriar Community Church*

Bible Truth Behind the Quote:
Jesus said, "Why do you see the speck that is in your brother's eye, but do not notice the log that is in your own eye?" (Matthew 7:3).

— 575 —

The proud are ever most provoked by pride.
—*William Cowper (1731-1800), English poet, hymnodist*

Bible Truth Behind the Quote:
"You have no excuse, O man, every one of you who judges. For in passing judgment on another you condemn yourself, because you, the judge, practice the very same things" (Romans 2:1).

— 576 —

It is a vital moment of truth when a man discovers
that what he condemns most vehemently in
others is that to which he is himself prone.

—*Anonymous*

Bible Truth Behind the Quote:
"The heart is deceitful above all things, and desperately sick; who can understand it?" (Jeremiah 17:9).

JUDGMENT

— 577 —

Every man shall give an account of his own works, a full and
true account of all that he ever did while alive, whether it was
good or evil…God will bring to light every circumstance that
accompanied each word and action. He will judge whether
they lessened or increased the goodness or badness of them.

—*John Wesley (1703-1791), founder of the Methodist church*

Bible Truth Behind the Quote:
"We must all appear before the judgment seat of Christ, so that each one may receive what is due for what he has done in the body, whether good or evil" (2 Corinthians 5:10).

— 578 —

All true believers who stand before the judgment seat will
qualify for heaven, but not all will receive the same reward.

—*J. Oswald Sanders (1902-1992), director, Overseas Missionary Fellowship*

Bible Truth Behind the Quote:
"If the work that anyone has built on the foundation survives, he will receive a reward. If anyone's work is burned up, he will suffer loss, though he himself will be saved, but only as through fire" (1 Corinthians 3:14-15).

— 579 —

The judgment seat of Christ might be compared to a
commencement ceremony. At graduation there is some measure
of disappointment and remorse that one did not do better and
work harder. However, at such an event the overwhelming
emotion is joy, not remorse. The graduates do not leave the
auditorium weeping because they did not earn better grades.
Rather, they are thankful that they have been graduated, and
they are grateful for what they did achieve. To overdo the sorrow
aspect of the judgment seat of Christ is to make heaven hell. To
underdo the sorrow aspect is to make faithfulness inconsequential.

—*Herman Hoyt, theologian, author*

Bible Truth Behind the Quote:
Heaven is the destiny for all Christians (Philippians 3:20), the heavily rewarded and the
minimally rewarded.

KINDNESS

— 580 —

Often the only thing a child can remember about an
adult in later years, when he or she is grown, is whether
or not that person was kind to him or her.

—*Billy Graham (born 1918), evangelist*

Bible Truth Behind the Quote:
We ought always to be kind and compassionate (Ephesians 4:32).

— 581 —

Kindness has converted more sinners than
zeal, eloquence or learning.

—*Frederick W. Faber (1814-1863), British hymn writer, theologian*

Bible Truth Behind the Quote:
You should always be "prepared to make a defense to anyone who asks you for a reason for
the hope that is in you; *yet do it with gentleness and respect*" (1 Peter 3:15-16).

— 582 —

He who throws dirt always loses ground.

—*Anonymous*

Bible Truth Behind the Quote:
"A man who is kind benefits himself, but a cruel man hurts himself" (Proverbs 11:17).

KNOWING GOD

— 583 —

What were we made for? To know God! What aim
should we set ourselves in life? To know God. What is the
"eternal life" that Jesus gives? Knowledge of God…What
is the best thing in life, bringing more joy, delight, and
contentment, than anything else? Knowledge of God.

—*J.I. Packer (born 1926), author, theologian*

Bible Truth Behind the Quote:
"This is eternal life, that they know you the only true God, and Jesus Christ whom you
have sent" (John 17:3).

— 584 —

We have no greater need than to know Christ better.

—*Andrew Murray (1828-1917), South African writer, pastor*

Bible Truth Behind the Quote:
"I count everything as loss because of the surpassing worth of knowing Christ Jesus my
Lord. For his sake I have suffered the loss of all things and count them as rubbish, in order
that I may gain Christ" (Philippians 3:8).

— 585 —

Bestow on me, O Lord my God,
understanding to know You,
diligence to seek You,
and a faithfulness
that may finally embrace You,
through Jesus Christ our Lord.

—*Thomas Aquinas (1225-1274), Italian philosopher, theologian*

Bible Truth Behind the Quote:
May we all "grow in the grace and knowledge of our Lord and Savior Jesus Christ"
(2 Peter 3:18).

LABOR

— 586 —

Labor: a powerful medicine.

—*Chrysostom (347-407), early church father*

Bible Truth Behind the Quote:
People who work hard sleep well (Ecclesiastes 5:12).

Laughter

— 587 —

If you're not allowed to laugh in heaven, I don't want to go there.

—*Martin Luther (1483-1546), priest, professor of theology, reformer*

Bible Truth Behind the Quote:
God "will wipe away every tear from their eyes, and death shall be no more, neither shall there be mourning nor crying nor pain anymore, for the former things have passed away" (Revelation 21:4). With such a wondrous environment, how can we not laugh?

— 588 —

A retired surgeon said to me on a plane, "I've practiced medicine for fifty-eight years and I've never known a person to die from laughter."

—*Roy B. Zuck, professor, Dallas Theological Seminary*

Bible Truth Behind the Quote:
"A joyful heart is good medicine" (Proverbs 17:22).

Laziness

— 589 —

God will not do for you what he has given you strength to do for yourself.

—*Bob Jones (1883-1968), American evangelist*

Bible Truth Behind the Quote:
While God rendered assistance, it was Noah who built the ark (Genesis 6–7).

— 590 —

Our confidence in Christ does not make us lazy, negligent, or careless, but on the contrary it awakens us, urges us on, and makes us active in living righteous lives and doing good. There is no self-confidence to compare with this.

—*Ulrich Zwingli (1484-1531), Swiss reformer*

Bible Truth Behind the Quote:
"Whatever you do, work heartily, as for the Lord and not for men" (Colossians 3:23).

LEADERSHIP

— 591 —

Anyone who influences others is a leader.

—Anonymous

Bible Truth Behind the Quote:
Leaders lead by a good example (1 Peter 5:3).

— 592 —

Leaders need to cultivate two things: a
righteous heart and rhinoceros skin.

—Charles Swindoll (born 1934), pastor, Stonebriar Community Church

Bible Truth Behind the Quote:
Joseph is a good example of a good leader (Genesis 47:13-26).

LET YOUR LIGHT SHINE

— 593 —

What other people think of me is becoming less and less
important; what they think of Jesus because of me is critical.

—Cliff Richards (born 1940), recording artist

Bible Truth Behind the Quote:
Jesus urged His followers, "Let your light shine before others, so that they may see your good works and give glory to your Father who is in heaven" (Matthew 5:16).

LIBERTY

— 594 —

Liberty has brought us the freedom to
be the slaves of righteousness.

—Charles Ryrie (born 1925), theologian, Dallas Theological Seminary

Bible Truth Behind the Quote:
The apostle Paul explains that "you are slaves of the one whom you obey, either of sin, which leads to death, or of obedience, which leads to righteousness...and, having been set free from sin, have become slaves of righteousness" (Romans 6:16,18).

Life and Death

— 595 —

Take care of your life; and the Lord will take care of your death.

—*George Whitefield (1714-1770), itinerant minister, Great Awakening*

Bible Truth Behind the Quote:
Jesus told a parable of a man who cared not for the important things of life, but only for the accumulation of wealth while on earth. Then without warning, God said to him, "Fool! This night your soul is required of you" (Luke 12:20). He was not prepared for death. If, however, we seek the Lord in life, death is nothing to fear of (1 Corinthians 15:55).

Longevity

— 596 —

Like anybody, I would like to live a long life. Longevity has its place. But I'm not concerned about that now. I just want to do God's will. And he's allowed me to go up to the mountain. I looked over, and I've seen the promised land.

—*Martin Luther (1483-1546), priest, professor of theology, reformer*

Bible Truth Behind the Quote:
"Set your minds on things that are above, not on things that are on earth" (Colossians 3:2).

— 597 —

If life be long I will be glad,
That I may long obey;
If short—yet why should I be sad
To welcome to endless day?

—*Richard Baxter (1615-1691), English Puritan church leader*

Bible Truth Behind the Quote:
"My times are in your hand" (Psalm 31:15).

Longings of the Heart

— 598 —

None but God can satisfy the longings of an immortal soul;
that as the heart was made for Him, so He only can fill it.

—*Richard Chenevix Trench (1807-1886), Anglican poet*

Bible Truth Behind the Quote:
Ecclesiastes 3:11 tells us that God "has put eternity into man's heart." Only God can satisfy the human heart. As the psalmist put it, "As a deer pants for flowing streams, so pants my soul for you, O God" (Psalm 42:1).

LOVE

— 599 —

Humility and patience are the surest proofs of the increase of love.
—*John Wesley (1703-1791), founder of the Methodist church*

Bible Truth Behind the Quote:
"Finally, all of you, have unity of mind, sympathy, brotherly love, a tender heart, and a humble mind" (1 Peter 3:8).

— 600 —

To love means loving the unlovable. To forgive means pardoning
the unpardonable. Faith means believing the unbelievable.
Hope means hoping when everything seems hopeless.
—*Gilbert Keith Chesterton (1874-1936), English author, apologist*

Bible Truth Behind the Quote:
"So now faith, hope, and love abide, these three; but the greatest of these is love" (1 Corinthians 13:13).

— 601 —

You can give without loving. But you cannot love without giving.
—*Amy Carmichael (1867-1951), missionary in India*

Bible Truth Behind the Quote:
Our love should motivate us to give to those in need (Luke 11:41; 12:33; Hebrews 13:16).

— 602 —

Faith deals with invisibles, but God hates
that love which is invisible.
—*Thomas Watson (1620-1686), Puritan preacher, author*

Bible Truth Behind the Quote:
Do not just pretend to love others (Romans 12:9-10).

— 603 —

The cold world needs warm-hearted Christians.
—*Anonymous*

Bible Truth Behind the Quote:
We ought to do everything with love (1 Corinthians 16:14).

— 604 —

The Bible tells us to love our neighbors, and also to love our
enemies; probably because generally they are the same people.
—*Gilbert Keith Chesterton (1874-1936), English author, apologist*

Bible Truth Behind the Quote:
Love your enemies (Luke 6:27).

— 605 —

God loves the world. Go thou and do likewise.
—*Erwin Lutzer (born 1941), pastor, Moody Church, Chicago*

Bible Truth Behind the Quote:
"Beloved, if God so loved us, we also ought to love one another" (1 John 4:11).

— 606 —

Darkness cannot drive out darkness; only light can do
that. Hate cannot drive out hate; only love can do that.
—*Martin Luther King, Jr. (1929-1968), clergyman,
activist in the African-American Civil Rights Movement*

Bible Truth Behind the Quote:
"You have heard that it was said, 'You shall love your neighbor and hate your enemy.' But I
say to you, Love your enemies and pray for those who persecute you" (Matthew 5:43-44).

— 607 —

Love that reaches up is adoration.
Love that reaches across is affection.
Love that reaches down is grace.
—*Donald Grey Barnhouse (1895-1960), preacher, pastor, theologian*

Bible Truth Behind the Quote:
"God is love, and whoever abides in love abides in God, and God abides in him" (1 John
4:16).

— 608 —

Genuine love demands toughness in moments of crisis.
—*James Dobson (born 1936), founder, Focus on the Family*

Bible Truth Behind the Quote:
"The Lord disciplines the one he loves" (Hebrews 12:6). This is much like the tough love
of human fathers (verse 7).

— 609 —

We cannot love good if we do not hate evil.
—*Jerome (374-420), apologist, translator*

Bible Truth Behind the Quote:
"I hate and abhor falsehood, but I love your law" (Psalm 119:163).

— 610 —

The love of our neighbor is the only door
out of the dungeon of self.
—*George MacDonald (1824-1905), Scottish author, poet, minister*

Bible Truth Behind the Quote:
Jesus instructed His followers, "A new commandment I give to you, that you love one another: just as I have loved you, you also are to love one another" (John 13:34).

LOVE OF MONEY

— 611 —

It is not the fact that a man has riches which keeps him from
the kingdom of heaven, but the fact that riches have him.
—*John Caird (1820-1898), Scottish theologian*

Bible Truth Behind the Quote:
Jesus said to His followers, "Truly, I say to you, only with difficulty will a rich person enter the kingdom of heaven" (Matthew 19:23).

LUST

— 612 —

Love can wait to give; it is lust that can't wait to get.
—*Josh McDowell (born 1939), Christian apologist*

Bible Truth Behind the Quote:
Scripture is clear: "For this is the will of God, your sanctification: that you abstain from sexual immorality" (1 Thessalonians 4:3).

MALICE

— 613 —

Malice is mental murder.
—*Thomas Watson (1620-1686), Puritan preacher, author*

Bible Truth Behind the Quote:
From the heart comes murder (Matthew 15:19; Mark 7:21).

MASKING SIN

— 614 —

He that does one fault at first, and tries to hide it, makes it two.
—*Isaac Watts (1674-1748), hymn writer*

Bible Truth Behind the Quote:
David had an adulterous relationship with Bathsheba (2 Samuel 12:24), and instead of facing up to what he had done, he sent her husband, Uriah, to the front lines of a battle where David knew he would die (2 Samuel 11:15). One sin led to another.

MEEKNESS

— 615 —

Meekness is not weakness. It is power under control.
—*Warren Wiersbe (born 1929), pastor, author*

Bible Truth Behind the Quote:
Scripture instructs us to be clothed with humility (Colossians 3:12). God blesses the gentle and lowly (Matthew 5:5); indeed, He supports the humble (Psalm 147:6).

MERCY

— 616 —

He that demands mercy, and shows none, ruins
the bridge over which he himself is to pass.
—*Thomas Adams (1583-1652), English clergyman, preacher*

Bible Truth Behind the Quote:
"Judgment is without mercy to one who has shown no mercy" (James 2:13).

— 617 —

We count on God's mercy for our past mistakes, on God's love
for our present needs, on God's sovereignty for our future.
—*Augustine (354-430), bishop of Hippo*

Bible Truth Behind the Quote:
"Answer me, O Lord, for your steadfast love is good; according to your abundant mercy, turn to me" (Psalm 69:16).

MINISTER

— 618 —

If a man can preach a sermon without mentioning Christ's
name in it, it ought to be his last, certainly the last that
any Christian ought to go to hear him preach.

—*Charles Spurgeon (1834-1892), pastor, New Park Street Chapel, London*

Bible Truth Behind the Quote:
Paul said "we preach Christ crucified" (1 Corinthians 1:23) and "the gospel of Christ"
(2 Corinthians 2:12). We should do likewise.

— 619 —

Many a church thinks it needs a new pastor
when it needs the same pastor renewed.

—*Anonymous*

Bible Truth Behind the Quote:
Two life verses for every pastor and ministry worker are "Apart from me you can do nothing" (John 15:5) and "I can do all things through him who strengthens me" (Philippians 4:13).

— 620 —

The preacher's sharpest and strongest
preaching should be to himself.

—*E.M. Bounds (1835-1913), clergyman, author*

Bible Truth Behind the Quote:
God's overseer in the church must be "above reproach" (1 Timothy 3:2).

— 621 —

Some ministers would make good martyrs:
they are so dry they would burn well.

—*Charles Spurgeon (1834-1892), pastor, New Park Street Chapel, London*

Bible Truth Behind the Quote:
This is especially a travesty in view of the fact that "the word of God is living and active"
(Hebrews 4:12) and brings delight to those who hear it (Psalm 119:14,16,24).

— 622 —

No man preaches a sermon well to others if he
does not first preach it to his own heart.

—*John Owen (1616-1683), church leader, theologian*

Bible Truth Behind the Quote:
God's ministers, like all Christians, must "walk the walk" (James 1:22).

— 623 —

When you speak of heaven, let your face light up. When
you speak of hell—well, then your everyday face will do.
—*Charles Spurgeon (1834-1892), pastor, New Park Street Chapel, London*

Bible Truth Behind the Quote:
A glad heart makes for a happy face (Proverbs 15:13).

— 624 —

God sometimes raises up many faithful
ministers out of the ashes of one.
—*Matthew Henry (1662-1714), Bible commentator, Presbyterian minister*

Bible Truth Behind the Quote:
One result of the apostle Paul's imprisonment was that "most of the brothers, having
become confident in the Lord by my imprisonment, are much more bold to speak the
word without fear" (Philippians 1:14).

— 625 —

I preach as though Christ was crucified yesterday, rose
from the dead today, and was coming back tomorrow.
—*Martin Luther (1483-1546), priest, professor of theology, reformer*

Bible Truth Behind the Quote:
We ought always to be enthusiastic about the Lord's work (1 Corinthians 15:58).

— 626 —

No man should preach on hell who can do so with dry eyes.
—*Charles Spurgeon (1834-1892), pastor, New Park Street Chapel, London*

Bible Truth Behind the Quote:
Paul often shed tears in preaching. "For three years I did not cease night or day to admonish everyone with tears" (Acts 20:31).

— 627 —

Once in seven years I burn all my sermons for it is a shame if I
cannot write better sermons now than I did seven years ago.
—*John Wesley (1703-1791), founder of the Methodist church*

Bible Truth Behind the Quote:
The accumulative effect of both old and new sermons should be the declaring of "the
whole counsel of God" (Acts 20:27).

— 628 —

I believe that the most damnable thing a man can do
is to preach the gospel merely as an actor and turn the
worship of God into a kind of theatrical performance.

—*Charles Spurgeon (1834-1892), pastor, New Park Street Chapel, London*

Bible Truth Behind the Quote:
We will answer for all pretense and hypocrisy at the judgment seat of Christ (2 Corinthians 5:10).

MIRACLES

— 629 —

Miracles are not contrary to nature but only
contrary to what we know about nature.

—*Augustine (354-430), bishop of Hippo*

Bible Truth Behind the Quote:
God "bore witness by signs and wonders and various miracles" (Hebrews 2:4).

MISSION WORK

— 630 —

There are three qualifications for missionaries:
patience, patience, patience.

—*J. Hudson Taylor (1832-1905), founder, China Inland Mission*

Bible Truth Behind the Quote:
We ought to clothe ourselves in patience (Colossians 3:12).

— 631 —

Every life without Christ is a mission field;
every life with Christ is a missionary.

—*Anonymous*

Bible Truth Behind the Quote:
Always be ready with an answer to everyone who asks (1 Peter 3:15).

MODESTY

— 632 —

Let us learn to lay upon ourselves the restraint of modesty.
—*John Calvin (1509-1564), French reformer*

Bible Truth Behind the Quote:
Scripture provides fine examples of modesty (1 Samuel 9:21; Esther 1:11-12; Job 32:4-7).

MONEY AND MATERIALISM

— 633 —

To "lay up treasure on earth" is a thing as expressly and clearly
forbidden by our Master as either adultery or murder.
—*John Wesley (1703-1791), founder of the Methodist church*

Bible Truth Behind the Quote:
"Those who desire to be rich fall into temptation, into a snare, into many senseless and
harmful desires that plunge people into ruin and destruction" (1 Timothy 6:9).

— 634 —

Riches are not forbidden, but the pride of them is.
—*Chrysostom (347-407), early church father*

Bible Truth Behind the Quote:
Abram was very rich (Genesis 13:2) but had no pride in it.

— 635 —

Money, in truth, is one of the most unsatisfying of possessions.
It takes away some cares, no doubt; but it brings with it quite as
many cares as it takes away. There is the trouble in the getting
of it. There is anxiety in the keeping of it. There are temptations
in the use of it. There is guilt in the abuse of it. There is sorrow
in the losing of it. There is perplexity in the disposing of it.
—*J.C. Ryle (1816-1900), Anglican bishop, Liverpool*

Bible Truth Behind the Quote:
Money lovers are never satisfied (Ecclesiastes 5:10).

— 636 —

I value all things only by the price they shall gain in eternity.
—*John Wesley (1703-1791), founder of the Methodist church*

Bible Truth Behind the Quote:
"Lay up for yourselves treasures in heaven, where neither moth nor rust destroys and where thieves do not break in and steal" (Matthew 6:20).

— 637 —

Depend on it. God's work done in God's way will never lack
God's supply. He is too wise a God to frustrate His purposes
for lack of funds, and He can just as easily supply them ahead
of time as afterwards, and He much prefers doing so.

—J. Hudson Taylor (1832-1905), founder, China Inland Mission

Bible Truth Behind the Quote:
"My God will supply every need of yours according to his riches in glory in Christ Jesus" (Philippians 4:19).

— 638 —

Materialism may be called "affluenza."

—Mrs. Ray Stedman, wife of the famous pastor

Bible Truth Behind the Quote:
We simply cannot have two masters—God and money (Matthew 6:24).

— 639 —

We may love money without having it, just as
we may have money without loving it.

—J.C. Ryle (1816-1900), Anglican bishop, Liverpool

Bible Truth Behind the Quote:
Whether we are rich or poor, we must not be greedy for money (1 Peter 5:2).

— 640 —

If we were given all we wanted here, our hearts would settle for
this world rather than the next. God is forever luring us up and
away from this one, wooing us to Himself and His still invisible
Kingdom, where we will certainly find what we so keenly long for.

—Elisabeth Elliot (born 1926), author, wife of Jim Elliot

Bible Truth Behind the Quote:
God "has put eternity into man's heart" (Ecclesiastes 3:11).

— 641 —

God judges what we give by what we keep.

—George Müller (1805-1898), director of orphanages in Bristol, England

Bible Truth Behind the Quote:
Jesus spoke of rich people putting large sums of money into the treasury box. He also noted that "a poor widow came and put in two small copper coins, which make a penny" (Mark 12:41-42). The rich gave out of their abundance, Jesus said, but she gave "everything she had, all she had to live on" (verse 44).

— 642 —

Wealth is no mark of God's favor. Poverty
is no mark of God's displeasure.
—*J.C. Ryle (1816-1900), Anglican bishop, Liverpool*

Bible Truth Behind the Quote:
"For you say, I am rich, I have prospered, and I need nothing, not realizing that you are wretched, pitiable, poor, blind, and naked" (Revelation 3:17).

— 643 —

Nothing that is God's is obtainable by money.
—*Tertullian (160-220), early apologist*

Bible Truth Behind the Quote:
"When Simon saw that the Spirit was given through the laying on of the apostles' hands, he offered them money, saying, 'Give me this power also, so that anyone on whom I lay my hands may receive the Holy Spirit.' But Peter said to him, 'May your silver perish with you, because you thought you could obtain the gift of God with money!'" (Acts 8:18-20).

— 644 —

I will place no value on anything I have or may possess,
except in relation to the kingdom of Christ.
—*David Livingstone (1813-1873), medical missionary*

Bible Truth Behind the Quote:
God owns everything, and we are merely stewards of God's possessions (Exodus 19:5; Psalm 50:10).

— 645 —

When I have money, I get rid of it quickly,
lest it find a way into my heart.
—*John Wesley (1703-1791), founder of the Methodist church*

Bible Truth Behind the Quote:
Money can bring temptations, snares, and harmful desires—even leading to ruin and destruction (1 Timothy 6:9).

— 646 —

He is rich enough who is poor with Christ.

—Jerome (374-420), apologist, translator

Bible Truth Behind the Quote:
"I have learned in whatever situation I am to be content" (Philippians 4:11).

— 647 —

The use of our possessions shows us up for what we actually are.

—Charles Ryrie (born 1925), theologian, Dallas Theological Seminary

Bible Truth Behind the Quote:
Let nothing take God's place in your heart (1 John 5:21).

— 648 —

Make all you can, save all you can, give all you can.

—John Wesley (1703-1791), founder of the Methodist church

Bible Truth Behind the Quote:
Give to the poor (Deuteronomy 15:7,8; Matthew 19:21; Galatians 2:10) and to all those in need (Luke 11:41; 12:33; Hebrews 13:16).

MUSIC

— 649 —

Next to theology I give to music the highest place and honor. Music is the art of the prophets, the only art that can calm the agitations of the soul; it is one of the most magnificent and delightful presents God has given us.

—Martin Luther (1483-1546), priest, professor of theology, reformer

Bible Truth Behind the Quote:
God can be praised with musical instruments (Psalm 43:4; 71:22; 98:5; 144:9; 147:7; 149:3; 150:3-4).

— 650 —

One man's music is another's noise.

—Erwin Lutzer (born 1941), pastor, Moody Church, Chicago

Bible Truth Behind the Quote:
Christians may have different opinions on some matters (Romans 14:2), but we still maintain unity (verses 3-4).

OBEDIENCE

— 651 —

If any kingdom has ever advanced totalitarian claims it is the kingdom of Christ and God. Authority and obedience, leading and following, command and subjection, this is its order. This is a totalitarian King, kingdom, and church. All half-heartedness and lukewarmness is an abomination to the King.

—*Erich Sauer (1898-1959), Wiedenest Bible School, West Germany*

Bible Truth Behind the Quote:
Jesus asserted, "If anyone would come after me, let him deny himself and take up his cross and follow me" (Matthew 16:24).

— 652 —

It might be well if we stopped using the words "victory" and "defeat" to describe our progress in holiness. Rather we should use the words "obedience" and "disobedience."

—*Jerry Bridges (born 1929), author, affiliated with The Navigators*

Bible Truth Behind the Quote:
Obedience is far more important than external religious rituals (1 Samuel 15:22). Our obedience to God ought to be perpetual (Psalm 119:44).

— 653 —

More depends on my walk than talk.

—*Dwight L. Moody (1837-1899), evangelist*

Bible Truth Behind the Quote:
"Be doers of the word, and not hearers only, deceiving yourselves" (James 1:22).

— 654 —

We cannot rely on God's promises without obeying his commandments.

—*John Calvin (1509-1564), French reformer*

Bible Truth Behind the Quote:
Obedience brings blessing (Deuteronomy 7:12; 11:17; 1 Kings 8:35-36; Zechariah 3:7).

— 655 —

We do not meditate that we may rest in contemplation, but in order to render obedience.

—*Thomas Manton (1620-1667), English Puritan clergyman*

Bible Truth Behind the Quote:
"I have stored up your word in my heart, that I might not sin against you" (Psalm 119:11).

— 656 —

Many crowd to get into the church, but make
no room for the sermon to get into them.
—*Thomas Adams (1583-1652), English clergyman, preacher*

Bible Truth Behind the Quote:
"Let the word of Christ dwell in you richly, teaching and admonishing one another in all wisdom, singing psalms and hymns and spiritual songs, with thankfulness in your hearts to God" (Colossians 3:16).

— 657 —

Only where there is trust and devotion, will God's
fountains be opened. Only upon a life, fully surrendered,
will He pour out His abundant blessings.
—*Erich Sauer (1898-1959), Wiedenest Bible School, West Germany*

Bible Truth Behind the Quote:
God's blessing is always contingent on obedience to Him (Exodus 19:5; 23:22; Leviticus 26:3; Deuteronomy 4:40; 12:28; 15:5; 28:1; 1 Kings 2:3; Zechariah 3:7; Hebrews 3:14).

— 658 —

Obedience to God is the most infallible evidence
of sincere and supreme love to him.
—*Nathanael Emmons (1745-1840), American theologian*

Bible Truth Behind the Quote:
Jesus instructed His followers, "If you love me, you will keep my commandments" (John 14:15).

— 659 —

The believer is not redeemed by obedience to
the law but he is redeemed unto it.
—*John Murray (1898-1975), Scottish-born Calvinist theologian*

Bible Truth Behind the Quote:
We are saved by grace through faith (Ephesians 2:8-9) but "unto good works" (Ephesians 2:10). Likewise, in Titus we are told that "he saved us, not because of righteous things we had done, but because of his mercy" (Titus 3:5). Then he says immediately that "those who have trusted in God may be careful to devote themselves to doing what is good" (verse 8).

— 660 —

Love of the creature toward the Creator must
include obedience or it is meaningless.
—*Francis Schaeffer (1912-1984), theologian, philosopher, pastor*

Bible Truth Behind the Quote:
Scripture tells us that God loves the obedient (Deuteronomy 5:10; Psalm 25:10), and that from His perspective, obedience is better than sacrifice (1 Samuel 15:22). Thus, we ought to obey God wholeheartedly (Joshua 24:14; Romans 6:17).

PAIN

— 661 —

God whispers to us in our joys, speaks to us in our
difficulties, and shouts to us in our pain.
—*C.S. Lewis (1898-1963), author, professor, Oxford University*

Bible Truth Behind the Quote:
"It is good for me that I was afflicted, that I might learn your statutes" (Psalm 119:71).

— 662 —

Pain is God's megaphone to rouse a deaf world.
—*C.S. Lewis (1898-1963), author, professor, Oxford University*

Bible Truth Behind the Quote:
"Before I was afflicted I went astray, but now I keep your word" (Psalm 119:67).

PARENTAL LOVE

— 663 —

We never know the love of a parent until
we become parents ourselves.
—*Henry Ward Beecher (1813-1887), Congregationalist clergyman*

Bible Truth Behind the Quote:
Once we become parents, we are given just a slight glimpse of the awesome love that God the Father has for His children—only His is infinitely deeper than that of any human parent (see Hebrews 12:7-11; 1 John 4:18,16).

PATIENCE

— 664 —

Teach us, O Lord, the disciplines of patience,
for to wait is often harder than to work.

—*Peter Marshall (1902-1949), Scottish-American preacher*

Bible Truth Behind the Quote:
Wisdom gives patience (Proverbs 19:11).

— 665 —

Be not angry that you cannot make others as you wish them
to be since you cannot make yourself as you wish to be.

—*Thomas à Kempis (1380-1471), author,* The Imitation of Christ

Bible Truth Behind the Quote:
Paul was patient with others because he so well knew his own frailties (Romans 7:15; 1 Timothy 1:15).

— 666 —

Prayer of the modern American: "Dear God, I
pray for patience. And I want it right now!"

—*Anonymous*

Bible Truth Behind the Quote:
We are to be clothed with patience (Colossians 3:12), being patient with virtually everyone (Ephesians 4:2). One result of walking in dependence on the Holy Spirit is patience (see Galatians 5:22). In times of trouble, we are to wait patiently on the Lord (Psalm 37:7).

PEACE

— 667 —

There can never be peace in the bosom of a believer.
There is peace with God, but constant war with sin.

—*Robert Murray M'Cheyne (1813-1843), minister, Church of Scotland*

Bible Truth Behind the Quote:
Even the great apostle Paul said, "I do not understand my own actions. For I do not do what I want, but I do the very thing I hate…I know that nothing good dwells in me, that is, in my flesh. For I have the desire to do what is right, but not the ability to carry it out. For I do not do the good I want, but the evil I do not want is what I keep on doing.

Now if I do what I do not want, it is no longer I who do it, but sin that dwells within me" (Romans 7:15,18-20).

PERSEVERANCE

— 668 —

By perseverance the snail reached the ark.
—*Charles Spurgeon (1834-1892), pastor, New Park Street Chapel, London*

Bible Truth Behind the Quote:
Never tire of doing good (Galatians 6:9; 2 Thessalonians 3:13), and seek to run with endurance (Hebrews 12:1).

PERSEVERANCE OF THE SAINTS

— 669 —

The perseverance of the saints is only possible
because of the perseverance of God.
—*J. Oswald Sanders (1902-1992), director, Overseas Missionary Fellowship*

Bible Truth Behind the Quote:
Scripture says of God, "Those whom he foreknew he also predestined to be conformed to the image of his Son, in order that he might be the firstborn among many brothers. And those whom he predestined he also called, and those whom he called he also justified, and those whom he justified he also glorified" (Romans 8:29-30). There's an unbroken chain from God's foreknowledge all the way through glorification. God perseveres!

POPULARITY

— 670 —

Nothing is so fickle and uncertain as popularity. It is
here today and gone tomorrow. It is a sandy foundation,
and sure to fail those who build upon it.
—*J.C. Ryle (1816-1900), Anglican bishop, Liverpool*

Bible Truth Behind the Quote:
It is unwise and ultimately unfulfilling to seek the praise of men (John 12:43).

POVERTY

— 671 —

World poverty is a hundred million mothers weeping...
because they cannot feed their children.
—*Ronald Sider (born 1939), theologian, Christian activist*

Bible Truth Behind the Quote:
Abject poverty should move Christians to give to the poor whenever there is opportunity (Matthew 19:21; Luke 11:41; 12:33; 1 John 3:17). We ought to use money for good (1 Timothy 6:17-18) and do so generously (Romans 12:8).

POWER IN MINISTRY

— 672 —

Nearness to Christ, intimacy with him, assimilation to his
character—these are the elements of a ministry of power.
—*Horatius Bonar (1808-1889), Scottish churchman, poet*

Bible Truth Behind the Quote:
Why is it important for the minister to stay near to Christ? Because without Christ we can do nothing (John 15:4), but with Christ we can do all things (Philippians 4:13).

PRACTICING THE PRESENCE OF GOD

— 673 —

Shall I tell you what supported me through all these years of exile,
among the people whose language I could not understand and whose
attitude toward me was always uncertain and often hostile? It was
this: "Lo, I am with you always even unto the end of the world."
—*David Livingstone (1813-1873), medical missionary*

Bible Truth Behind the Quote:
"Behold, I am with you always, to the end of the age" (Matthew 28:20).

— 674 —

When Jesus is present, all is good and nothing seems
difficult; but when Jesus is absent, all is hard.
—*Thomas à Kempis (1380-1471), author,* The Imitation of Christ

Bible Truth Behind the Quote:
"Whoever abides in me and I in him, he it is that bears much fruit, for apart from me you can do nothing" (John 15:5).

— 675 —

Lord, make yourself always present to my mind, and let
your love fill and rule my soul in all those places, companies,
and employments to which You call me. Amen.
—*John Wesley (1703-1791), founder of the Methodist church*

Bible Truth Behind the Quote:
"Seek the LORD and his strength; seek his presence continually!" (Psalm 105:4).

— 676 —

All our life is a celebration for us; we are convinced,
in fact, that God is always everywhere. We sing
while we work, we sing hymns while we sail, we pray
while we carry out all life's other occupations.
—*Clement of Alexandria (150-215), theologian, philosopher*

Bible Truth Behind the Quote:
"Let the word of Christ dwell in you richly, teaching and admonishing one another in all wisdom, singing psalms and hymns and spiritual songs, with thankfulness in your hearts to God" (Colossians 3:16).

— 677 —

The Christian finds safety not in the absence
of danger but in the presence of God.
—*Anonymous*

Bible Truth Behind the Quote:
"Keep me as the apple of your eye; hide me in the shadow of your wings" (Psalm 17:8).

— 678 —

Practice the presence of Christ in thy life. Think
of this: Where thou art, He also is. He sees every
situation. He can help daily and hourly.
—*Erich Sauer (1898-1959), Wiedenest Bible School, West Germany*

Bible Truth Behind the Quote:
Jesus is "Immanuel," which means "God with us" (Matthew 1:23).

— 679 —

Live near to God, and all things will appear little
to you in comparison with eternal realities.
—*Robert Murray M'Cheyne (1813-1843), minister, Church of Scotland*

Bible Truth Behind the Quote:
"Draw near to God, and he will draw near to you" (James 4:8).

PRAISE

— 680 —

O for a thousand tongues to sing my great Redeemer's praise!
—*Charles Wesley (1707-1788), leader of Methodist Movement, hymn writer*

Bible Truth Behind the Quote:
"Praise our God, all you his servants, you who fear him, small and great" (Revelation 19:5).

— 681 —

Be not afraid of saying too much in the praises of
God; all the danger is of saying too little.
—*Matthew Henry (1662-1714), Bible commentator, Presbyterian minister*

Bible Truth Behind the Quote:
"Then I heard what seemed to be the voice of a great multitude, like the roar of many waters and like the sound of mighty peals of thunder, crying out, Hallelujah!" (Revelation 19:6).

PRAYER

— 682 —

Many pray with their lips for that for
which their hearts have no desire.
—*Jonathan Edwards (1703-1758), American theologian*

Bible Truth Behind the Quote:
We ought to pray earnestly from the heart (Matthew 9:38).

— 683 —

Prayer is not overcoming God's reluctance,
but laying hold of His willingness.
—*Martin Luther (1483-1546), priest, professor of theology, reformer*

Bible Truth Behind the Quote:
"You do not have, because you do not ask" (James 4:2).

— 684 —

All our perils are nothing, so long as we have prayer.
—*Charles Spurgeon (1834-1892), pastor, New Park Street Chapel, London*

Bible Truth Behind the Quote:
"Do not be anxious about anything, but in everything by prayer and supplication with thanksgiving let your requests be made known to God" (Philippians 4:6).

— 685 —

Yank some of the gloom out of your
prayers, and put in some shouts.

—*Billy Sunday (1862-1935), American athlete, evangelist*

Bible Truth Behind the Quote:
"Enter his gates with thanksgiving" (Psalm 100:4).

— 686 —

Secret, fervent, believing prayer lies at the
root of all personal godliness.

—*William Carey (1761-1834), English Baptist missionary*

Bible Truth Behind the Quote:
"You, beloved, build yourselves up in your most holy faith; pray in the Holy Spirit" (Jude 1:20).

— 687 —

Keep praying, and be thankful that God's
answers are wiser than your prayers!

—*William Culbertson (1905-1971), president, Moody Bible Institute*

Bible Truth Behind the Quote:
Father knows best (Psalm 139:1-4; Matthew 11:21; 1 John 3:20).

— 688 —

Let prayer be the key of the morning and the bolt of the evening.

—*Matthew Henry (1662-1714), Bible commentator, Presbyterian minister*

Bible Truth Behind the Quote:
"Pray without ceasing" (1 Thessalonians 5:17).

— 689 —

A prayerless Christian is a powerless Christian.

—*Billy Graham (born 1918), evangelist*

Bible Truth Behind the Quote:
"Save us, we pray, O Lord! O Lord, we pray, give us success!" (Psalm 118:25).

— 690 —

I have so much to do today that I must set
apart more time than usual to pray.
—*Martin Luther (1483-1546), priest, professor of theology, reformer*

Bible Truth Behind the Quote:
We ought to follow Jesus' example, who often prayed early in the morning, before the
day started (Mark 1:35).

— 691 —

If you have no prayer life yourself, it is rather a useless
gesture to make your child say his prayers every night.
—*Peter Marshall (1902-1949), Scottish-American preacher*

Bible Truth Behind the Quote:
Parents can set a very good example for their children (see 1 Kings 9:4; 2 Chronicles 17:3;
2 Timothy 1:5).

— 692 —

Beware in your prayer, above everything, of limiting God, not
only by unbelief, but by fancying that you know what he can do.
—*Andrew Murray (1828-1917), South African writer, pastor*

Bible Truth Behind the Quote:
"Trust in the LORD with all your heart, and do not lean on your own understanding"
(Proverbs 3:5).

— 693 —

In prayer it is better to have a heart without
words, than words without a heart.
—*John Bunyan (1628-1688), English Christian writer, preacher*

Bible Truth Behind the Quote:
We ought to engage in "earnest prayer" (Acts 12:5).

— 694 —

Fight all your battles on your knees and you win every time.
—*Charles Stanley (born 1932), senior pastor, First Baptist Church of Atlanta*

Bible Truth Behind the Quote:
We ought always to cast all our anxieties on God, for He cares for us (1 Peter 5:7).

— 695 —

Prayer is the most important thing in my life. If I should neglect
prayer for a single day, I should lose a great deal of the fire of faith.
—*Martin Luther (1483-1546), priest, professor of theology, reformer*

Bible Truth Behind the Quote:
"Continue steadfastly in prayer" (Colossians 4:2).

— 696 —

We stand tallest and strongest on our knees.
—*Charles Stanley (born 1932), senior pastor, First Baptist Church of Atlanta*

Bible Truth Behind the Quote:
"The prayer of a righteous person has great power as it is working" (James 5:16).

— 697 —

Trouble and perplexity drive us to prayer, and
prayer driveth away trouble and perplexity.
—*Phillip Melanchton (1497-1560), German reformer*

Bible Truth Behind the Quote:
"Call upon me in the day of trouble; I will deliver you, and you shall glorify me" (Psalm
50:15).

— 698 —

Life is fragile…Handle with prayer.
—*Anonymous*

Bible Truth Behind the Quote:
"Do not be anxious about anything, but in everything by prayer and supplication with
thanksgiving let your requests be made known to God" (Philippians 4:6).

— 699 —

God has not always answered my prayers. If he had, I
would've married the wrong man—several times!
—*Ruth Bell Graham (1920-2007), wife of Billy Graham*

Bible Truth Behind the Quote:
Father always knows best (Psalm 139:1-4; Matthew 11:21; 1 John 3:20).

— 700 —

I live in the spirit of prayer. I pray as I walk about, when I lie
down, and when I rise up. And the answers are always coming.
—*George Müller (1805-1898), director of orphanages in Bristol, England*

Bible Truth Behind the Quote:
"Pray without ceasing" (1 Thessalonians 5:17).

— 701 —

Prayer will make a man cease from sin, or sin
will entice a man to cease from prayer.
—*John Bunyan (1628-1688), English Christian writer, preacher*

Bible Truth Behind the Quote:
"Lead us not into temptation, but deliver us from evil" (Matthew 6:13).

— 702 —

The angel fetched Peter out of prison, but
it was prayer fetched the angel.
—*Thomas Watson (1620-1686), Puritan preacher, author*

Bible Truth Behind the Quote:
"Peter was kept in prison, but earnest prayer for him was made to God by the church"
(Acts 12:5).

— 703 —

The more godly a man is, and the more graces and blessings
of God are upon him, the more need he hath to pray,
because Satan is busiest against him, and because he is
readiest to be puffed up with a conceited holiness.
—*Richard Greenham (1535-1594), English Puritan*

Bible Truth Behind the Quote:
"Continue steadfastly in prayer" (Colossians 4:2).

— 704 —

Dealing in generalities is the death of prayer.
—*J.H. Evans*

Bible Truth Behind the Quote:
We are privileged to make specific requests of God in prayer (Philippians 4:6).

— 705 —

He who has learned to pray has learned the
greatest secret of a holy and a happy life.
—*William Law (1686-1761), English cleric, author*

Bible Truth Behind the Quote:
The Lord's Prayer is an excellent place to begin (Matthew 6:9-13).

— 706 —

The men who have done the most for God in
this world have been early on their knees.

—*E.M. Bounds (1835-1913), clergyman, author*

Bible Truth Behind the Quote:
Such individuals follow the example of Jesus (Mark 1:35).

— 707 —

The neglect of prayer is a grand hindrance to holiness.

—*John Wesley (1703-1791), founder of the Methodist church*

Bible Truth Behind the Quote:
One cannot realistically expect deliverance from sin without specifically asking for God's
help (see Matthew 6:13).

— 708 —

Most Christians expect little from God, ask little, and
therefore receive little, and are content with little.

—*A.W. Pink (1886-1952), Calvinist evangelist, Bible scholar*

Bible Truth Behind the Quote:
God is "able to do far more abundantly than all that we ask or think" (Ephesians 3:20)
and stands ready to do so.

— 709 —

Nothing lies beyond the reach of prayer except
that which lies outside the will of God.

—*Anonymous*

Bible Truth Behind the Quote:
"This is the confidence that we have toward him, that if we ask anything according to his
will he hears us" (1 John 5:14).

— 710 —

When life knocks you on your knees, you're
in the perfect position to pray!

—*Anonymous*

Bible Truth Behind the Quote:
God promises, "When he calls to me, I will answer him; I will be with him in trouble"
(Psalm 91:15).

— 711 —

Pray often; for prayer is a shield to the soul, a
sacrifice to God, and a scourge for Satan.

—*John Bunyan (1628-1688), English Christian writer, preacher*

Bible Truth Behind the Quote:
We ought to pray "at all times in the Spirit, with all prayer and supplication" (Ephesians 6:18).

— 712 —

The activities we do for God are secondary. God is looking
for people who long for communication with him.

—*Erwin Lutzer (born 1941), pastor, Moody Church, Chicago*

Bible Truth Behind the Quote:
"O God, you are my God; earnestly I seek you; my soul thirsts for you; my flesh faints for you, as in a dry and weary land where there is no water" (Psalm 63:1).

— 713 —

Our-Father-who-art-in-heaven-gimme-gimme-gimme.

—*Calvin Miller, author, artist*

Bible Truth Behind the Quote:
"You ask and do not receive, because you ask wrongly, to spend it on your passions" (James 4:3).

— 714 —

We need more Christians for whom prayer
is the first resort, not the last.

—*John Blanchard, preacher, apologist, author*

Bible Truth Behind the Quote:
We "ought always to pray and not lose heart" (Luke 18:1).

— 715 —

The mightier any is in the Word, the more
mighty he will be in prayer.

—*William Gurnall (1617-1679), English author*

Bible Truth Behind the Quote:
"We will devote ourselves to prayer and to the ministry of the word" (Acts 6:4).

— 716 —

Be careful for nothing, prayerful for
everything, thankful for anything.

—*Dwight L. Moody (1837-1899), evangelist*

Bible Truth Behind the Quote:
We ought always to give thanks (Ephesians 5:20; Colossians 3:15).

— 717 —

God does nothing but in answer to prayer; and even they who
have been converted to God without praying for it themselves
(which is exceeding rare) were not without the prayers of others.
Every new victory, which a soul gains, is the effect of a new prayer.

—*John Wesley (1703-1791), founder of the Methodist church*

Bible Truth Behind the Quote:
"You do not have, because you do not ask" (James 4:2).

— 718 —

Do not work so hard for Christ that you have no
strength to pray, for prayer requires strength.

—*J. Hudson Taylor (1832-1905), founder, China Inland Mission*

Bible Truth Behind the Quote:
Epaphras prayed so diligently that Scripture describes him as "always struggling" (or wrestling) in prayer for the church at Colossae (Colossians 4:12).

— 719 —

We are never more like Christ than in prayers of intercession.

—*Austin Phelps (1820-1890), American Congregational minister*

Bible Truth Behind the Quote:
Jesus "always lives to make intercession" for us (Hebrews 7:25). We are exhorted to "pray for one another" (James 5:16).

— 720 —

The great tragedy of life is not unanswered
prayer but unoffered prayer.

—*F.B. Meyer (1847-1929), Baptist pastor, evangelist*

Bible Truth Behind the Quote:
James 4:2 tells us, "You do not have, because you do not ask." No Christian should be prayerless.

— 721 —

Prayer is happy company with God.

—Clement of Alexandria (150-215), theologian, philosopher

Bible Truth Behind the Quote:
The psalmist refers to God as "God my exceeding joy" (Psalm 43:4). Spending time with God in prayer naturally involves happy company with God.

— 722 —

Prayer is not wrestling with God's reluctance to bless
us; it is laying hold of his willingness to do so.

—John Blanchard (born 1932), preacher, apologist, author

Bible Truth Behind the Quote:
This desire on God's part to bless us lies behind Paul's instruction on prayer: "Do not be anxious about anything, but in everything by prayer and supplication with thanksgiving let your requests be made known to God. And the peace of God, which surpasses all understanding, will guard your hearts and your minds in Christ Jesus" (Philippians 4:6-7).

— 723 —

The measure of our love for others can largely be determined
by the frequency and earnestness of our prayers for them.

—A. W. Pink (1886-1952), Calvinist evangelist, Bible scholar

Bible Truth Behind the Quote:
Jesus loves us, and "he always lives to make intercession" for us (Hebrews 7:25). Likewise, those who are His followers show their love by interceding to God on their behalf (see James 5:16; Colossians 1:9-11).

PRAYER FOR BIBLE STUDY

— 724 —

Grant me grace, O merciful God, to desire ardently
all that is pleasing to Thee, to examine it prudently, to
acknowledge it truthfully, and to accomplish it perfectly,
for the praise and glory of Thy name. Amen.

—Thomas Aquinas (1225-1274), Italian philosopher, theologian

Bible Truth Behind the Quote:
"Open my eyes, that I may behold wondrous things out of your law" (Psalm 119:18).

PRAYER FOR TENDER MERCY

— 725 —

Gentle Jesus, meek and mild,
look upon a little child,
pity my simplicity,
suffer me to come to thee.

—Charles Wesley (1707-1788), leader of Methodist Movement, hymn writer

Bible Truth Behind the Quote:
"Come to me, all who labor and are heavy laden, and I will give you rest. Take my yoke upon you, and learn from me, for I am gentle and lowly in heart, and you will find rest for your souls" (Matthew 11:28-29).

PRAYER OF HUMILITY

— 726 —

When we are wrong,
make us willing to change.
And when we are right,
make us easy to live with.

—Peter Marshall (1902-1949), Scottish-American preacher

Bible Truth Behind the Quote:
"If my people who are called by my name humble themselves, and pray and seek my face and turn from their wicked ways, then I will hear from heaven and will forgive their sin and heal their land" (2 Chronicles 7:14).

PRAYER OF SERENITY

— 727 —

God, grant me the serenity to accept the things I
cannot change; the courage to change the things I
can; and the wisdom to know the difference.

—Reinhold Niebuhr (1892-1971), Protestant theologian

Bible Truth Behind the Quote:
Praying for wisdom is wise. "If any of you lacks wisdom, let him ask God, who gives generously to all without reproach, and it will be given him" (James 1:5).

PRAYING HARD

— 728 —

You should find this to be God's usual course:
not to give his children the taste of his delights till
they begin to sweat in seeking after them.
—*Richard Baxter (1615-1691), English Puritan church leader*

Bible Truth Behind the Quote:
Luke 11:5-10 records Jesus' parable about prayer in which a person knocked on a friend's door at midnight in need of three loaves of bread, asking persistently until the request was finally granted.

PREACHING

— 729 —

To love to preach is one thing; to love to
whom you preach is quite another.
—*D. Martyn Lloyd-Jones (1899-1981), Welsh Protestant minister*

Bible Truth Behind the Quote:
"This is the message that you have heard from the beginning, that we should love one another" (1 John 3:11).

— 730 —

I preach as never sure to preach again the
message of a dying man to dying men.
—*Richard Baxter (1615-1691), English Puritan church leader*

Bible Truth Behind the Quote:
"Preach the word; be ready in season and out of season" (2 Timothy 4:2).

— 731 —

No man ought to be in a Christian pulpit
who fears man more than God.
—*William Still (1839-1900), Scottish pastor, author*

Bible Truth Behind the Quote:
The apostle Paul emphasized that he sought the approval not of human beings but of God (see Galatians 1:10). The same must be true of every preacher of the truth.

PRIDE

— 732 —

God sends no one away empty except
those who are full of themselves.

—Dwight L. Moody (1837-1899), evangelist

Bible Truth Behind the Quote:
God mocks proud mockers (Proverbs 3:34).

— 733 —

He who sings his own praise is usually off-key.

—Anonymous

Bible Truth Behind the Quote:
Shun self-confident boasting (2 Corinthians 11:17).

— 734 —

Pride loves to climb up, not as Zaccheus
to see Christ, but to be seen.

—William Gurnall (1617-1679), English author

Bible Truth Behind the Quote:
Better to be lowly in spirit (Proverbs 16:19).

— 735 —

A man is never so proud as when striking an attitude of humility.

—C.S. Lewis (1898-1963), author, professor, Oxford University

Bible Truth Behind the Quote:
Do not be conceited (Romans 12:16).

— 736 —

Poverty and affliction take away the fuel that feeds pride.

—Richard Sibbes (1577-1635), English theologian

Bible Truth Behind the Quote:
God humbles the proud (Isaiah 13:11; Daniel 4:37).

— 737 —

The proud man lives halfway down the slope to hell.

—Anonymous

Bible Truth Behind the Quote:
Pride goes before destruction (Proverbs 16:18; 18:12).

— 738 —

Conceit is a weird disease—it makes
everybody sick except the guy who has it.

—*James Dobson (born 1936), founder, Focus on the Family*

Bible Truth Behind the Quote:
Boasting is evil (James 4:16).

— 739 —

It was pride that changed angels into devils; it
is humility that makes men as angels.

—*Augustine (354-430), bishop of Hippo*

Bible Truth Behind the Quote:
Walk humbly with your God (Micah 6:8).

— 740 —

The labor of self-love is a heavy one indeed. Think for
yourself whether much of your sorrow has not arisen from
someone speaking slightingly of you. As long as you set
yourself up as a little god to which you must be loyal there
will be those who will delight to offer affront to your idol.

—*A. W. Tozer (1897-1963), American pastor, author*

Bible Truth Behind the Quote:
"Do nothing from rivalry or conceit, but in humility count others more significant than
yourselves" (Philippians 2:3).

— 741 —

He who thinks too much of his virtues
bids others to think of his vices.

—*Anonymous*

Bible Truth Behind the Quote:
"If anyone thinks he is something, when he is nothing, he deceives himself" (Galatians
6:3).

— 742 —

The gate of heaven, though it is so wide that the
greatest sinner may enter, is nevertheless so low
that pride can never pass through it.

—*Charles Spurgeon (1834-1892), pastor, New Park Street Chapel, London*

Bible Truth Behind the Quote:
It is good for us to reflect on Jesus' words about the proud Pharisee ("God, I thank you that I am not like other men...") and the humble, repentant tax collector ("Be merciful to me...") in Luke 18:10-14. It was the humble man who found salvation, not the self-inflated Pharisee.

— 743 —

Boasting is the outward form of the inner condition of pride.

—John Piper (born 1936), Evangelical Calvinist preacher, author

Bible Truth Behind the Quote:
The arrogant have a boastful tongue (Psalm 12:3-4).

— 744 —

Pride is the ground in which all the other sins grow,
and the parent from which all the other sins come.

—William Barclay (1907-1978), professor, University of Glasgow

Bible Truth Behind the Quote:
"When pride comes, then comes disgrace" (Proverbs 11:2).

— 745 —

You can have no greater sign of a confirmed pride
than when you think you are humble enough.

—William Law (1686-1761), English cleric, author

Bible Truth Behind the Quote:
"Do nothing from rivalry or conceit, but in humility count others more significant than yourselves" (Philippians 2:3).

— 746 —

The cure of boasting is to boast in the Lord all the day long.

—Charles Spurgeon (1834-1892), pastor, New Park Street Chapel, London

Bible Truth Behind the Quote:
"Let the one who boasts, boast in the Lord" (1 Corinthians 1:31).

— 747 —

It's ludicrous for any Christian to believe that he or she is
the worthy object of public worship; it would be like the
donkey carrying Jesus into Jerusalem believing the crowds
were cheering and laying down their garments for him.

—Chuck Colson (born 1931), founder, Prison Fellowship

Bible Truth Behind the Quote:
Can an ax boast over the person who uses it? (Isaiah 10:15).

— 748 —

God has humbled himself, but man is still proud.
—Augustine (354-430), bishop of Hippo

Bible Truth Behind the Quote:
Christ humbled himself by becoming a man (Philippians 2:5-11), but many humans arrogantly reject Him (John 1:11).

— 749 —

Pride is the devil's dragnet in which he takes more
fish than in any other, except procrastination.
—Charles Spurgeon (1834-1892), pastor, New Park Street Chapel, London

Bible Truth Behind the Quote:
The Lord warns of those who become "trapped in their pride" (Psalm 59:12).

Priesthood of the Believer

— 750 —

No church or a priest can stand between God and man.
—Martin Luther (1483-1546), priest, professor of theology, reformer

Bible Truth Behind the Quote:
We have direct access through Christ. "Let us then with confidence draw near to the throne of grace, that we may receive mercy and find grace to help in time of need" (Hebrews 4:16).

Promises of God

— 751 —

God's promises are like the stars; the darker
the night the brighter they shine.
—David Nicholas, pastor, founder of The Church Planting Network

Bible Truth Behind the Quote:
Let us not forget that "he who promised is faithful" (Hebrews 10:23). Indeed, "not one word has failed of all his good promise" (1 Kings 8:56).

PROSPERITY

— 752 —

We can stand affliction better than we can
prosperity, for in prosperity we forget God.
—*Dwight L. Moody (1837-1899), evangelist*

Bible Truth Behind the Quote:
Jesus affirmed, "How difficult it is for those who have wealth to enter the kingdom of
God" (Luke 18:24).

QUARRELING

— 753 —

Few things demoralize, discourage, and weaken a church
as much as bickering, backbiting and fighting among its
members...Because of quarreling the Father is dishonored, the
Son is disgraced, His people are demoralized and discredited,
and the world is turned off and confirmed in unbelief.
—*John MacArthur (born 1939), pastor, Grace Community Church*

Bible Truth Behind the Quote:
We are exhorted to act quickly to settle quarrels (Matthew 5:25).

— 754 —

Discord and division become no Christian. For wolves
to worry the lambs is no wonder, but for one lamb to
worry another, this is unnatural and monstrous.
—*Thomas Brooks (1608-1680), minister, London*

Bible Truth Behind the Quote:
We must seek to avoid contentiousness among believers (Psalm 120:7; 140:2; Proverbs
15:18; 17:19; 18:6; 26:21).

— 755 —

What! At peace with the Father, and at war
with His children? It cannot be.
—*John Flavel (1627-1691), English Presbyterian clergyman*

Bible Truth Behind the Quote:
Among God's people, there ought never to be quarreling, jealousy, and outbursts of anger
(2 Corinthians 12:20).

— 756 —

Division has done more to hide Christ from the view of
men than all the infidelity that has ever been spoken.

—*George MacDonald (1824-1905), Scottish author, poet, minister*

Bible Truth Behind the Quote:
There ought to be no division in the body of Christ (1 Corinthians 12:25).

— 757 —

Nothing does so much harm to the cause of
religion as the quarrels of Christians.

—*J.C. Ryle (1816-1900), Anglican bishop, Liverpool*

Bible Truth Behind the Quote:
It is better to "maintain the unity of the Spirit in the bond of peace" (Ephesians 4:3).

— 758 —

The devil's master stroke is that of dividing
forces that ought to stand.

—*G. Campbell Morgan (1863-1945), pastor, Westminster Chapel, London*

Bible Truth Behind the Quote:
We must constantly be alert to the devil's schemes (Ephesians 6:11).

— 759 —

The more fractured we are, the greater we become
spectacles to the world. The more we are united
in love, the more the world sees Christ.

—*Curtis C. Thomas (born 1937), author*

Bible Truth Behind the Quote:
We are exhorted to "be united in the same mind and the same judgment" (1 Corinthians
1:10).

RACIAL EQUALITY

— 760 —

I have a dream that my four little children will one day
live in a nation where they will not be judged by the color
of their skin but by the content of their character.

—*Martin Luther King, Jr. (1929-1968), clergyman,
activist in the African-American Civil Rights Movement*

Bible Truth Behind the Quote:
God "made from one man every nation of mankind to live on all the face of the earth" (Acts 17:26).

RELATIONSHIPS

— 761 —

Life is not a solo but a chorus. We live in
relationships from cradle to grave.

—Anonymous

Bible Truth Behind the Quote:
We live in relationships with family members (Matthew 15:4; 19:19; Luke 18:20), friends (Proverbs 27:10), and members of the family of God (Matthew 25:40; Luke 8:21; John 21:23).

REPENTANCE

— 762 —

To do so no more is the truest repentance.

—Martin Luther (1483-1546), priest, professor of theology, reformer

Bible Truth Behind the Quote:
"Bear fruit in keeping with repentance" (Matthew 3:8).

— 763 —

Let us beware of a repentance without evidence.

—J.C. Ryle (1816-1900), Anglican bishop, Liverpool

Bible Truth Behind the Quote:
Believers should engage in "deeds in keeping with their repentance" (Acts 26:20).

— 764 —

An unrepentant sin is a continued sin.

—Corrie ten Boom (1892-1983), Dutch Christian Holocaust survivor

Bible Truth Behind the Quote:
"Turn away from evil" (Proverbs 3:7).

— 765 —

To those whom God finds impenitent sinners he
will be found to be an implacable judge.

—Matthew Henry (1662-1714), Bible commentator, Presbyterian minister

Bible Truth Behind the Quote:
"We will all stand before the judgment seat of God" (Romans 14:10).

— 766 —

By delay of repentance, sin strengthens, and the heart hardens.
The longer ice freezeth, the harder it is to be broken.
—*Thomas Watson (1620-1686), Puritan preacher, author*

Bible Truth Behind the Quote:
"They have become callous and have given themselves up to sensuality, greedy to practice every kind of impurity" (Ephesians 4:19).

— 767 —

True repentance has a double aspect; it looks upon things past
with a weeping eye, and upon the future with a watchful eye.
—*Robert South (1634-1716), English churchman*

Bible Truth Behind the Quote:
Let us "lay aside every weight, and sin which clings so closely, and let us run with endurance the race that is set before us" (Hebrews 12:1).

— 768 —

The devil would make us wade so far in the waters
of repentance that we should get beyond our depth
and be drowned in the gulf of despair.
—*Thomas Watson (1620-1686), Puritan preacher, author*

Bible Truth Behind the Quote:
Scripture warns of "the schemes of the devil" (Ephesians 6:11). We must be sober-minded and watchful (1 Peter 5:8).

— 769 —

The chief mark of authentic revival is enduring repentance.
—*Erroll Hulse (born 1931), author*

Bible Truth Behind the Quote:
Repent and turn to God "that times of refreshing may come from the presence of the Lord" (Acts 3:19-20).

— 770 —

Hardening of the heart ages people more
quickly than hardening of the arteries.
—*Anonymous*

Bible Truth Behind the Quote:
"Today, if you hear his voice, do not harden your hearts" (Hebrews 3:15).

RESOLUTION

— 771 —

Resolved, to endeavor to my utmost to act as I
can think I should do, if I had already seen the
happiness of heaven, and hell torments.

—Jonathan Edwards (1703-1758), American theologian

Bible Truth Behind the Quote:
"Set your minds on things that are above, not on things that are on earth" (Colossians 3:2).

— 772 —

Resolved, to endeavor to obtain for myself as much
happiness, in the other world, as I possibly can, with all
the might, power, vigor, and vehemence, yea, violence,
I am capable of, or can bring myself to exert, in any way.

—Jonathan Edwards (1703-1758), American theologian

Bible Truth Behind the Quote:
Be motivated by this recognition, "Our citizenship is in heaven" (Philippians 3:20).

— 773 —

Resolved, that I will live so as I shall
wish I had done when I come to die.

—Jonathan Edwards (1703-1758), American theologian

Bible Truth Behind the Quote:
"Teach us to number our days that we may get a heart of wisdom" (Psalm 90:12).

— 774 —

Resolved, never to do anything, which I should
be afraid to do, if it were the last hour of my life.

—Jonathan Edwards (1703-1758), American theologian

Bible Truth Behind the Quote:
"O LORD, make me know my end and what is the measure of my days; let me know how fleeting I am!" (Psalm 39:4).

— 775 —

Resolved, to live with all my might while I do live. Resolved,
never to lose one moment of time, to improve it in the
most profitable way I can. Resolved, never to do anything
which I should despise or think meanly in another.

—Jonathan Edwards (1703-1758), American theologian

Bible Truth Behind the Quote:
Let us make "the best use of the time, because the days are evil" (Ephesians 5:16).

RESURRECTION

— 776 —

Taking all the evidence together, it is not too much
to say that there is no historic incident better or more
variously supported than the resurrection of Christ.

—Canon Westcott (1825-1901), Cambridge scholar

Bible Truth Behind the Quote:
"He presented himself alive after his suffering by many proofs, appearing to them during forty days" (Acts 1:3).

— 777 —

As a lawyer, I have made a prolonged study of the evidences
for the events of the first Easter Day. To me, the evidence is
conclusive, and over and over again in the High Court I have
secured the verdict on evidence not nearly so compelling.

—Sir Edward Clarke (1841-1931), British Lawyer

Bible Truth Behind the Quote:
"He appeared to more than five hundred brothers at one time" (1 Corinthians 15:6).

— 778 —

I know of no one fact in the history of mankind which is
proved by better and fuller evidence of every sort, to the
understanding of a fair inquiry, than the great sign which God
has given us that Christ died and rose again from the dead.

—Thomas Arnold (1795-1842), Oxford University

Bible Truth Behind the Quote:
An angel told the women at the tomb, "He is not here, for he has risen, as he said. Come, see the place where he lay" (Matthew 28:6).

RESURRECTION POWER

— 779 —

The same power that brought Christ back from
the dead is operative within those who are Christ's.
The resurrection is an ongoing thing.
—*Leon Morris (1914-2006), Australian New Testament scholar*

Bible Truth Behind the Quote:
Paul affirmed, "We were buried therefore with him by baptism into death, in order that, just as Christ was raised from the dead by the glory of the Father, we too might walk in newness of life" (Romans 6:4). Christ's resurrection power is available to us even now.

RIGHTEOUSLY, LIVE

— 780 —

Be dogmatically true, obstinately holy, immovably
honest, desperately kind, fixedly upright.
—*Charles Spurgeon (1834-1892), pastor, New Park Street Chapel, London*

Bible Truth Behind the Quote:
Let us remember that virtue leads to honor (Proverbs 3:16; 8:18; 13:18; 21:21; 22:4).

RIGHTEOUSNESS

— 781 —

Right is right, even if everyone is against it; and
wrong is wrong, even if everyone is for it.
—*William Penn (1644-1718), English Quaker, founder of Pennsylvania*

Bible Truth Behind the Quote:
Right and wrong are never to be confused. The dividing line between the two must remain distinct and clear. As Isaiah the prophet put it, "Woe to those who call evil good and good evil, who put darkness for light and light for darkness" (Isaiah 5:20).

RIGHTEOUSNESS, INSUFFICIENT FOR SALVATION

— 782 —

If there be ground for you to trust in your own righteousness,
then all that Christ did to purchase salvation, and all
that God did to prepare the way for it, is in vain.
—*Jonathan Edwards (1703-1758), American theologian*

Bible Truth Behind the Quote:
Scripture is clear: "All have sinned and fall short of the glory of God" (Romans 3:23). Indeed, "None is righteous, no, not one; no one understands; no one seeks for God. All have turned aside; together they have become worthless; no one does good, not even one" (Romans 3:10-12). Most certainly, Christ's sacrifice was not in vain!

SALVATION

— 783 —

What was eternally determined in Him *before* the ages
will in the ages be carried through and perfected.
—*Erich Sauer (1898-1959), Wiedenest Bible School, West Germany*

Bible Truth Behind the Quote:
God's plan of salvation is called by Paul His "eternal purpose" (Ephesians 3:11), carried out by the "King of ages" (1 Timothy 1:17).

— 784 —

Christ took our hell so that we might take His heaven.
—*Donald Grey Barnhouse (1895-1960), preacher, pastor, theologian*

Bible Truth Behind the Quote:
"For our sake he made him to be sin who knew no sin, so that in him we might become the righteousness of God" (2 Corinthians 5:21).

— 785 —

He who works in an orderly way in nature has not left the
salvation of man to haphazard and uncertain experimentation.
Scripture shows us that he has a definite plan of salvation. This
plan includes the means by which salvation is to be provided,
the objectives that are to be realized, the persons that are to
benefit by it, the conditions on which it is to be available,
and the agents and means by which it is to be applied.
—*Henry C. Thiessen, theologian, author*

Bible Truth Behind the Quote:
The plan of salvation was conceived before the foundation of the world (1 Peter 1:20).

— 786 —

As God did not at first choose you because you were
high, so He will not forsake you because you are low.
—*John Flavel (1627-1691), English Presbyterian clergyman*

Bible Truth Behind the Quote:
"He has said, 'I will never leave you nor forsake you'" (Hebrews 13:5).

— 787 —

Heaven is large but the way to heaven must be narrow.
—*Henry Smith (1560-1591), English Puritan preacher*

Bible Truth Behind the Quote:
"There is salvation in no one else [other than Jesus], for there is no other name under heaven given among men by which we must be saved" (Acts 4:12, insert added for clarification).

SALVATION, ASSURANCE OF

— 788 —

The greatest thing that we can desire, next to the glory of God, is our own salvation; and the sweetest thing we can desire is the assurance of our salvation…All saints shall enjoy a heaven when they leave this earth; some saints enjoy a heaven while they are here on earth.
—*Joseph Caryl (1602-1673), English preacher*

Bible Truth Behind the Quote:
"Who shall separate us from the love of Christ? Shall tribulation, or distress, or persecution, or famine, or nakedness, or danger, or sword?" (Romans 8:35).

SAVIOR

— 789 —

I remember two things: that I am a great sinner
and that Christ is a great Savior.
—*John Newton (1725-1807), Anglican clergyman*

Bible Truth Behind the Quote:
The apostle Paul emphasized that "Christ Jesus came into the world to save sinners, of whom I am the foremost" (1 Timothy 1:15). Paul recognized that even he was a great sinner, but he also knew he had a great Savior (see Titus 2:13-14).

SCRIPTURE

— 790 —

We owe to Scripture the same reverence which we owe to God.
—*John Calvin (1509-1564), French reformer*

Bible Truth Behind the Quote:
All Scripture is "breathed out" by God (2 Timothy 3:16).

— 791 —

The source of all our troubles is in not knowing the Scriptures.
—Chrysostom (347-407), early church father

Bible Truth Behind the Quote:
Scripture is "profitable for teaching, for reproof, for correction, and for training in righteousness" (2 Timothy 3:16).

— 792 —

If you wish to know God, you must know His Word. If you
wish to perceive His power, you must see how He works
by His Word. If you wish to know His purpose before it
comes to pass, you can only discover it by His Word.
—Charles Spurgeon (1834-1892), pastor, New Park Street Chapel, London

Bible Truth Behind the Quote:
All God's words are true (Psalm 119:160).

— 793 —

I believe that even now, when we cannot explain alleged
difficulties in Holy Scripture, the wisest course is to blame
the interpreter and not the text, to suspect our own ignorance
to be in fault, and not any defect in God's Word.
—J.C. Ryle (1816-1900), Anglican bishop, Liverpool

Bible Truth Behind the Quote:
Every word of God is flawless (Proverbs 30:5-6).

— 794 —

I am much afraid that the universities will prove to be the great
gates to hell, unless they diligently labor to explain the Holy
Scriptures and to engrave them on the hearts of youth. I advise
no one to place his child where the Scriptures do not reign
paramount. Every institution where men are not unceasingly
occupied with the Word of God must become corrupt.
—Martin Luther (1483-1546), priest, professor of theology, reformer

Bible Truth Behind the Quote:
God's Word is truth (John 17:17).

— 795 —

Read the Scripture, not only as a history, but
as a love-letter sent to you from God.

—*Thomas Watson (1620-1686), Puritan preacher, author*

Bible Truth Behind the Quote:
The Scriptures are God's words to us; God personally speaking to us (Matthew 4:4).

— 796 —

It is a great thing, this reading of the Scriptures! For
it is not possible ever to exhaust the mind of the
Scriptures. It is a well that has no bottom.

—*Chrysostom (347-407), early church father*

Bible Truth Behind the Quote:
God's Word is wonderful (Psalm 119:129-130).

— 797 —

Any teaching which does not square with the Scriptures
is to be rejected even if it shows miracles every day.

—*Martin Luther (1483-1546), priest, professor of theology, reformer*

Bible Truth Behind the Quote:
The Christians in Berea were in the habit of "examining the Scriptures daily to see if these
things were so" (Acts 17:11). We ought to follow their example.

— 798 —

The Scriptures teach us the best way of living, the noblest
way of suffering, and the most comfortable way of dying.

—*John Flavel (1627-1691), English Presbyterian clergyman*

Bible Truth Behind the Quote:
"All Scripture is breathed out by God and profitable for teaching, for reproof, for correction, and for training in righteousness" (2 Timothy 3:16).

— 799 —

There is only one real inevitability: it is necessary
that the Scriptures be fulfilled.

—*Carl F.H. Henry (1913-2003), American evangelical theologian*

Bible Truth Behind the Quote:
This inevitability is affirmed numerous times in Scripture (Luke 4:21; 22:37; John 13:18;
17:12; 19:36; Acts 1:16; James 2:23).

— 800 —

Ignorance of the Scripture is ignorance of Christ.

—Jerome (374-420), apologist, translator

Bible Truth Behind the Quote:
Jesus told some Jewish leaders, "You search the Scriptures because you think that in them you have eternal life; and it is they that bear witness about me" (John 5:39).

— 801 —

God the Father is the giver of Holy Scripture; God the Son
is the theme of Holy Scripture; and God the Spirit is the
author, authenticator, and interpreter of Holy Scripture.

—J.I. Packer (born 1926), author, theologian

Bible Truth Behind the Quote:
How awesome is our triune God (Matthew 28:19; 2 Corinthians 13:14)!

— 802 —

Neglect the Word and you neglect the Lord.

—Anonymous

Bible Truth Behind the Quote:
Jesus flatly asserted that the Scriptures bear witness of Him (John 5:39).

— 803 —

Scripture is the royal chariot in which Jesus rides.

—Charles Spurgeon (1834-1892), pastor, New Park Street Chapel, London

Bible Truth Behind the Quote:
The Old Testament points to the coming of Jesus (see Isaiah 7:14; 9:6; 40:3). The New Testament represents the fulfillment of Jesus (Matthew 5:17; Luke 24:27,44; John 5:39; Hebrews 10:7).

— 804 —

Against all the sayings of the Fathers, against all the
arts and words of the angels, men, and devils, I set the
Scriptures and the Gospel...Here I take my stand.

—Martin Luther (1483-1546), priest, professor of theology, reformer

Bible Truth Behind the Quote:
Scripture was the final court of appeal for Jesus, for He often said "It is written..." (Matthew 4:4,6,7,10).

SECOND COMING

— 805 —

Christ hath told us He will come, but not when, that we
might never put off our clothes, or put out the candle.

—*William Gurnall (1617-1679), English author*

Bible Truth Behind the Quote:
Scripture affirms that no one knows the day or hour of Christ's coming (Matthew 24:42,
44, 46-50).

— 806 —

If the Lord is coming soon, is this not a very practical
motive for greater missionary effort? I know of no other
motive that has been so stimulating to myself.

—*J. Hudson Taylor (1832-1905), founder, China Inland Mission*

Bible Truth Behind the Quote:
"The Lord is not slow to fulfill his promise as some count slowness, but is patient toward
you, not wishing that any should perish, but that all should reach repentance" (2 Peter 3:9).

— 807 —

We should live our lives as though Christ
were coming this afternoon.

—*Jimmy Carter (born 1924), thirty-ninth president of the United States*

Bible Truth Behind the Quote:
The "crown of righteousness" will be given to all who have "loved his appearing" or look
forward to His coming (2 Timothy 4:8).

— 808 —

The best way to prepare for the coming of Christ
is never to forget the presence of Christ.

—*William Barclay (1907-1978), professor, University of Glasgow*

Bible Truth Behind the Quote:
"Behold, I am with you always, to the end of the age" (Matthew 28:20).

SELF-DENIAL

— 809 —

They that deny themselves for Christ shall
enjoy themselves in Christ.

—*Anonymous*

Bible Truth Behind the Quote:
Jesus affirmed, "If anyone would come after me, let him deny himself and take up his cross and follow me. For whoever would save his life will lose it, but whoever loses his life for my sake will find it" (Matthew 16:24-25). Truly the secret of true life—the life brimming with spiritual blessing—is found in unreserved commitment to Jesus Christ.

SELF-DEPENDENCE

— 810 —

God-dependence only begins when self-dependence ends.
And self-dependence only comes to its end, with some of us,
when sorrow, suffering, affliction, broken plans and hopes
bring us to that place of self-helplessness and defeat.

—*Miles Stanford (1914-1999), American Deeper-Life author*

Bible Truth Behind the Quote:
"It is good for me that I was afflicted, that I might learn your statutes" (Psalm 119:71).

SELF-FOCUS

— 811 —

Self-adoration is the death of the soul.

—*William Barclay (1907-1978), professor, University of Glasgow*

Bible Truth Behind the Quote:
We ought to be clothed with humility (Colossians 3:12; 1 Peter 5:5-6).

— 812 —

All the sin of heathendom, all the sin of Christendom,
is but the outgrowth of the one root—God
dethroned, self enthroned in the heart of man.

—*Andrew Murray (1828-1917), South African writer, pastor*

Bible Truth Behind the Quote:
"Where jealousy and selfish ambition exist, there will be disorder and every vile practice" (James 3:16).

— 813 —

Seeking to perpetuate one's name on earth is like
writing on the sand by the seashore; to be perpetual
it must be written on eternal shores.

—*Dwight L. Moody (1837-1899), evangelist*

Bible Truth Behind the Quote:
It is better to be lowly in spirit (Proverbs 16:19).

— 814 —

Above all the grace and the gifts that Christ gives
to his beloved is that of overcoming self.
—*St. Francis of Assisi (1181-1226), founder of Franciscans*

Bible Truth Behind the Quote:
The importance of this lies in how human beings are prone to self-importance (Galatians 6:3), self-pity (Psalm 37), self-righteousness (Luke 18:9), self-seeking (1 Corinthians 13:5), self-confidence (Matthew 26:35), being self-willed (Acts 7:51), and engaging in self-confident boasting (2 Corinthians 11:17).

— 815 —

If the only way I can make myself look good is to
criticize you, something is seriously wrong with me.
—*Warren Wiersbe (born 1929), pastor, author*

Bible Truth Behind the Quote:
Christians ought always to encourage each other (1 Thessalonians 4:18; Hebrews 10:24-25).

Self-Knowledge

— 816 —

He who knows himself best esteems himself least.
—*Anonymous*

Bible Truth Behind the Quote:
The apostle Paul not only considered himself the "foremost" among sinners (1 Timothy 1:15) but referred to himself as "the very least of all the saints" (Ephesians 3:8) and "the least of the apostles, unworthy to be called an apostle" (1 Corinthians 15:9). No wonder he rejoiced in the wondrous grace of God (Ephesians 2:8-9).

Serving Others

— 817 —

God is not looking for more stars; he's looking for more servants.
—*Howard Hendricks (born 1924), professor, Dallas Theological Seminary*

Bible Truth Behind the Quote:
"As each has received a gift, use it to serve one another, as good stewards of God's varied grace" (1 Peter 4:10).

— 818 —

You may be sure that being a blessing to others brings blessing
to yourself. If we work for the revival of others we are ourselves
revived. You will overcome the signs of fatigue in yourself if
you give yourself up wholly to the Lord to be commissioned
by Him to overcome paralysis and feebleness in others. He
who loves and nurses his Ego makes himself spiritually old.
Selfishness makes weary. The service of love keeps us young.

—*Erich Sauer (1898-1959), Wiedenest Bible School, West Germany*

Bible Truth Behind the Quote:
"It is more blessed to give than to receive" (Acts 20:35).

SHINE AS A LIGHT

— 819 —

You may be the only Bible some will ever read.

—*Anonymous*

Bible Truth Behind the Quote:
"By this all people will know that you are my disciples, if you have love for one another"
(John 13:35).

— 820 —

There is no argument like a holy life.

—*Robert Murray M'Cheyne (1813-1843), minister, Church of Scotland*

Bible Truth Behind the Quote:
"As he who called you is holy, you also be holy in all your conduct" (1 Peter 1:15).

— 821 —

The Christian should stand out like a sparkling diamond.

—*Billy Graham (born 1918), evangelist*

Bible Truth Behind the Quote:
"Let your light shine before others, so that they may see your good works and give glory
to your Father who is in heaven" (Matthew 5:16).

— 822 —

A godly life is always the best advertisement for Christianity.

—*Geoffrey B. Wilson*

Bible Truth Behind the Quote:
We ought to "lead a peaceful and quiet life, godly and dignified in every way" (1 Timothy 2:2).

— 823 —

Example is the most powerful rhetoric.

—*Thomas Brooks (1608-1680), minister, London*

Bible Truth Behind the Quote:
The Thessalonian Christians "became an example to all the believers in Macedonia and in Achaia" (1 Thessalonians 1:7).

— 824 —

You and I were created to tell the truth about God
by reflecting his likeness. That is normality. How
many lies have you told about God today?

—*Ian Thomas (1914-2007), theology teacher, author*

Bible Truth Behind the Quote:
"You were bought with a price. So glorify God in your body" (1 Corinthians 6:20).

SILENCE CAN BE WISE

— 825 —

Better to remain silent and be thought a fool than
to open your mouth and remove all doubt.

—*Anonymous*

Bible Truth Behind the Quote:
"Aspire to live quietly, and to mind your own affairs" (1 Thessalonians 4:11).

SIN

— 826 —

Those who seek most for God experience
the strongest opposition [from sin].

—*John Owen (1616-1683), church leader, theologian*

Bible Truth Behind the Quote:
The apostle Paul is an example, for sin caused him to do what he knew he should not do and hindered him from doing what he knew he should do (Romans 7:15-17).

— 827 —

To be sensible of our corruption and abhor our own
transgressions is the first symptom of spiritual health.

—*J.C. Ryle (1816-1900), Anglican bishop, Liverpool*

Bible Truth Behind the Quote:
Paul said, "Wretched man that I am! Who will deliver me from this body of death?" (Romans 7:24). The Deliverer is Jesus Christ (verse 25).

— 828 —

As the salt flavors every drop in the Atlantic, so
does sin affect every atom of our nature.

—*Charles Spurgeon (1834-1892), pastor, New Park Street Chapel, London*

Bible Truth Behind the Quote:
Our sin nature permeates our whole being and causes us to engage in a wide range of sinful acts (Galatians 5:19-21).

— 829 —

It is not the absence of sin but the grieving over it which
distinguishes the child of God from empty professors.

—*A. W. Pink (1886-1952), Calvinist evangelist, Bible scholar*

Bible Truth Behind the Quote:
Even the apostle Paul lamented, "Wretched man that I am! Who will deliver me from this body of death?" (Romans 7:24).

— 830 —

Sin is like quicksand. The man who walks on
it must ultimately sink and be lost.

—*Anonymous*

Bible Truth Behind the Quote:
Sin entraps us (Psalm 9:16; Proverbs 12:13; 29:6).

— 831 —

Prevent sin from negotiating with the soul.

—*John Owen (1616-1683), church leader, theologian*

Bible Truth Behind the Quote:
We ought to flee immorality (1 Corinthians 6:18) like Joseph did in Old Testament times (Genesis 39:12)

— 832 —

It is our wisest and our safest course to stand at the
farthest distance from sin…The best course to prevent
falling into the pit is to keep at the greatest distance.

—*Thomas Brooks (1608-1680), minister, London*

Bible Truth Behind the Quote:
Just as we keep a safe distance from fire so we don't get burned (Proverbs 6:26), so we ought to keep a safe distance from sin.

— 833 —

Beware of no man more than of yourself; we
carry our worst enemies within us.

—*Charles Spurgeon (1834-1892), pastor, New Park Street Chapel, London*

Bible Truth Behind the Quote:
Paul said, "I do not understand my own actions. For I do not do what I want, but I do the very thing I hate" (Romans 7:15).

— 834 —

I have more trouble with D.L. Moody than
with any other man I ever met.

—*Dwight L. Moody (1837-1899), evangelist*

Bible Truth Behind the Quote:
Paul said, "I know that nothing good dwells in me, that is, in my flesh" (Romans 7:18).

— 835 —

One leak will sink a ship; and one sin will destroy a sinner.

—*John Bunyan (1628-1688), English Christian writer, preacher*

Bible Truth Behind the Quote:
Any sin separates us from God (Ephesians 4:17-19).

— 836 —

When it is least felt, it is in fact most powerful.

—*John Owen (1616-1683), church leader, theologian*

Bible Truth Behind the Quote:
Scripture speaks of "the deceitfulness of sin" (Hebrews 3:13). It is a tricky beast.

— 837 —

Whatever weakens your reason, impairs the tenderness of
your conscience, obscures your sense of God, and takes
off the relish of spiritual things—that to you is sin.

—*Susanna Wesley (1669-1742), mother of John and Charles Wesley*

Bible Truth Behind the Quote:
Sin has many evil manifestations (Galatians 5:19).

— 838 —

We are not sinners because we sin; we sin because we are sinners.

—R.C. Sproul (born 1939), pastor, author

Bible Truth Behind the Quote:
"By the one man's [Adam's] disobedience the many were made sinners" (Romans 5:19, insert added for clarification).

— 839 —

Sin is the dare of God's justice, the rape of his mercy, the jeer of his patience, the slight of his power, and the contempt of his love.

—John Bunyan (1628-1688), English Christian writer, preacher

Bible Truth Behind the Quote:
Beware of a flippant attitude toward sin because "it is a fearful thing to fall into the hands of the living God" (Hebrews 10:31).

— 840 —

Worst of all my foes, I fear the enemy within.

—John Wesley (1703-1791), founder of the Methodist church

Bible Truth Behind the Quote:
The sin nature within gives rise to "sexual immorality, impurity, sensuality, idolatry, sorcery, enmity, strife, jealousy, fits of anger, rivalries, dissensions, divisions, envy, drunkenness, orgies, and things like these" (Galatians 5:19-21).

— 841 —

Take heed of abusing this mercy of God...To sin because mercy abounds is the devil's logic.

—Thomas Watson (1620-1686), Puritan preacher, author

Bible Truth Behind the Quote:
"Are we to sin because we are not under law but under grace? By no means!" (Romans 6:15).

— 842 —

A sin is two sins when it is defended.

—Henry Smith (1560-1591), English Puritan preacher

Bible Truth Behind the Quote:
After sinning, Adam offered this excuse to God, "The woman whom you gave to be with me, she gave me fruit of the tree, and I ate" (Genesis 3:12).

— 843 —

Those sins that seem most sweet in life
will prove most bitter in death.

—*Thomas Brooks (1608-1680), minister, London*

Bible Truth Behind the Quote:
We all will have to face God and give an account for all our sins (2 Corinthians 5:10).

— 844 —

Sin hath the devil for its father, shame for its
companion, and death for its wages.

—*Thomas Watson (1620-1686), Puritan preacher, author*

Bible Truth Behind the Quote:
"The wages of sin is death" (Romans 6:23).

— 845 —

Sin never ruins but where it reigns.

—*William Secker (died 1681), Church of England clergyman*

Bible Truth Behind the Quote:
"The way of the wicked he [God] brings to ruin" (Psalm 146:9, insert added for clarification).

— 846 —

Sins are like circles in the water when a stone is
thrown into it; one produces another. When anger
was in Cain's heart, murder was not far off.

—*Philip Henry (1631-1696), English clergyman*

Bible Truth Behind the Quote:
David first committed fornication in his heart when he watched Bathsheba. This then led him to commit physical adultery. Next he tried to deceive her husband into sleeping with her. Then he sent her husband to the front line of a battle so he'd surely die (2 Samuel 11). One sin led to another.

— 847 —

Be yourself is about the worst advice you could give some people.

—*Anonymous*

Bible Truth Behind the Quote:
"None is righteous, no, not one" (Romans 3:10).

— 848 —

He who doubts human depravity had better study himself.

—*Charles Spurgeon (1834-1892), pastor, New Park Street Chapel, London*

Bible Truth Behind the Quote:
"The heart is deceitful above all things, and desperately sick; who can understand it?" (Jeremiah 17:9).

— 849 —

The sin of our nature is like a sleeping lion, the least thing that awakens it makes it rage. The sin of our nature, though it seems quiet, and lies as fire hid under the embers, yet if it be a little stirred and blown up by a temptation, how quickly may it flame forth into scandalous evils?

—*Thomas Watson (1620-1686), Puritan preacher, author*

Bible Truth Behind the Quote:
"Sin is crouching at the door. Its desire is for you, but you must rule over it" (Genesis 4:7).

— 850 —

The recognition of sin is the beginning of salvation.

—*Martin Luther (1483-1546), priest, professor of theology, reformer*

Bible Truth Behind the Quote:
"God, be merciful to me, a sinner" (Luke 18:13).

— 851 —

Sin is always at work in the heart; a temporary lull in its assaults means not that it is dead, but that it is very much alive…Sin's strategy is to induce a false sense of security as a prelude to a surprise attack.

—*J.I. Packer (born 1926), author, theologian*

Bible Truth Behind the Quote:
Sin is "crouching at the door," ready to pounce (Genesis 4:7).

— 852 —

Dim or indistinct views of sin are the origin of most of the errors, heresies, and false doctrines of the present day. If a man does not realize the dangerous nature of his soul's disease, you cannot wonder if he is content with false or imperfect remedies.

—*J.C. Ryle (1816-1900), Anglican bishop, Liverpool*

Bible Truth Behind the Quote:
An example would be the Nicolaitans, who promoted license in Christian conduct (Revelation 2:6,15).

— 853 —

A former experience of sin is an advantage Satan uses
to make another, more spectacular assault. Without the
previous entry of sin, the greater assault is not possible.

—*John Owen (1616-1683), church leader, theologian*

Bible Truth Behind the Quote:
People can become ensnared in transgression, like being caught in a spider's web (Proverbs 29:6)

— 854 —

If you will not have death unto sin, you shall have sin unto
death. There is no alternative. If you do not die to sin, you
shall die for sin. If you do not slay sin, sin will slay you.

—*Charles Spurgeon (1834-1892), pastor, New Park Street Chapel, London*

Bible Truth Behind the Quote:
"The wages of sin is death" (Romans 6:23). Sin "leads to death" (verse 16) and will "result in death" (verse 21). "If you live according to the flesh you will die, but if by the Spirit you put to death the deeds of the body, you will live" (Romans 8:13).

— 855 —

The heart of the human problem is the
problem of the human heart.

—*Adrian Rogers (1931-2005), Baptist pastor, author*

Bible Truth Behind the Quote:
"The heart is deceitful above all things, and desperately sick; who can understand it?" (Jeremiah 17:9).

— 856 —

The very animals whose smell is most offensive to us
have no idea that they are offensive, and are not offensive
to one another. And man, fallen man, I believe, can
have no just idea what a vile thing sin is in the sight of
that God whose handiwork is absolutely perfect.

—*J.C. Ryle (1816-1900), Anglican bishop, Liverpool*

Bible Truth Behind the Quote:
Sin is grievous to God (Genesis 6:6; Ephesians 4:30).

— 857 —

We could weep our eyes out when we discover what a
palate for pleasurable sin our old nature still retains; yea, a
longing for the very sin of which we most bitterly repent
and from which we most eagerly long to be delivered.

—*Charles Spurgeon (1834-1892), pastor, New Park Street Chapel, London*

Bible Truth Behind the Quote:
Paul said, "I do not understand my own actions. For I do not do what I want, but I do
the very thing I hate" (Romans 7:15).

— 858 —

Kill sin before it kills you.

—*Richard Baxter (1615-1691), English Puritan church leader*

Bible Truth Behind the Quote:
Paul clearly stated, "The wages of sin is death" (Romans 6:23; 1 John 5:16), and "death
spread to all men because all sinned" (Romans 5:12). No wonder he emphasized the necessity of killing such evil propensities within us. He said, "Put to death therefore what is
earthly in you: sexual immorality, impurity, passion, evil desire, and covetousness, which
is idolatry...you must put them all away" (Colossians 3:5,8). He affirmed that "those
who belong to Christ Jesus have crucified the flesh with its passions and desires" (Galatians 5:24).

SIN, CONSEQUENCES OF

— 859 —

No marvel that our sorrows are multiplied when our sins are.

—*Matthew Henry (1662-1714), Bible commentator, Presbyterian minister*

Bible Truth Behind the Quote:
The good news for Christians is that a godly sorrow over sin can move one to repentance
(2 Corinthians 7:10).

SIN, PERSONAL

— 860 —

It's a good thing God chose me before I was born,
because he surely would not have afterwards.

—*Charles Spurgeon (1834-1892), pastor, New Park Street Chapel, London*

Bible Truth Behind the Quote:
God "chose us in him before the foundation of the world" (Ephesians 1:4).

Sin, Realistic Assessment of

— 861 —

We shall never come to the perfect man till
we come to the perfect world.
—*Matthew Henry (1662-1714), Bible commentator, Presbyterian minister*

Bible Truth Behind the Quote:
Heaven is the paradise of God (2 Corinthians 12:2-4), the city of glory (Revelation 21:23), the holy city (Revelation 21:1-2), and the kingdom of light (Colossians 1:12) where all will be perfect.

— 862 —

Let us not expect too much from our own hearts here below.
At our best we shall find in ourselves daily cause for humiliation,
and discover that we are needy debtors to mercy and grace every hour.
The more light we have, the more we shall see our own imperfection.
—*J.C. Ryle (1816-1900), Anglican bishop, Liverpool*

Bible Truth Behind the Quote:
Even the apostle Paul considered himself the foremost among sinners (1 Timothy 1:15).

— 863 —

The longer I live, the larger allowances I make for human
infirmities. I exact more from myself and less from others.
—*John Wesley (1703-1791), founder of the Methodist church*

Bible Truth Behind the Quote:
Recognizing our own shortcomings, we ought to be patient with everyone (Ephesians 4:2; 1 Thessalonians 5:14).

Sin, Remaining in

— 864 —

It is not falling into the water, but lying in the water that drowns.
—*Thomas Brooks (1608-1680), minister, London*

Bible Truth Behind the Quote:
The Christian who sins ought not remain in sin but confess that sin and be restored to fellowship with God (1 John 1:9). To remain in sin invites discipline (Hebrews 12:5-11).

SIN, SORROW FOR

— 865 —

Sorrow is given us on purpose to cure us of sin.

—*Chrysostom (347–407), early church father*

Bible Truth Behind the Quote:
A godly sorrow over sin can move us to repentance (2 Corinthians 7:10).

SINGLE-HEARTEDNESS

— 866 —

This world and that to come are two enemies. We cannot
therefore be friends to both; but we must resolve which
we would forsake and which we would enjoy.

—*Clement of Alexandria (150 -215), theologian, philosopher*

Bible Truth Behind the Quote:
"Do you not know that friendship with the world is enmity with God? Therefore whoever wishes to be a friend of the world makes himself an enemy of God" (James 4:4).

— 867 —

I have one passion only: It is he! It is he!

—*Nicolas von Zinzendorf (1700-1760), German religious reformer*

Bible Truth Behind the Quote:
Paul affirmed, "I count everything as loss because of the surpassing worth of knowing Christ Jesus my Lord" (Philippians 3:8).

SPIRIT WORLD

— 868 —

A spiritual kingdom lies all about us, enclosing us, embracing
us, altogether within reach of our inner selves, waiting
for us to recognize it. God Himself is here waiting our
response to His Presence. This eternal world will come alive
to us the moment we begin to reckon upon its reality.

—*A. W. Tozer (1897-1963), American pastor, author*

Bible Truth Behind the Quote:
"We look not to the things that are seen but to the things that are unseen. For the things that are seen are transient, but the things that are unseen are eternal" (2 Corinthians 4:17-18).

— 869 —

At the root of the Christian life lies belief in the invisible.
The object of the Christian's faith is unseen reality.

—Anonymous

Bible Truth Behind the Quote:
We must live by faith and not by sight (2 Corinthians 5:7).

— 870 —

The world of sense intrudes upon our attention day and night
for the whole of our lifetime. It is clamorous, insistent and
self-demonstrating. It does not appeal to our faith; it is here,
assaulting our five senses, demanding to be accepted as real
and final. But sin has so clouded the lenses of our hearts that
we cannot see that other reality, the City of God, shining
around us. The world of sense triumphs. The visible becomes
the enemy of the invisible; the temporal, of the eternal.

—A. W. Tozer (1897-1963), American pastor, author

Bible Truth Behind the Quote:
Elisha had to pray that God would open the eyes of his servant so the servant could behold their angelic protectors (2 Kings 6:17).

SPIRITUAL BLINDNESS

— 871 —

It is no advantage to be near the light if the eyes are closed.

—Augustine (354-430), bishop of Hippo

Bible Truth Behind the Quote:
Many who are exposed to the truth of Jesus Christ choose against Him and remain in spiritual darkness (Matthew 23:37).

— 872 —

The carnal mind sees God in nothing, not even in spiritual things.
The spiritual mind sees Him in everything, even in natural things.

—Robert Leighton (1611-1684), Scottish minister, bishop of Dunblane, Archbishop of Glasgow

Bible Truth Behind the Quote:
"The natural person does not accept the things of the Spirit of God, for they are folly to him, and he is not able to understand them because they are spiritually discerned" (1 Corinthians 2:14).

STRENGTH IN WEAKNESS

— 873 —

Do not ask God to give you a light burden; ask Him to
give you a strong shoulder to carry a heavy burden.
—*Bob Jones (1883-1968), American evangelist*

Bible Truth Behind the Quote:
Paul learned that God's "power is made perfect in weakness" (2 Corinthians 12:9).

— 874 —

God's giants have been weak men who did great things for
God, because they reckoned on God's being with them.
—*J. Hudson Taylor (1832-1905), founder, China Inland Mission*

Bible Truth Behind the Quote:
Paul could do anything through Christ who strengthened him (Philippians 4:13).

SUBMISSION TO GOD

— 875 —

Adam was created to be the friend and companion of God; he was
to have dominion over all the life in the air and earth and sea, but
one thing he was not to have dominion over, and that was himself.
—*Oswald Chambers (1874-1917), author,* My Utmost for His Highest

Bible Truth Behind the Quote:
Adam was under the dominion of God, who gave him moral commands which he failed
to obey (Genesis 2:17).

— 876 —

What does God require? Everything!
—*Erwin Lutzer (born 1941), pastor, Moody Church, Chicago*

Bible Truth Behind the Quote:
"Whoever would save his life will lose it, but whoever loses his life for my sake will find
it" (Matthew 16:25).

— 877 —

It seems amazingly difficult to put on the yoke of Christ, but
immediately we do put it on, everything becomes easy.
—*Oswald Chambers (1874-1917), author,* My Utmost for His Highest

Bible Truth Behind the Quote:
"Come to me, all who labor and are heavy laden, and I will give you rest. Take my yoke upon you, and learn from me, for I am gentle and lowly in heart, and you will find rest for your souls. For my yoke is easy, and my burden is light" (Matthew 11:28-30).

SUFFERING

— 878 —

The dark moments of our life will last only so long as is
necessary for God to accomplish His purpose in us.

—*Charles Stanley (born 1932), senior pastor, First Baptist Church of Atlanta*

Bible Truth Behind the Quote:
Joseph said to his brothers who had done wrong, "You meant evil against me, but God meant it for good, to bring it about that many people should be kept alive, as they are today" (Genesis 50:20).

— 879 —

All our heartaches and a great many of our physical ills spring
directly out of our sins. Pride, arrogance, resentfulness, evil
imaginings, malice, greed: these are the sources of more human
pain than all the diseases that ever afflicted mortal flesh.

—*A. W. Tozer (1897-1963), American pastor, author*

Bible Truth Behind the Quote:
In a confession of personal sin, David said, "When I kept silent, my bones wasted away through my groaning all day long" (Psalm 32:3).

— 880 —

The more spiritual a man desires to be, the more bitter does
this present life become to him, because he perceives better
and sees more clearly the defects of human corruption.

—*Thomas à Kempis (1380-1471), author,* The Imitation of Christ

Bible Truth Behind the Quote:
Paul affirmed, "nothing good dwells in me" and that sin "dwells within me" (Romans 7:18,20). He referred to himself as a "wretched man" (Romans 7:24).

— 881 —

Labor to grow better under all your afflictions,
lest your afflictions grow worse.

—*John Owen (1616-1683), church leader, theologian*

Bible Truth Behind the Quote:
God will not remove His discipline of the child of God until the discipline has accomplished its purpose (see Hebrews 12:5-11).

— 882 —

We learn more in our valley experiences
than on our mountaintops.

—Charles Stanley (born 1932), senior pastor, First Baptist Church of Atlanta

Bible Truth Behind the Quote:
"Count it all joy, my brothers, when you meet trials of various kinds, for you know that the testing of your faith produces steadfastness" (James 1:2-3).

— 883 —

I have often looked gratefully back to my sick chamber.
I am certain that I never did grow in grace one-half so
much anywhere as I have upon the bed of pain.

—Charles Spurgeon (1834-1892), pastor, New Park Street Chapel, London

Bible Truth Behind the Quote:
The psalmist affirmed, "It is good for me that I was afflicted, that I might learn your statutes" (Psalm 119:71).

SURRENDER ALL

— 884 —

We are often hindered from giving up our treasures to the Lord out
of fear for their safety; this is especially true when those treasures are
loved relatives and friends. But we need have no such fears. Our Lord
came not to destroy but to save. Everything is safe which we commit
to Him, and nothing is really safe which is not so committed.

—A. W. Tozer (1897-1963), American pastor, author

Bible Truth Behind the Quote:
"Trust in the LORD with all your heart, and do not lean on your own understanding. In all your ways acknowledge him, and he will make straight your paths" (Proverbs 3:5-6).

TAKE UP YOUR CROSS

— 885 —

What our Lord said about cross-bearing and obedience is not
in fine type. It is in bold print on the face of the contract.

—Vince Havner (1901-1986), Baptist pastor

Bible Truth Behind the Quote:
Jesus asserted in no uncertain terms, "If anyone would come after me, let him deny himself and take up his cross and follow me. For whoever would save his life will lose it, but whoever loses his life for my sake will find it" (Matthew 16:24-25).

TAMING THE TONGUE

— 886 —

One of the first things that happens when a man is really
filled with the Spirit is not that he speaks with tongues, but
that he learns to hold the one tongue he already has.

—J. Sidlow Baxter (1903-1999), pastor, theologian

Bible Truth Behind the Quote:
Paul noted that the fruit of the Holy Spirit included such virtues as love, kindness, goodness, gentleness, and self-control (Galatians 5:22-23). Such virtues play a critical role in controlling the tongue!

TEAMWORK

— 887 —

The human body is probably the most amazing example of
teamwork anywhere. Every part needs the other. When the
stomach is hungry, the eyes spot the hamburger. The nose smells
the onions, the feet run to the snack stand, the hands douse
the burger with mustard and shove it back into the mouth,
where it goes down to the stomach. Now that's cooperation!

—Joni Eareckson Tada (born 1949), founder, Joni and Friends

Bible Truth Behind the Quote:
God intends for the different parts of the body of Christ to work together (1 Corinthians 12:21-26).

TEMPER

— 888 —

I have no more right as a Christian to allow a bad temper to dwell
in me than I have to allow the devil himself to dwell there.

—Charles Spurgeon (1834-1892), pastor, New Park Street Chapel, London

Bible Truth Behind the Quote:
"Be angry and do not sin; do not let the sun go down on your anger, and give no opportunity to the devil" (Ephesians 4:26-27).

TEMPTATION

— 889 —

In no case must we permit sin to find a lodging in our mind. Learn to say "no" right in the moment sin approaches you. Only thus is victory possible.

—*Erich Sauer (1898-1959), Wiedenest Bible School, West Germany*

Bible Truth Behind the Quote:
We ought to flee immorality immediately (1 Corinthians 6:18), as Joseph did in Old Testament times (Genesis 39:12).

— 890 —

We must be watchful, especially in the beginning of the temptation. The enemy is then more easily overcome, if he is not permitted in any wise to enter the door of our hearts, but is resisted without the gate at his first knock…First there comes to the mind a bare thought of evil, then a strong imagination thereof, afterward delight, and an evil motion, and then consent. And so little by little our wicked enemy gets complete entrance, because he is not resisted in the beginning. And the longer a man is slow to resist, so much the weaker does he become daily in himself, and the enemy stronger against him.

—*Thomas à Kempis (1380-1471), author,* The Imitation of Christ

Bible Truth Behind the Quote:
"No temptation has overtaken you that is not common to man. God is faithful, and he will not let you be tempted beyond your ability, but with the temptation he will also provide the way of escape, that you may be able to endure it" (1 Corinthians 10:13).

— 891 —

We are too apt to forget that temptation to sin will rarely present itself to us in its true colors, saying, "I am your deadly enemy, and I want to ruin you forever in hell." Oh, no! sin comes to us, like Judas, with a kiss…Sin rarely seems sin at its first beginnings.

—*J.C. Ryle (1816-1900), Anglican bishop, Liverpool*

Bible Truth Behind the Quote:
"Watch and pray that you may not enter into temptation" (Mark 26:41).

— 892 —

In the greatest temptations, a single look to Christ, and the
barely pronouncing his name, suffices to overcome the wicked
one, so it be done with confidence and calmness of spirit.
—*John Wesley (1703-1791), founder of the Methodist church*

Bible Truth Behind the Quote:
Our Lord promises, "I will never leave you nor forsake you" (Hebrews 13:5).

— 893 —

It is possible to be full of Scripture and full of carnality.
—*Anonymous*

Bible Truth Behind the Quote:
Peter was well trained in the truth by Christ Himself, and yet—in a brief time of weakness—he denied Christ three times (John 13:38).

— 894 —

Set a strong guard about thy outward senses: these are
Satan's landing places, especially the eye and the ear.
—*William Gurnall (1617-1679), English author*

Bible Truth Behind the Quote:
The psalmist prayed, "Set a guard, O LORD, over my mouth; keep watch over the door of my lips!" (Psalm 141:3).

— 895 —

There is no way to kill a man's righteousness
but by his own consent.
—*John Bunyan (1628-1688), English Christian writer, preacher*

Bible Truth Behind the Quote:
Sin involves the will. Scripture speaks of those who "did not choose the fear of the LORD" (Proverbs 1:29) and who "do not choose any of his ways" (3:31).

— 896 —

Any unmortified desire which a man allows in will
effectually drive and keep Christ out of the heart.
—*Charles Wesley (1707-1788), leader of Methodist Movement, hymn writer*

Bible Truth Behind the Quote:
We are exhorted, "Put to death therefore what is earthly in you: sexual immorality, impurity, passion, evil desire, and covetousness, which is idolatry" (Colossians 3:5).

— 897 —

A heart in heaven will be a most excellent preservative against
temptations, a powerful means to kill thy corruptions.

—Richard Baxter (1615-1691), English Puritan church leader

Bible Truth Behind the Quote:
"Set your minds on things that are above, not on things that are on earth" (Colossians 3:2).

— 898 —

At every point right living begins with right thinking.

—Bruce Milne, American theologian

Bible Truth Behind the Quote:
We ought to fill our minds with good thoughts. "Whatever is true, whatever is honorable, whatever is just, whatever is pure, whatever is lovely, whatever is commendable, if there is any excellence, if there is anything worthy of praise, think about these things" (Philippians 4:8).

— 899 —

He who would believe, let him reconcile himself to
the fact that his faith will not stay untempted.

—Martin Luther (1483-1546), priest, professor of theology, reformer

Bible Truth Behind the Quote:
We should always turn to Christ "for because he himself has suffered when tempted, he is able to help those who are being tempted" (Hebrews 2:18).

— 900 —

If the heart be full of sinful thoughts, there is no
room for holy and heavenly thoughts. If the heart be
full of holy and heavenly thoughts by meditation,
there is no room for evil and sinful thoughts.

—William Bridge (1600-1670), English minister, preacher, religious writer

Bible Truth Behind the Quote:
"Do not be conformed to this world, but be transformed by the renewal of your mind" (Romans 12:2).

— 901 —

The spiritual battle, the loss of victory, is
always in the thought world.

—Francis Schaeffer (1912-1984), theologian, philosopher, pastor

Bible Truth Behind the Quote:
You are "to be renewed in the spirit of your minds" (Ephesians 4:23).

— 902 —

Temptation is to see the tempter standing outside the
back door of your heart. Sin is to unlock that door so
that he may have his desire. Victory is to open wide the
front door of your heart, inviting the Savior to enter
and give you strength to bar tight the back door.
—*E. Schuyler, English Bible scholar*

Bible Truth Behind the Quote:
God can keep you from falling (Jude 24) and will make a way of escape (1 Corinthians
10:13).

THANKS-LIVING

— 903 —

Thanksgiving is good but thanks-living is better.
—*Matthew Henry (1662-1714), Bible commentator, Presbyterian minister*

Bible Truth Behind the Quote:
Our thanks to God should show itself in the way we live. We can follow Christ's example
in this regard (Matthew 14:19; 15:36; 26:26; Mark 6:41; 8:6; 14:22; Luke 9:16).

THANKSGIVING

— 904 —

The more we count the blessings we have, the
less we crave the luxuries we haven't.
—*William Arthur Ward (1921–1994), Methodist leader, author*

Bible Truth Behind the Quote:
Paul commented, "I have learned in whatever situation I am to be content. I know how
to be brought low, and I know how to abound. In any and every circumstance, I have
learned the secret of facing plenty and hunger, abundance and need. I can do all things
through him who strengthens me" (Philippians 4:11-13). For Paul, his primary "blessing"
was his relationship with Jesus Christ.

THEOLOGY

— 905 —

My entire theology can be condensed into
four words: "Jesus died for me."

—*Charles Spurgeon (1834-1892), pastor, New Park Street Chapel, London*

Bible Truth Behind the Quote:
"Christ died for our sins" (1 Corinthians 15:3).

— 906 —

Theological truth is useless until it is obeyed.

—*A.W. Tozer (1897-1963), American pastor, author*

Bible Truth Behind the Quote:
"Be doers of the word, and not hearers only, deceiving yourselves" (James 1:22).

— 907 —

Biblical orthodoxy without compassion is
surely the ugliest thing in the world.

—*Francis Schaeffer (1912-1984), theologian, philosopher, pastor*

Bible Truth Behind the Quote:
We should always be prepared "to make a defense to anyone who asks you for a reason for
the hope that is in you; *yet do it with gentleness and respect*" (1 Peter 3:15-16).

— 908 —

A man may be theologically knowing and spiritually ignorant.

—*Stephen Charnock (1628-1680), Puritan clergyman*

Bible Truth Behind the Quote:
Such individuals are "always learning and never able to arrive at a knowledge of the truth"
(2 Timothy 3:7).

THIRSTING FOR GOD

— 909 —

God thirsts to be thirsted after.

—*Augustine (354-430), bishop of Hippo*

Bible Truth Behind the Quote:
"As a deer pants for flowing streams, so pants my soul for you, O God. My soul thirsts for
God, for the living God" (Psalm 42:1-2).

TIME, USE OF

— 910 —

Remember always your end, and how that time lost returns not.
—*Thomas à Kempis (1380-1471), author,* The Imitation of Christ

Bible Truth Behind the Quote:
It is wise to be mindful of how brief time is on earth (Psalm 39:4) and then make the most of the remaining time (Psalm 90:12).

— 911 —

Though I am always in a haste, I am never in a hurry,
because I never undertake more work than I can
go through with perfect calmness of spirit.
—*John Wesley (1703-1791), founder of the Methodist church*

Bible Truth Behind the Quote:
Busy rushing ends in nothing (Psalm 39:6).

— 912 —

The tragedy of life is not that it ends so soon,
but that we wait so long to begin it.
—*W. M. Lewis*

Bible Truth Behind the Quote:
"Our citizenship is in heaven, and from it we await a Savior, the Lord Jesus Christ" (Philippians 3:20).

TODAY, LIVE FOR

— 913 —

God never built a Christian strong enough to carry today's
duties and tomorrow's anxieties piled on top of them.
—*Theodore Ledyard Cuyler (1822-1909), Presbyterian minister*

Bible Truth Behind the Quote:
"Do not be anxious about tomorrow, for tomorrow will be anxious for itself. Sufficient for the day is its own trouble" (Matthew 6:34).

— 914 —

Never try to carry tomorrow's burdens with today's grace.
—*Anonymous*

Bible Truth Behind the Quote:
Moment by moment, we will find God's grace fully sufficient (1 Corinthians 15:10; 2 Corinthians 12:9).

— 915 —

Tomorrow, tomorrow, tomorrow! Alas, tomorrow never
comes! It is in no calendar except the almanac of fools.
—*Charles Spurgeon (1834-1892), pastor, New Park Street Chapel, London*

Bible Truth Behind the Quote:
We ought to make the "best use of the time" (Colossians 4:5).

— 916 —

He who governed the world before I was born
shall take care of it likewise when I am dead. My
part is to improve the present moment.
—*John Wesley (1703-1791), founder of the Methodist church*

Bible Truth Behind the Quote:
Each and every moment, we ought to "serve the LORD with gladness!" (Psalm 100:2).

— 917 —

Don't waste your time waiting and longing for large
opportunities which may never come. But faithfully handle
the little things that are always claiming your attention.
—*F.B. Meyer (1847-1929), Baptist pastor, evangelist*

Bible Truth Behind the Quote:
We ought to "work heartily, as for the Lord and not for men" (Colossians 3:23).

— 918 —

Today is mine. Tomorrow is none of my business. If I peer
anxiously into the fog of the future, I will strain my spiritual
eyes so that I will not see clearly what is required of me now.
—*Elisabeth Elliot (born 1926), author, wife of Jim Elliot*

Bible Truth Behind the Quote:
"Do not be anxious about tomorrow" (Matthew 6:34).

— 919 —

The past exists in our memory, the future in our expectancy; what
we possess is the present. Mastering the ever-present moment

means mastering life. And if you do not serve the Lord today
there is no guarantee that you will serve Him tomorrow.
—*Erich Sauer (1898-1959), Wiedenest Bible School, West Germany*

Bible Truth Behind the Quote:
Live in the present moment (Matthew 6:34; James 4:14).

— 920 —

Happy is he who makes daily progress and who considers not
what he did yesterday but what advance he can make today.
—*Jerome (374-420), apologist, translator*

Bible Truth Behind the Quote:
"Blessed be the Lord, who daily bears us up" (Psalm 68:19).

— 921 —

Today is the tomorrow you worried about yesterday.
—*Anonymous*

Bible Truth Behind the Quote:
Don't worry! Instead, cast all anxieties on the Lord (1 Peter 5:7).

— 922 —

Yesterday's hits won't win today's game.
—*Anonymous*

Bible Truth Behind the Quote:
"The steadfast love of the LORD never ceases; his mercies never come to an end; they are
new every morning; great is your faithfulness" (Lamentations 3:22-23).

— 923 —

Some people go back into the past and rake up all the
troubles they ever had, and then they look into the future
and anticipate that they will have still more trouble, and
then they go reeling and staggering all through life.
—*Dwight L. Moody (1837-1899), evangelist*

Bible Truth Behind the Quote:
"Do not be anxious about anything, but in everything by prayer and supplication with
thanksgiving let your requests be made known to God. And the peace of God, which
surpasses all understanding, will guard your hearts and your minds in Christ Jesus" (Philippians 4:6-7).

TONGUE

— 924 —

The tongue is but three inches long, yet
it can kill a man six feet high.

—*Anonymous*

Bible Truth Behind the Quote:
The tongue can cut like a sharp razor (Psalm 52:2), sting like a snake (Psalm 140:3), and can kill (Proverbs 18:21). No one can tame it (James 3:8).

— 925 —

The tongue is a slave of the heart. So let's
be sure the heart is a good master.

—*Stanley Toussaint, professor, Dallas Theological Seminary*

Bible Truth Behind the Quote:
"What comes out of the mouth proceeds from the heart, and this defiles a person" (Matthew 15:18).

TRANQUILITY

— 926 —

He has great tranquility of heart who cares neither for the praises
nor the fault-finding of men. He will easily be content and
pacified, whose conscience is pure. You are not holier if you are
praised, nor the more worthless if you are found fault with.

—*Thomas à Kempis (1380-1471), author,* The Imitation of Christ

Bible Truth Behind the Quote:
"Just as we have been approved by God to be entrusted with the gospel, so we speak, not to please man, but to please God who tests our hearts" (1 Thessalonians 2:4).

TRAVELING

— 927 —

Traveling is one of the devil's special opportunities for tempting
us. Seek always to know the mind of God before you do anything,
but even more so before going on a trip. Don't needlessly expose
yourself and give the devil an opportunity to ensnare you.

—*George Müller (1805-1898), director of orphanages in Bristol, England*

Bible Truth Behind the Quote:
Scripture warns of "the schemes of the devil" (Ephesians 6:11). One such scheme is no doubt to distract believers from Scripture. We are thus to be sober-minded and watchful (1 Peter 5:8).

TRIALS

— 928 —

Each problem is a God-appointed instructor.
—*Charles Swindoll (born 1934), pastor, Stonebriar Community Church*

Bible Truth Behind the Quote:
"Count it all joy, my brothers, when you meet trials of various kinds, for you know that the testing of your faith produces steadfastness" (James 1:2-3).

— 929 —

Take those road hazards—the potholes, ruts, detours, and all the rest—as evidence that you were on the right route. It's when you find yourself on that big, broad, easy road that you ought to worry.
—*Joni Eareckson Tada (born 1949), founder, Joni and Friends*

Bible Truth Behind the Quote:
"Through many tribulations we must enter the kingdom of God" (Acts 14:22).

— 930 —

Everything that God brings into our life is directed to one purpose: that we might be conformed to the image of Christ.
—*Erwin Lutzer (born 1941), pastor, Moody Church, Chicago*

Bible Truth Behind the Quote:
"We know that for those who love God all things work together for good, for those who are called according to his purpose" (Romans 8:28).

— 931 —

We should not be upset when unexpected and upsetting and discouraging things happen. God in his wisdom means to make something of us which we have not yet attained and is dealing with us accordingly.
—*J.I. Packer (born 1926), author, theologian*

Bible Truth Behind the Quote:
"It is good for me that I was afflicted, that I might learn your statutes" (Psalm 119:71).

— 932 —

I believe in getting into hot water. I think it keeps you clean.

—*Gilbert Keith Chesterton (1874-1936), English author, apologist*

Bible Truth Behind the Quote:
"We rejoice in our sufferings, knowing that suffering produces endurance, and endurance produces character, and character produces hope" (Romans 5:3-4).

— 933 —

Sickness is God's messenger to call us to meet with God.

—*Thomas Manton (1620-1667), English Puritan clergyman*

Bible Truth Behind the Quote:
The repentant psalmist prayed, "For when I kept silent, my bones wasted away through my groaning all day long. For day and night your hand was heavy upon me; my strength was dried up as by the heat of summer" (Psalm 32:3-4).

— 934 —

I would...suggest that some form of suffering
is virtually indispensable to holiness.

—*John Stott (born 1921), Anglican clergyman*

Bible Truth Behind the Quote:
Trials test our faith and produce steadfastness (1 Peter 1:6-7).

— 935 —

Affliction is the badge of adoption.

—*Thomas Watson (1620-1686), Puritan preacher, author*

Bible Truth Behind the Quote:
"It has been granted to you that for the sake of Christ you should not only believe in him but also suffer for his sake" (Philippians 1:29).

— 936 —

God's heavenly plan doesn't always make earthly sense.

—*Charles Swindoll (born 1934), pastor, Stonebriar Community Church*

Bible Truth Behind the Quote:
God affirms, "For my thoughts are not your thoughts, neither are your ways my ways, declares the LORD. For as the heavens are higher than the earth, so are my ways higher than your ways and my thoughts than your thoughts" (Isaiah 55:8-9).

— 937 —

The diamonds cannot be polished without friction,
nor the man perfected without trials.

—*Anonymous*

Bible Truth Behind the Quote:

"Rejoice, though now for a little while, if necessary, you have been grieved by various trials, so that the tested genuineness of your faith—more precious than gold that perishes though it is tested by fire—may be found to result in praise and glory and honor at the revelation of Jesus Christ" (1 Peter 1:6-7).

— 938 —

We find it hard to understand the detours along
which God takes us, and it is often only afterwards
that we see that we had to go that way.

—*Paul Tournier (1898-1986), Swiss physician, author*

Bible Truth Behind the Quote:

Joseph was betrayed and sold into slavery by his own brothers. At the time, he had no idea what God was doing in his life. Only later could he look back and say, "God meant it for good" (Genesis 50:20).

— 939 —

God tests us so that we might stand; the devil
tests us so that we might stumble.

—*Adrian Rogers (1931-2005), Baptist pastor, author*

Bible Truth Behind the Quote:

Jesus warned Peter, "Simon, Simon, behold, Satan demanded to have you, that he might sift you like wheat" (Luke 22:31). Jesus prayed that Peter's faith would not fail. While Peter did end up denying Christ three times (John 13:38), he repented and became a great leader of the church.

— 940 —

Christ's followers cannot expect better treatment
in the world than their Master had.

—*Matthew Henry (1662-1714), Bible commentator, Presbyterian minister*

Bible Truth Behind the Quote:

"If the world hates you, know that it has hated me before it hated you. If you were of the world, the world would love you as its own; but because you are not of the world, but I chose you out of the world, therefore the world hates you" (John 15:18-19).

— 941 —

Trials are medicines which our gracious and wise Physician
prescribes because we need them; and he proportions the
frequency and weight of them to what the case requires.
Let us trust his skill and thank him for his prescription.

—*John Newton (1725-1807), English Anglican clergyman*

Bible Truth Behind the Quote:
"Count it all joy, my brothers, when you meet trials of various kinds" (James 1:2).

— 942 —

Beware of succumbing to failure as inevitable;
make it a stepping stone to success.

—*Oswald Chambers (1874-1917), author,* My Utmost for His Highest

Bible Truth Behind the Quote:
Peter sank in the water when he attempted to walk on it (Matthew 14:28-31). By this failure, he learned to maintain faith and not take his eyes off of Jesus.

— 943 —

God never allows pain without a purpose in the lives of
His children. He never allows Satan, nor circumstances,
nor any ill-intending person to afflict us unless He uses
that affliction for our good. God never wastes pain.

—*Jerry Bridges (born 1929), author, affiliated with The Navigators*

Bible Truth Behind the Quote:
God always causes our circumstances to work together for our ultimate good—the good of conforming us more to the likeness of His Son (see Romans 8:28-29).

— 944 —

If God sends us on stony paths, he will
provide us with strong shoes.

—*Alexander Maclaren (1826-1910), English minister*

Bible Truth Behind the Quote:
God's power is "made perfect in weakness" (2 Corinthians 12:9).

— 945 —

If God has made your cup sweet, drink it with grace. If he
has made it bitter, drink it in communion with Him.

—*Oswald Chambers (1874-1917), author,* My Utmost for His Highest

Bible Truth Behind the Quote:
"I have learned in whatever situation I am to be content" (Philippians 4:11).

— 946 —

The Lord gets His best soldiers out of the highlands of affliction.

—*Charles Spurgeon (1834-1892), pastor, New Park Street Chapel, London*

Bible Truth Behind the Quote:
Paul is an example. "Five times I received at the hands of the Jews the forty lashes less one. Three times I was beaten with rods. Once I was stoned. Three times I was shipwrecked; a night and a day I was adrift at sea; on frequent journeys, in danger from rivers, danger from robbers, danger from my own people, danger from Gentiles, danger in the city, danger in the wilderness, danger at sea, danger from false brothers; in toil and hardship, through many a sleepless night, in hunger and thirst, often without food, in cold and exposure" (2 Corinthians 11:24-27). Through all this, Paul's faith was tested and grew.

— 947 —

No man, without trials and temptations, can attain
a true understanding of the Holy Scriptures.

—*John Bunyan (1628-1688), English Christian writer, preacher*

Bible Truth Behind the Quote:
"It is good for me that I was afflicted, that I might learn your statutes" (Psalm 119:71).

TRINITY

— 948 —

If I believe everything the Bible says about topic X and use
a term not found in the Bible to describe the full teaching
of Scripture on that point, am I not being more truthful
to the Word than someone who limits themselves to only
biblical terms, but rejects some aspect of God's revelation?

—*James White in reference to cults who say the word "Trinity"*
is not in the Bible (born 1962), director, Alpha and Omega Ministries

Bible Truth Behind the Quote:
There is one God, and within the unity of the godhead, there are three co-eternal and co-equal persons: the Father, the Son, and the Holy Spirit (see Matthew 28:19; 2 Corinthians 13:14).

TROUBLES

— 949 —

God will not permit any troubles to come upon us, unless He has a
specific plan by which great blessing can come out of the difficulty.

—*Peter Marshall (1902-1949), Scottish-American preacher*

Bible Truth Behind the Quote:
Paul affirmed, "We know that for those who love God all things work together for good, for those who are called according to his purpose" (Romans 8:28). Paul certainly understood his imprisonment this way, for he said that "what has happened to me has really served to advance the gospel" (Philippians 1:12). Indeed, he said, "most of the brothers, having become confident in the Lord by my imprisonment, are much more bold to speak the word without fear" (verse 14).

Trust in Jesus

— 950 —

How sweet the Name of Jesus sounds in a believer's ear! It
soothes his sorrows, heals his wounds, and drives away his fear!
—*John Newton (1725-1807), Anglican clergyman*

Bible Truth Behind the Quote:
Scripture reveals that "God has highly exalted him [Jesus] and bestowed on him the name that is above every name, so that at the name of Jesus every knee should bow, in heaven and on earth and under the earth, and every tongue confess that Jesus Christ is Lord, to the glory of God the Father" (Philippians 2:9-11, insert added for clarification).

— 951 —

Let us never despair while we have Christ as our leader!
—*George Whitefield (1714-1770), itinerant minister, Great Awakening*

Bible Truth Behind the Quote:
The writer to the Hebrews urged, "Let us run with endurance the race that is set before us, looking to Jesus, the founder and perfecter of our faith" (Hebrews 12:1-2). Never give up!

— 952 —

God incarnate is the end of fear; and the heart that realizes
that He is in the midst…will be quiet in the midst of alarm.
—*F.B. Meyer (1847-1929), Baptist pastor, evangelist*

Bible Truth Behind the Quote:
Scripture reveals, "The Lord is at hand; do not be anxious about anything, but in everything by prayer and supplication with thanksgiving let your requests be made known to God. And the peace of God, which surpasses all understanding, will guard your hearts and your minds in Christ Jesus" (Philippians 4:5-7).

TRUSTING GOD

— 953 —

I lay my "whys"
before your cross
in worship kneeling,
my mind too numb
for thought,
my heart beyond
all feeling:
And worshiping,
realize that I
in knowing you
don't need a "why."

—*Ruth Bell Graham (1920-2007), wife of Billy Graham*

Bible Truth Behind the Quote:
"Trust in the LORD with all your heart, and do not lean on your own understanding. In all your ways acknowledge him, and he will make straight your paths" (Proverbs 3:5-6).

— 954 —

Never be afraid to trust an unknown future to a known God.

—*Corrie ten Boom (1892-1983), Dutch Christian Holocaust survivor*

Bible Truth Behind the Quote:
"My times are in your hand" (Psalm 31:15).

— 955 —

The more we know of God the more unreservedly we
will trust him; the greater our progress in theology,
the simpler and more childlike will be our faith.

—*John Gresham Machen (1881-1937), American Presbyterian theologian*

Bible Truth Behind the Quote:
"Blessed is the man who makes the LORD his trust" (Psalm 40:4).

— 956 —

I have held many things in my hands, and I have lost them all;
but whatever I have placed in God's hands, that I still possess.

—*Martin Luther (1483-1546), priest, professor of theology, reformer*

Bible Truth Behind the Quote:
God guards all that we entrust to Him (2 Timothy 1:12). Everything God does is worthy of trust (Psalm 33:4).

— 957 —

Trusting means drawing on the inexhaustible resources of God.

—*Anonymous*

Bible Truth Behind the Quote:
God is "able to do far more abundantly than all that we ask or think" (Ephesians 3:20).

— 958 —

Trust involves letting go and knowing God will catch you.

—*James Dobson (born 1936), founder, Focus on the Family*

Bible Truth Behind the Quote:
The moment Peter began to sink after walking on water, "Jesus immediately reached out his hand and took hold of him" (Matthew 14:31). The Lord promises, "I will never leave you nor forsake you" (Hebrews 13:5).

— 959 —

It is not difficult for me to remember that the little ones need breakfast in the morning, dinner at midday, and something before they go to bed at night. Indeed I could not forget it. And I find it impossible to suppose that our heavenly Father is less tender or mindful than I…I do not believe that our heavenly Father will ever forget His children. I am a very poor father, but it is not my habit to forget my children. God is a very, very good Father. It is not His habit to forget His children.

—*J. Hudson Taylor (1832-1905), founder, China Inland Mission*

Bible Truth Behind the Quote:
We ought to daily affirm, "In God I trust" (Psalm 56:11).

TRUTH

— 960 —

If all of this world falls from the truth, I will stand!

—*Athanasius (293-373), theologian, bishop of Alexandria, church father*

Bible Truth Behind the Quote:
"Contend for the faith that was once for all delivered to the saints" (Jude 3).

— 961 —

From the Liberality which says that everybody is right;
From the Charity which forbids us to say that anybody is wrong;
From the Peace which is bought at the expense of Truth—
May the good Lord deliver us.

—J.C. Ryle (1816-1900), Anglican bishop, Liverpool

Bible Truth Behind the Quote:
We must set forth the truth plainly (2 Corinthians 4:2) and speak the truth in love (Ephesians 4:15).

— 962 —

Peace if possible, but truth at any rate.

—Martin Luther (1483-1546), priest, professor of theology, reformer

Bible Truth Behind the Quote:
We should always be "prepared to make a defense to anyone who asks you for a reason for the hope that is in you; yet do it with gentleness and respect" (1 Peter 3:15-16).

UNBELIEVERS

— 963 —

The seeming peace a sinner has is not from the knowledge
of his happiness but the ignorance of his danger.

—Thomas Watson (1620-1686), Puritan preacher, author

Bible Truth Behind the Quote:
"The god of this world has blinded the minds of the unbelievers" (2 Corinthians 4:4).

UNITY ON THE ESSENTIALS

— 964 —

In necessary things, unity;
in doubtful things, liberty;
in all things, charity.

—Richard Baxter (1615-1691), English Puritan church leader

Bible Truth Behind the Quote:
"Be watchful, stand firm in the faith" (1 Corinthians 16:13). ("The faith" refers to that apostolic body of truth communicated to the early church.)

USED BY GOD

— 965 —

If you are not willing to be used by God, ask
God to make you willing to be willing.

—F.B. Meyer (1847-1929), Baptist pastor, evangelist

Bible Truth Behind the Quote:
The Lord has the unique ability to turn the human heart (Proverbs 21:1). Ask Him to change yours!

USEFUL, BEING

— 966 —

O Lord, let me not live to be useless.

—John Wesley (1703-1791), founder of the Methodist church

Bible Truth Behind the Quote:
"Do not neglect the gift you have" (1 Timothy 4:14). "Fan into flame the gift" God gave you (2 Timothy 1:6).

VACUUM IN HEART

— 967 —

O God, Thou hast made us for Thyself, and our
hearts find no rest until they rest in Thee.

—Augustine (354-430), bishop of Hippo

Bible Truth Behind the Quote:
God "has put eternity into man's heart" (Ecclesiastes 3:11).

— 968 —

There is a God-shaped vacuum in every heart.

—Blaise Pascal (1623-1662), French mathematician, physicist, religious philosopher

Bible Truth Behind the Quote:
"Behold, I stand at the door and knock. If anyone hears my voice and opens the door, I will come in to him and eat with him, and he with me" (Revelation 3:20).

— 969 —

When you empty yourself, God Almighty rushes in!

—A.W. Tozer (1897-1963), American pastor, author

Bible Truth Behind the Quote:
"It is no longer I who live, but Christ who lives in me. And the life I now live in the flesh I live by faith in the Son of God, who loved me and gave himself for me" (Galatians 2:20).

Vanity

— 970 —

It is vanity to seek after perishing riches and to trust in them. Also it is vanity to hunt after honors and to climb to high degree. It is vanity to follow the desires of the flesh, and to long after that for which you must afterward suffer grievous punishment.

—*Thomas à Kempis (1380-1471), author,* The Imitation of Christ

Bible Truth Behind the Quote:
Psalm 90:12 informs us that by numbering our days, we gain a heart of wisdom. The psalmist prayed, "O LORD, make me know my end and what is the measure of my days; let me know how fleeting I am!" (Psalm 39:4).

Victory

— 971 —

God is never defeated. Though He may be opposed, attacked, resisted, still the ultimate outcome can never be in doubt.

—*Brother Andrew (born 1928), Christian missionary, Bible smuggler*

Bible Truth Behind the Quote:
"The horse is made ready for the day of battle, but the victory belongs to the LORD" (Proverbs 21:31).

— 972 —

There is no more dangerous moment in our lives than that which follows a great victory.

—*Stephen Olford (1918-2004), pastor, author*

Bible Truth Behind the Quote:
Scripture soberly warns, "Let anyone who thinks that he stands take heed lest he fall" (1 Corinthians 10:12).

VIRTUE

— 973 —

The strength of a man's virtue should not be measured
by his special exertions, but by his habitual acts.

—Blaise Pascal (1623-1662), French mathematician, physicist, religious philosopher

Bible Truth Behind the Quote:
"A healthy tree cannot bear bad fruit, nor can a diseased tree bear good fruit" (Matthew 7:18).

WAITING

— 974 —

There is no place for faith if we expect God to
fulfill immediately what he promises.

—John Calvin (1509-1564), French reformer

Bible Truth Behind the Quote:
"Wait for the LORD; be strong, and let your heart take courage; wait for the LORD!" (Psalm 27:14).

WALKING WITH GOD

— 975 —

I would rather walk with God in the dark
than go alone in the light.

—Mary Gardiner Brainard (1837-1905), American writer of religious poetry

Bible Truth Behind the Quote:
"I am the light of the world. Whoever follows me will not walk in darkness, but will have the light of life" (John 8:12).

WAR

— 976 —

Since 3600 BC the world has known only 292 years
of peace. In that period, stretching more than 55
centuries, there have been an incredible 14,531 wars in
which over 3.6 billion people have been killed.

—John Ankerberg (born 1945) and John Weldon, apologists

Bible Truth Behind the Quote:
"Deliver me, O LORD, from evil men; preserve me from violent men, who plan evil things in their heart and stir up wars continually" (Psalm 140:1-2).

WEAKNESS

— 977 —

We have no power from God unless we live in the
persuasion that we have none of our own.

—*John Owen (1616-1683), church leader, theologian*

Bible Truth Behind the Quote:
God instructed Paul, "My power is made perfect in weakness" (2 Corinthians 12:9).

WEALTH

— 978 —

In this world it is not what we take up, but
what we give up that makes us rich.

—*Henry Ward Beecher (1813-1887), Congregationalist clergyman*

Bible Truth Behind the Quote:
Jesus spoke of rich people putting large sums of money into the treasury box. He then noted that "a poor widow came and put in two small copper coins, which make a penny" (Mark 12:41-42). The rich gave out of their abundance, Jesus said, but she gave "everything she had, all she had to live on" (verse 44).

— 979 —

It ill disposes the servant to seek to be rich and great and honored
in this world where his Lord was poor and mean and despised.

—*George Müller (1805-1898), director of orphanages in Bristol, England*

Bible Truth Behind the Quote:
"Those who desire to be rich fall into temptation, into a snare, into many senseless and harmful desires that plunge people into ruin and destruction" (1 Timothy 6:9).

WILL OF GOD

— 980 —

There are no disappointments to those whose
wills are buried in the will of God.

—*Frederick W. Faber (1814-1863), British hymn writer, devotional writer*

Bible Truth Behind the Quote:
Those who truly seek God's will can say even of troublemakers, as Joseph did in regard to his brothers who had sinned against him, "You meant evil against me, but God meant it for good" (Genesis 50:20).

— 981 —

I can say from experience that 95% of knowing the will of God
consists in being prepared to do it before you know what it is.
—Donald Grey Barnhouse (1895-1960), pastor, theologian

Bible Truth Behind the Quote:
In the Old Testament, God affirmed, "Be careful to obey all these words that I command you, that it may go well with you and with your children after you forever, when you do what is good and right in the sight of the LORD your God" (Deuteronomy 12:28). God is basically saying, "Whatever I reveal my will to be in the Law, that is precisely what I expect you to obey without hesitation." This ought to be our attitude today!

WISE WAGER

— 982 —

Belief is a wise wager. Granted that faith cannot be proved,
what harm will come to you if you gamble on its truth and it
proves false?…If you gain, you gain all; if you lose, you lose
nothing. Wager, then, without hesitation, that he exists.
—Blaise Pascal (1623-1662), French mathematician, physicist, religious philosopher

Bible Truth Behind the Quote:
Because none of us knows the day we will die, is it not the height of folly to put off turning to Christ for salvation today (Luke 12:20; 2 Corinthians 6:2)?

WITNESS

— 983 —

We are the Bibles the world is reading; we are the creeds the
world is needing; we are the sermons the world is heeding.
—Billy Graham (born 1918), evangelist

Bible Truth Behind the Quote:
"Let your light shine before others, so that they may see your good works and give glory to your Father who is in heaven" (Matthew 5:16).

— 984 —

The world is far more ready to receive the Gospel
than Christians are to hand it out.

—*George W. Peters, professor of world missions, Dallas Theological Seminary*

Bible Truth Behind the Quote:
"Go therefore and make disciples of all nations, baptizing them in the name of the Father and of the Son and of the Holy Spirit" (Matthew 28:19).

WONDER AND AWE

— 985 —

There is a hint of the everlasting in the vastness of the sea.

—*J.B. Phillips (1906-1982), Bible translator, author, clergyman*

Bible Truth Behind the Quote:
God's "invisible attributes, namely, his eternal power and divine nature, have been clearly perceived, ever since the creation of the world, in the things that have been made" (Romans 1:20).

WONDERFUL PSALM

— 986 —

The twenty-third psalm is the nightingale of the psalms. It is
small, of a homely feather, singing shyly out of obscurity; but
it has filled the air of the whole world with melodious joy.

—*Henry Ward Beecher (1813-1887), Congregationalist clergyman*

Bible Truth Behind the Quote:
"The LORD is my shepherd; I shall not want..." (Psalm 23:1).

WORD OF GOD

— 987 —

Wherever we see the Word of God purely preached and heard,
there a church of God exists, even if it swarms with many faults.

—*John Calvin (1509-1564), French reformer*

Bible Truth Behind the Quote:
"Preach the word; be ready in season and out of season; reprove, rebuke, and exhort, with complete patience and teaching" (2 Timothy 4:2).

WORDS

— 988 —

Cold words freeze people, and hot words scorch them,
and bitter words make them bitter, and wrathful words
make them wrathful. Kind words also produce their
image on men's souls; and a beautiful image it is. They
smooth, and quiet, and comfort the hearer.

—Blaise Pascal (1623-1662), French mathematician, physicist, religious philosopher

Bible Truth Behind the Quote:
As Paul put it, "Let your speech always be gracious, seasoned with salt, so that you may
know how you ought to answer each person" (Colossians 4:6).

WORK

— 989 —

Let us work as if success depended on ourselves
alone, but with the heartfelt conviction that we
are doing nothing and God everything.

—Ignatius of Antioch (35-117), third Bishop and Patriarch of Antioch

Bible Truth Behind the Quote:
Let us not forget that "it is God who works in you, both to will and to work for his good
pleasure" (Philippians 2:13).

WORKS-BASED SALVATION?

— 990 —

The most damnable and pernicious heresy that has ever plagued
the mind of man was the idea that somehow he could make
himself good enough to deserve to live with an all-holy God.

—Martin Luther (1483-1546), priest, professor of theology, reformer

Bible Truth Behind the Quote:
"For by grace you have been saved through faith. And this is not your own doing; it is the
gift of God, not a result of works, so that no one may boast" (Ephesians 2:8-9). "A person is not justified by works of the law but through faith in Jesus Christ" (Galatians 2:16).

WORLD

— 991 —

Anything that cools my love for Christ is the world.

—John Wesley (1703-1791), founder of the Methodist church

Bible Truth Behind the Quote:
"All that is in the world—the desires of the flesh and the desires of the eyes and pride in possessions—is not from the Father but is from the world" (1 John 2:16).

WORRY

— 992 —

You can tell the size of your God by looking at the size of your worry list. The longer your list, the smaller your God.

—Anonymous

Bible Truth Behind the Quote:
"Do not be anxious about anything, but in everything by prayer and supplication with thanksgiving let your requests be made known to God. And the peace of God, which surpasses all understanding, will guard your hearts and your minds in Christ Jesus" (Philippians 4:6-7).

— 993 —

Bear not a single care thyself,
One is too much for thee;
The work is Mine, and Mine alone;
Thy work—to rest in Me.

—Anonymous

Bible Truth Behind the Quote:
"Cast your burden on the LORD, and he will sustain you; he will never permit the righteous to be moved" (Psalm 55:22).

— 994 —

All our fret and worry is caused by calculating without God.

—Oswald Chambers (1874-1917), author, My Utmost for His Highest

Bible Truth Behind the Quote:
You should cast "all your anxieties on him, because he cares for you" (1 Peter 5:7).

— 995 —

Half our miseries are caused by things that
we think are coming upon us.

—*J.C. Ryle (1816-1900), Anglican bishop, Liverpool*

Bible Truth Behind the Quote:
"Do not be anxious about tomorrow, for tomorrow will be anxious for itself. Sufficient for the day is its own trouble" (Matthew 6:34).

WORSHIP

— 996 —

Worship God in the difficult circumstances, and when
He chooses, He will alter them in two seconds.

—*Oswald Chambers (1874-1917), author,* My Utmost for His Highest

Bible Truth Behind the Quote:
"The Lord knows how to rescue the godly from trials" (2 Peter 2:9).

— 997 —

To worship God is to realize the purpose for which God created us.

—*Herbert M. Carson, Christian author*

Bible Truth Behind the Quote:
"Ascribe to the LORD the glory due his name; worship the LORD in the splendor of holiness" (Psalm 29:2).

YIELDED TO GOD

— 998 —

I am no longer my own, but Yours. Put me to what You will,
rank me with whom You will; put me to doing, put me to
suffering; let me be employed for You or laid aside for You,
exalted for You or brought low for You; let me be full, let me be
empty; let me have all things, let me have nothing; I freely and
wholeheartedly yield all things to Your pleasure and disposal.

—*John Wesley (1703-1791), founder of the Methodist church*

Bible Truth Behind the Quote:
Jesus affirmed, "Whoever finds his life will lose it, and whoever loses his life for my sake will find it" (Matthew 10:39).

YOU ARE SPECIAL

— 999 —

You aren't an accident. You weren't mass-produced. You aren't an assembly-line product. You were deliberately planned, specifically gifted, and lovingly positioned on this earth by the Master Craftsman.

—*Max Lucado (born 1955), author, minister, Oak Hills Church*

Bible Truth Behind the Quote:
"You formed my inward parts; you knitted me together in my mother's womb. I praise you, for I am fearfully and wonderfully made" (Psalm 139:13-14).

— 1000 —

Christ loves you so much it hurts.

—*Anonymous*

Bible Truth Behind the Quote:
Paul tells us, "For our sake he made him to be sin who knew no sin, so that in him we might become the righteousness of God" (2 Corinthians 5:21). Christ loves you so much that He took your sin upon Himself so that you might have the righteousness of God.

ZEAL

— 1001 —

Enthusiasm, like fire, must not only burn but must be controlled.

—*A.H. Strong*

Bible Truth Behind the Quote:
There are some who "have a zeal for God, but not according to knowledge" (Romans 10:2). Enthusiasm should be passionate but also tempered by godly knowledge.

TOPICAL INDEX

Abundant Living—1

Acronym to Remember—2

Aging—3, 4

Angels—5, 6

Anger—7, 8, 9, 10, 11, 12, 13, 14

Anxiety—15

Apology—16

Apostasy—17

Atheists—18, 19

Attitude—20, 21, 22, 23

Authenticity—24

Authority—25

Availability to God—26

Awe and Wonder—27

Backsliding—28, 29, 30, 31

Bearing Fruit—32

Beauty—33

Belittling—34

Bible—35, 36, 37, 38, 39, 40, 41, 42, 43, 44, 45, 46, 47, 48, 49, 50, 51, 52, 53, 54, 55, 56, 57, 58

Bible Application—59

Bible Interpretation—60, 61, 62, 63, 64, 65, 66, 67

Bible Promises—68

Bible Study—69

Blessing—70, 71

Busyness—72, 73

Change Is Coming—74

Character—75, 76, 77, 78, 79, 80, 81

Charity—82, 83, 84, 85

Child of God—86

Christ, Deity of—87

Christ, Love of—88

Christianity—89, 90, 91, 92, 93, 94, 95, 96, 97, 98, 99, 100, 101, 102, 103

Christmas—104

Church—105, 106, 107, 108, 109, 110, 111, 112, 113, 114, 115, 116, 117, 118, 119, 120

Church Attendance—121, 122

Church Influence—123

Church—Perfect?—124, 125

Citizen of Heaven—126

Citizenship—127

Comfort—128

Commitment—129, 130, 131, 132, 133, 134, 135, 136

Compassion—137

Confession—138, 139

Conscience—140, 141, 142, 143, 144, 145, 146, 147, 148, 149, 150, 151, 152, 153, 154

Consequences—155

Consistency—156

Contamination—157

Conversion—158, 159, 160

Convictions—161

Cooperation—162

Covetousness—163

Criticism—164

Cross—165

Crucified with Christ—166, 167

Darkness to Light—168

Death and Dying—169, 170, 171, 172,
173, 174, 175, 176, 177, 178, 179, 180,
181, 182, 183, 184, 185, 186, 187, 188,
189, 190, 191, 192, 193, 194, 195, 196,
197, 198

Death, Moment of—199, 200, 201, 202,
203

Defeat—204

Dependability—205

Dependence on God—206

Dependence on the Spirit—207

Devil—208, 209, 210, 211, 212, 213,
214, 215, 216, 217, 218, 219, 220,
221, 222, 223

Devil's Lies—224

Difficulties—225, 226

Diligence—227

Disappointments—228

Discernment—229, 230

Discipline, God's—231, 232, 233, 234,
235, 236, 237, 238

Discouragement—239, 240, 241

Disgracing Others—242

Dishonesty—243

Disillusionment with Christians—244

Doctrine—245

Doers of the Word—246, 247

Earth—248

Encouragement—249, 250, 251

Endurance—252

Enthusiasm About Faith—253

Envy—254

Epitaph—255

Eternal Life—256

Eternal Perspective—257, 258, 259,
260, 261, 262, 263, 264, 265, 266,
267, 268, 269, 270, 271, 272, 273,
274, 275, 276, 277, 278, 279, 280,
281, 282, 283, 284, 285, 286, 287,
288, 289, 290, 291, 292, 293, 294

Eternal Security—295

Evangelism—296, 297, 298, 299, 300,
301, 302, 303

Evil—304, 305, 306, 307, 308, 309

Evolution—310, 311

Failure—312

Faith—313, 314, 315, 316, 317, 318, 319,
320, 321, 322, 323, 324, 325, 326,
327, 328, 329, 330, 331, 332, 333,
334, 335, 336, 337, 338, 339, 340,
341, 342, 343, 344

Faith, The—345

Faith and Works—346

Faithfulness—347, 348

Falling Away—349

Falling Short—350, 351, 352

Family—353, 354, 355, 356, 357

Fasting—358, 359

Fatherhood—360

Fathers and Sons—361

Fear—362, 363, 364

Fear of the Lord—365, 366, 367, 368,
369

Feelings—370

Fellowship—371

First Impressions—372

Forgiveness—373, 374, 375, 376, 377,
378, 379, 380

Friends—381

Future—382

Gaining Christ—383

Giving—384, 385, 386, 387, 388

God, Awesome—389, 390, 391

God, Beauty of—392

God, Blessing of—393

God, Dependability of—394

God, False Concept of—395

God, Glory of—396, 397, 398

God, Good—399

God Helps His Children—400, 401,

402, 403, 404, 405, 406, 407, 408, 409, 410

God, Holiness of—411, 412

God, Immanence of—413, 414

God, Infinite in Perfections—415

God, Loving—416

God, Merciful—417, 418

God, Omnipotent—419, 420

God, Omnipresent—421, 422

God, Patience of—423

God, Proof of—424

God, Providential—425, 426, 427, 428, 429, 430, 431

God, Silences of—432, 433, 434, 435

God, Sovereign—436, 437

God, Will of—438, 439, 440, 441, 442

Godliness—443

Good and Evil—444

Good Ideas—445

Good Works, Doing—446, 447, 448, 449, 450, 451

Gospel—452, 453, 454

Gospel, Urgency of the—455

Gossip—456

Government—457

Grace—458, 459, 460, 461, 462

Grace, Growing in—463

Grace, Perceived Need for—464

Gratitude—465

Great Opportunities—466

Greatness—467

Grief—468

Guilt—469

Habits—470

Happiness—471, 472, 473, 474, 475, 476, 477, 478, 479, 480, 481

Health and Wealth—482

Health for the Soul—483

Heaven—484, 485, 486, 487, 488, 489, 490, 491, 492, 493, 494, 495, 496, 497, 498, 499, 500, 501

Heaven and Hell—502, 503, 504, 505

Hell—506, 507

History—508

Holiness—509, 510, 511, 512, 513, 514, 515, 516

Holy Spirit—517, 518, 519, 520, 521, 522

Hope—523, 524, 525, 526, 527, 528

Humility—529, 530, 531, 532, 533, 534, 535, 536, 537, 538, 539, 540, 541, 542

Husband and Wife—543, 544

Hypocrisy—545, 546

Idleness—547, 548

Idolatry—549

Ignorance—550, 551

Imitate the Lord—552

Immature Christians—553

Injustice—554

Intentions, Important—555

Jealousy—556, 557, 558

Jesus—559, 560

Jesus, Claims of—561

Jesus, God-Man—562

Jesus Our Intercessor—563

Jesus, Looking to—564

Jesus, Sufficiency of—565, 566, 567, 568, 569

Jesus Died for You and Me—570, 571, 572

Joy—573

Judging Others—574, 575, 576

Judgment—577, 578, 579

Kindness—580, 581, 582

Knowing God—583, 584, 585

Labor—586

Laughter—587, 588

Laziness—589, 590

Leadership—591, 592

Let Your Light Shine—593

Liberty—594

Life and Death—595
Longevity—596, 597
Longings of the Heart—598
Love—599, 600, 601, 602, 603, 604,
    605, 606, 607, 608, 609, 610
Love of Money—611
Lust—612
Malice—613
Masking Sin—614
Meekness—615
Mercy—616, 617
Minister—618, 619, 620, 621, 622, 623,
    624, 625, 626, 627, 628
Miracles—629
Mission Work—630, 631
Modesty—632
Money and Materialism—633, 634,
    635, 636, 637, 638, 639, 640, 641,
    642, 643, 644, 645, 646, 647, 648
Music—649, 650
Obedience—651, 652, 653, 654, 655,
    656, 657, 658, 659, 660
Pain—661, 662
Parental Love—663
Patience—664, 665, 666
Peace—667
Perseverance—668
Perseverance of the Saints—669
Popularity—670
Poverty—671
Power in Ministry—672
Practicing the Presence of God—673,
    674, 675, 676, 677, 678, 679
Praise—680, 681
Prayer—682, 683, 684, 685, 686, 687,
    688, 689, 690, 691, 692, 693, 694,
    695, 696, 697, 698, 699, 700, 701,
    702, 703, 704, 705, 706, 707, 708,
    709, 710, 711, 712, 713, 714, 715,
    716, 717, 718, 719, 720, 721, 722,
    723
Prayer for Bible Study—724

Prayer for Tender Mercy—725
Prayer of Humility—726
Prayer of Serenity—727
Praying Hard—728
Preaching—729, 730, 731
Pride—732, 733, 734, 735, 736, 737,
    738, 739, 740, 741, 742, 743, 744,
    745, 746, 747, 748, 749
Priesthood of the Believer—750
Promises of God—751
Prosperity—752
Quarreling—753, 754, 755, 756, 757,
    758, 759
Racial Equality—760
Relationships—761
Repentance—762, 763, 764, 765, 766,
    767, 768, 769, 770
Resolution—771, 772, 773, 774, 775
Resurrection—776, 777, 778
Resurrection Power—779
Righteously, Live—780
Righteousness—781
Righteousness, Insufficient for Salva-
    tion—782
Salvation—783, 784, 785, 786, 787
Salvation, Assurance of—788
Savior—789
Scripture—790, 791, 792, 793, 794,
    795, 796, 797, 798, 799, 800, 801,
    802, 803, 804
Second Coming—805, 806, 807, 808
Self-Denial—809
Self-Dependence—810
Self-Focus—811, 812, 813, 814, 815
Self-Knowledge—816
Serving Others—817, 818
Shine as a Light—819, 820, 821, 822,
    823, 824
Silence Can Be Wise—825
Sin—826, 827, 828, 829, 830, 831, 832,
    833, 834, 835, 836, 837, 838, 839,

840, 841, 842, 843, 844, 845, 846, 847, 848, 849, 850, 851, 852, 853, 854, 855, 856, 857, 858

Sin, Consequences of—859

Sin, Personal—860

Sin, Realistic Assessment of—861, 862, 863

Sin, Remaining in—864

Sin, Sorrow for—865

Single-Heartedness—866, 867

Spirit World—868, 869, 870

Spiritual Blindness—871, 872

Strength in Weakness—873, 874

Submission to God—875, 876, 877

Suffering—878, 879, 880, 881, 882, 883

Surrender All—884

Take Up Your Cross—885

Taming the Tongue—886

Teamwork—887

Temper—888

Temptation—889, 890, 891, 892, 893, 894, 895, 896, 897, 898, 899, 900, 901, 902

Thanks-Living—903

Thanksgiving—904

Theology—905, 906, 907, 908

Thirsting for God—909

Time, Use of—910, 911, 912

Today, Live for—913, 914, 915, 916, 917, 918, 919, 920, 921, 922, 923

Tongue—924, 925

Tranquility—926

Traveling—927

Trials—928, 929, 930, 931, 932, 933, 934, 935, 936, 937, 938, 939, 940, 941, 942, 943, 944, 945, 946, 947

Trinity—948

Troubles—949

Trust in Jesus—950, 951, 952

Trusting God—953, 954, 955, 956, 957, 958, 959

Truth—960, 961, 962

Unbelievers—963

Unity on the Essentials—964

Used by God—965

Useful, Being—966

Vacuum in Heart—967, 968, 969

Vanity—970

Victory—971, 972

Virtue—973

Waiting—974

Walking with God—975

War—976

Weakness—977

Wealth—978, 979

Will of God—980, 981

Wise Wager—982

Witness—983, 984

Wonder and Awe—985

Wonderful Psalm—986

Word of God—987

Words—988

Work—989

Works-Based Salvation?—990

World—991

Worry—992, 993, 994, 995

Worship—996, 997

Yielded to God—998

You Are Special—999, 1000

Zeal—1001

BIBLIOGRAPHY

PRIMARY BOOKS

Carter, Tom, comp. *Spurgeon At His Best.* Grand Rapids: Baker, 1988.

Comfort, Ray, comp. *Spurgeon Gold.* Gainesville, FL: Bridge-Logos, 2005.

Comfort, Ray, comp. *Wesley Gold.* Gainesville, FL: Bridge-Logos, 2005.

Comfort, Ray, comp. *Whitefield Gold.* Gainesville, FL: Bridge-Logos, 2005.

Cook, John, comp. and arr. *The Book of Positive Quotations.* Minneapolis: Fairview Press, 1993.

Doan, Eleanor Lloyd, ed. *The Complete Speakers Sourcebook: 8,000 Illustrations and Quotations for Every Occasion.* Grand Rapids, MI: Zondervan, 1996.

Draper, Edythe, ed. *Draper's Book of Quotations for the Christian World.* Wheaton, IL: Tyndale, 1992.

Kelly, Bob. *Quotes Worth Repeating.* Grand Rapids: Kregel, 2003.

Manser, Martin, comp. *The Westminster Collection of Christian Quotations.* Louisville, KY: Westminster John Knox, 2001.

Martindale, Wayne and Jerry Root, eds. *The Quotable Lewis.* Wheaton, IL: Tyndale, 1989.

Mencken, Henry Louis, ed. *A New Dictionary of Quotations.* New York: Knopf, 1942.

Pederson, Randall J., comp. and ed. *Day by Day with Jonathan Edwards.* Peabody, MA: Hendrickson Publishers, 2005.

Pentz, Croft. *The Complete Book of Zingers.* Wheaton: Tyndale, 1990.

Rukin, Joe, comp. *Look at the Bees: Quotes for Life.* United Kingdom: Buzzing Books, 2007.

Singh, M.P., comp. *Quote Unquote: A Handbook of Famous Quotations.* New Delhi: Lotus Press, 2006.

Summers, William T., ed. *The Quotable Matthew Henry.* Grand Rapids: Revell, 1990.

Sweeting, George, comp. *Great Quotes and Illustrations.* Waco, TX: Word, 1985.

Tan, Paul Lee, comp. *Encyclopedia of 7700 Illustrations.* Rockville, MD: Assurance, 1979.

Water, Mark, ed. *The New Encyclopedia of Christian Quotations.* Grand Rapids: Baker, 1995.

Zuck, Roy, ed. *The Speaker's Quote Book.* Grand Rapids, MI: Kregel, 2009.

SUPPLEMENTAL BOOKS

Alcorn, Randy. *Heaven.* Wheaton: Tyndale, 2004.

Baxter, J. Sidlow. *The Other Side of Death.* Grand Rapids: Kregel, 1997.

Buchanan, Mark. *Things Unseen.* Sisters: Multnomah, 2002.

Calvin, John. *Institutes of the Christian Religion.* Edited by John McNeill. Louisville: Westminster John Knox Press, 1960.

Edwards, Jonathan. *The Works of Jonathan Edwards, Vol. 1.* Edinburgh: Banner of Truth, 1976.

Elliot, Elisabeth. *In The Shadow of the Almighty.* New York: Harper and Row, 1958.

Flavel, John. *Keeping the Heart.* New York: Cosimo: 2007.

Grosart, Alexander, ed. *Works of Richard Sibbes: Miscellaneous Sermons.* Carlisle: Banner of Truth Trust, 1982.

Gurnall, William. *The Christian in Complete Armor.* Carlisle: Banner of Truth Trust, 1964.

Kempis, Thomas à. *The Imitation of Christ.* Chicago: Moody Press, n.d.

Lewis, C.S. *A Grief Observed.* New York: HarperOne, 2001.

Lewis, C.S. *Mere Christianity.* San Francisco: HarperSanFrancisco, 2001.

Lewis, C.S. *Screwtape Letters.* New York: HarperCollins, 2001.

Lewis, C.S. *The Problem of Pain.* New York: HarperOne, 2001.

Lewis, C.S. *The Weight of Glory.* New York: HarperCollins, 2001.

Owen, John. *Sin and Temptation.* Portland: Multnomah, 1983.

Packer, J.I. *Knowing God.* Downers Grove: InterVarsity, 1979.

Piper, John. *Desiring God.* Colorado Springs: Multnomah, 1996.

Piper, John. *Don't Waste Your Life.* Wheaton: Crossway, 2010.

Ryle, J.C. *Holiness.* Moscow: Charles Nolan, 2001.

Ryle, J.C. *Practical Religion.* Cambridge: James Clarke, 1977.

Ryle, J.C. *Shall We Know One Another in Heaven.* Greenville: Emerald House Group, 1997.

Sanders, J. Oswald. *Heaven: Better by Far.* Grand Rapids: Discovery House, 1993.

Sauer, Erich. *From Eternity to Eternity.* Grand Rapids: Eerdmans, 1979.

Sauer, Erich. *In the Arena of Faith.* Grand Rapids: Eerdmans, 1977.

Sauer, Erich. *The Triumph of the Crucified.* Grand Rapids: Eerdmans, 1977.

Stanford, Miles. *Principles of Spiritual Growth.* Lincoln: Back to the Bible, 1976.

Stanley, Charles F., ed. *The Charles F. Stanley Life Principles Bible.* Nashville: Thomas Nelson, 2009.

Swindoll, Charles. *The Mystery of God's Will.* Nashville: Thomas Nelson, 2002.

Tada, Joni Eareckson. *Heaven: Your Real Home.* Grand Rapids: Zondervan, 1995.

Taylor, Dr. and Mrs. Howard. *Hudson Taylor's Spiritual Secret.* Chicago, Moody Press, n.d.

Tozer, A.W. *The Knowledge of the Holy.* New York: HarperOne, 1992.

Tozer, A. W. *The Pursuit of God.* Harrisburg: Christian Publications, n.d.

Wesley, John, and Charles Wesley. *Selected Writings and Hymns.* Mahwah: Paulist Press, 1981.

Wiersbe, Warren, comp. *The Best of A. W. Tozer.* Camp Hill: Christian Publications, 1993.

If you have any questions or comments, feel free to contact Reasoning from the Scriptures Ministries.

RON RHODES
Reasoning from the Scriptures Ministries

PHONE:	214-618-0912
EMAIL:	ronrhodes@earthlink.net
WEB:	www.ronrhodes.org

Free newsletter available upon request

Other Great Harvest House Reading

by Ron Rhodes

The 10 Most Important Things
You Can Say to a Catholic

The 10 Most Important Things
You Can Say to a Jehovah's Witness

The 10 Most Important Things
You Can Say to a Mason

The 10 Most Important Things
You Can Say to a Mormon

10 Things You Need to Know
About Islam

5-Minute Apologetics for Today

Angels Among Us

Answering the Objections of Atheists,
Agnostics, and Skeptics

Archaeology and the Bible:
What You Need to Know

The Book of Bible Promises

Christian Views of War:
What You Need to Know

Christianity According to the Bible

Commonly Misunderstood Bible Verses

The Complete Guide to Bible Translations

The Complete Guide to Christian
Denominations

Conviction Without Compromise
(with Norman Geisler)

Find It Fast in the Bible

Halloween: What You Need to Know

Homosexuality:
What You Need to Know

Islam: What You Need to Know

Jehovah's Witnesses:
What You Need to Know

The Middle East Conflict:
What You Need to Know

Northern Storm Rising

The Popular Dictionary of Bible Prophecy

Reasoning from the Scriptures
with Catholics

Reasoning from the Scriptures
with the Jehovah's Witnesses

Reasoning from the Scriptures
with Masons

Reasoning from the Scriptures
with the Mormons

Reasoning from the Scriptures
with Muslims

The Topical Handbook of Bible Prophecy

The Truth Behind Ghosts, Mediums, and
Psychic Phenomena

Understanding the Bible from A to Z

What Does the Bible Say About...?

Why Do Bad Things Happen
If God Is Good?

The Wonder of Heaven

World Religions:
What You Need to Know

To learn more about Harvest House books and
to read sample chapters, log on to our website:

www.harvesthousepublishers.com

HARVEST HOUSE PUBLISHERS

EUGENE, OREGON